*Interpretation and Explanation
in the Human Sciences*

*SUNY Series in the Philosophy
of the Social Sciences*

Lenore Langsdorf, editor

Interpretation and Explanation in the Human Sciences

DAVID K. HENDERSON

STATE UNIVERSITY OF NEW YORK PRESS

Published by
State University of New York Press, Albany

© 1993 State University of New York

For information, address State University of New York
Press, State University Plaza, Albany, N.Y., 12246

Production by Diane Ganeles
Marketing by Dana E. Yanulavich

Library of Congress Cataloguing-in-Publication Data
Henderson, David K., 1954–
    Interpretation and explanation in the human sciences /
David K. Henderson.
        p.   cm.   —(SUNY series in the philosophy of the
social sciences)
    Includes bibliographical references and index.
    ISBN 0–7914–1405–1 (CH : acid free). ISBN 0–7914–1406–X
(PB : acid-free)
    1. Social sciences—Philosophy. I. Title. II. Series.
H61.H438 1993
300—dc20   92–8608
                                                                CIP

10 9 8 7 6 5 4 3 2 1

Contents

Acknowledgments

I am indebted to Deborah Soles, Robert Barrett, and Roger Gibson for encouragement and helpful criticism from the earliest history of this work through to its present form. Conversations with Terry Horgan, John Tienson, and Dennis Bradshaw have been invaluable; their willingness to read and comment on the manuscript was exploited. The later chapters were much improved by spending the summer of 1991 at a National Endowment for the Humanities Summer Seminar at the University of Virginia. There, Paul Humphreys provided helpful discussions on causation and explanation. My wife, Carlotta, provided unwavering understanding and support.

Portions of earlier papers have been woven into this text, although I have consistently deepened the presentation, drawn connections more fully than I was able to do previously, and sometimes modified central aspects of my earlier understandings. Portions of my second and third chapters are descendents of "The Principle of Charity and the Problem of Irrationality," *Synthese* 73 (1987), pp. 225–52, and "A Solution to Davidson's Problem of Irrationality," *Erkenntnis* 27 (1987), pp. 359–69, reprinted by permission of Kluwer Academic Publishers. My fifth and sixth chapters draw upon related material in "Rationalizing Explanation in the Human Sciences: Its Role and Limitation," *Canadian Journal of Philosophy* 19 (1989), pp. 267–88, and "Rationalizing Explanation, Normative Principles, and Descriptive Generalizations," *Behavior and Philosophy* 19 (1992), 1–20. My seventh chapter incorporates much of "On the Testability of Psychological Generalizations," *Philosophy of Science* 58 (1991), pp. 586–606. (In this last case, the presentation in the book remains particularly close to that found in the article.)

1

Interpretation and Explanation: Claims and Concerns

This book is devoted to developing complementary accounts of both interpretation and explanation in the human sciences. This is undertaken with the conviction that an account of either interpretation or explanation will be inadequate and incomplete without a supporting account of the other. Accounts of either matter ultimately will need to appeal to, or suppose, important points regarding the other. On the one hand, explanatory success is itself the central desideratum of correctness in interpretation, and thus an account of explanation figures directly in articulating adequacy conditions for interpretation. On the other hand, explanations in the human sciences typically make reference to conditions described in intentional terms, and thus are dependent on interpretations. In view of this, philosophers have often attempted to repudiate accounts of explanation in the human sciences by advancing an account of interpretation that precludes certain things supposed in the account of explanation under attack. A satisfactory account of explanation must have the resources to deflect such criticisms.

In view of these connections, one could almost say that accounts of interpretation and explanation in the human sciences describe two faces of the same coin. However, writers who would make this claim have often been *methodological separatists*, holding that, as a result, the logic of explanation (and testing) in the human sciences is fundamentally different from what we employ in natural sciences. They have held that the constraints on interpretation are unique and quite disanalogous to the constraints on the description of phenomena of interest in the natural sciences. This is thought to foreclose the possibility of the sort of explanation appropriate to the natural sciences. For example, the possibility of such explanations is sometimes thought to be foreclosed by interpretive constraints rendering generalizations regarding intentional states inherently non-nomic. Such a view is suggested by Davidson's (1980c, 1980d) doctrine of the anomalousness of the mental, the separatist implications of which have been pointed out by Rosenberg (1985b). Alternatively, it is sometimes argued that such explanations become superfluous in view of the intimate relation between intentional interpretation and a distinctly intentional form of explanation, (Winch 1958; McDowell 1985). What remains, it is said, is the possibility of a distinct sort of explanation, sometimes called empathetic understanding or rationalizing explanation, which is thought not to rely on nomic generalizations in the way characteristic of explanations in the natural sciences.

I, however, deny such separatist claims. I defend the *methodological naturalist* thesis that, at an important and fundamental level of analysis, the logic of inquiry (including explanation and testing) in the human sciences is the same as that informing the natural sciences. I do this, not by ignoring what is surely the strength of the separatist's position—the concern for interpretive understanding and a sensitivity to its central role in the human sciences—but by developing a methodological naturalist account of such interpretation. I show how debates over interpretations in the human sciences reflect a concern for the explicability of those interpreted, where "explicability" can best be understood in terms of a generic notion of explanation appropriate to the natural sciences as well as the human sciences. I proceed to develop the needed account of explanation in the human sciences, including an account of the much misunderstood status of rationalizing explanations in particular.

The point of the present chapter is to provide the reader with an overview of my position, which must be elaborated by a serial consideration of a set of interdependent issues: the nature of interpretation and the constraints on interpretation; the nature of mental states and whether it is a priori that, within any individual, they are preponderantly rational; the place of rationalizing explanations in the human sciences and the limitations of such explanations in these contexts; the nature of nomic generalizations and their place in explanation; the relations between the special sciences and the more fundamental sciences; the relation of psychological states to physical states; and so on. However, due to the intimate interrelations between such issues, and the interdependence of positions taken on such issues, dealing first with any one is bound to give rise to worries concerning the others, and to a resulting unease regarding the point then under discussion. My strategy here is simply to let the reader know what my general position on the interrelated issues is, without defending that position at any length. As I then focus on particular issues in the chapters to follow, the reader can at least envision how I would seek to address threatening problems arising from the perspective of the other issues. Accordingly, this chapter is not intended to convince my readers, but only to inform them of what to expect. What I give here is a series of "I.O.U.s," which I discharge in later chapters.

In the next two chapters, I will provide my basic account of interpretation. This is a particularly important discussion, for it will undercut important separatist arguments. As noted above, it is commonly held that interpretation is alien to the general scientific method. There are constraints on interpretation as the attribution of intentional states; these are (more or less implicit) adequacy criteria reflected in interpretive practice. Such constraints have to do with what it is to "make sense" of behavior, what it is to find what is done "intelligible." It is these constraints that are often thought to give rise to a fundamental difference between the human sciences and the natural sciences, for they are thought to be essentially unlike constraints on the description of physical and biological systems. After discussing, in chapter 2, what has come to be the standard or common account of the constraints on interpretation, I will argue, in chapter 3, that a superior account of such constraints is possible, and that such an account does not have the threatened separatist implications.

There is, of course, some disagreement regarding the nature of these constraints, but two general points seem to enjoy a fair consensus. First, interpretation is a holistic matter—what interpretation is proper for a particular bit of text or behavior is dependent on what interpretation can be settled on for the larger text or range of the agent's behavior, of which the particular bit is a part. This, of course, is a familiar orthodoxy in hermeneutics; it is acknowledged in discussions of the "hermeneutical circle" in which the constructions placed on the parts and on the whole are "played off" each against the other in a continual process of refining interpretation. It is also orthodox in contemporary analytic philosophy of language and mind, where Quine and Davidson, among others, have described how the content of a belief is dependent on its place in a pattern of other beliefs and attitudes. It is also an integral feature of any philosophy of psychology and mind that is influenced by functionalist accounts of cognitive processes. I am convinced both that this first point is correct and that it need not give rise to separatist results. Holism, after all, is not unique to interpretation.

In fact, it is characteristic of the analysis of systems. For example, it is found in the analysis of biological systems, and functionally characterized systems generally, as well as in the treatment of intentional or cognitive systems.

Second, it is commonly suggested that in "finding intelligible" and "making sense" of a range of behavior, the holistic pattern employed is, of necessity, a *fundamentally charitable* one. This is to claim that interpreters are under a *basic methodological constraint* to interpret so as to construe people as predominantly rational in thought and deed, and as largely correct in their beliefs. Such a "principle of charity" is, I believe, best understood as a proffered codification of interpretive practice. Again, I think there is wide agreement on the claim that interpretation is constrained by such a principle. Indeed, it is easy enough to understand "making intelligible" and "making sense" to mean "finding the rationality in" the behavior at issue. This fits comfortably with the view that interpretation automatically leads us to rationalizing explanations of the thought and deeds of those interpreted. Such views find expression in the writings of Davidson, Winch, Turner, and Taylor, among others.

This second point of substantial consensus regarding the constraints on interpretation is particularly significant. For it is what gives rise to the view that interpretation is really fundamentally distinct from all other sorts of inquiry. Were the principle of charity really a fundamental methodological constraint on adequate interpretation, this would make for a deep difference between interpretation and the description of phenomena in the other sciences. After all, it is said, such a constraint "has no echo" in other contexts (Davidson 1980d, p. 231). Sure, the scientific description of phenomena is "theory laden" in all contexts, and is thus constrained by extant theoretical understandings. But this theoretical background is supposedly responsive to standard scientific concerns, for explanatory power, for example. As our theory changes, our descriptions of phenomena come to be informed by different theoretical principles, and thus different constraints, without thereby putting us in violation of any fundamental methodological constraint. In contrast, interpretive description is commonly thought to be constrained by the principle of charity in a more fundamental way. These constraints are thought not to be just a matter of interpretation being theory-laden description, for this would make such constraints subject to the shifting sands of theory. Instead, the constraints are more a matter of interpretation being wedded to an a priori restricted range of psychological theories, those that view people as preponderantly rational (Root 1986). Or perhaps it is preferable to say that the constraints on interpretation themselves force that range of theory on us. On this view, one might say that it is not that our descriptions must lead to explanations, but that they must lead to (mostly) *rationalizing* explanations.

I have no quarrel with the principle of charity when it is understood as a crude codification of interpretive practice and thus subject to substantial refinement. For it certainly captures important aspects of that practice. However, I argue that it is a *derivative principle*, a general rule of thumb, the place for, and limitations of, which can be understood in terms of a yet more fundamental constraint that I have (1987a) called the principle of explicability. The principle of explicability councils us to so interpret as to construe people as doing explicable things, in view of their beliefs and desires, and as believing and desiring explicable things in view of their other beliefs and desires and their training.

There are a range of considerations supporting this view of charity in interpretation as derivative, and thus not a fundamental methodological constraint. To begin with, when one considers refinements philosophers have come to make in formulating versions of the principle of charity, one finds that these ultimately are tailored to what is explicable in the way of cognitive and practical successes and failures, not to degrees of normative propriety. Those cases in which the principle of charity seems most constraining are just those where error would be generally most inexplicable, and attributions of error would most tend to violate the principle of explicability. Further, when one attends to anthropological controversies concerning what is an ultimately acceptable interpretation in cases of apparent irrationality or egregious error, one finds that the issue quickly comes to be the explicability of what is said and done according to the competing interpretations, not the normative propriety of what is attributed in the competing accounts. Such observations (to be defended later) show that the principle of charity is tailored to fit the dictates of the principle of explicability, given present general descriptive information about psychological and sociological processes. This indicates the derivative character of the principle of charity. When properly qualified, it can thus be recognized as just a reflection of the theory-laden nature of description, given present theoretical resources. (Of course, the notion of explanation supposed here is the standard one: roughly, explicability in terms of causal antecedents, where these are picked out in terms of background nomic generalizations—here regarding human cognitive capacities, learning and socialization, and so forth.)

I believe that the sort of argument suggested just now (and developed in chapters 2 and 3) demonstrates that the adequacy of an interpretation turns on the explicability of what is attributed to those interpreted. Obviously, this is an encouraging result for a methodological naturalist. For, if the methodology of interpretation is compliant to the concerns for explanation, and the relevant sort of explanation is a generic sort that is also instanced in the natural sciences, then what once appeared to be deep methodological differences turn out to be just central bits of psychological theory reflected in theory-laden descriptions. However, a survey of the literature will show that there remain two related sources of misgivings, both of which are variants of the general claim that while interpretation may follow explicability in many cases, it is still subject to a special constraint to attribute rationality (and perhaps correctness) at some minimal level.

First, an a priori minimal rationality requirement on interpretation is sometimes defended by arguing that it is "constitutive of the concept" of intentional states, and thus an adequacy criterion for the attribution of such states, that those states be minimally rational (Davidson 1980c, 1980d, 1980e; Root 1986; Stich 1985). Here the suggestion is that, explicability aside, if our attributions do not uncover enough rationality, then whatever we are identifying simply are not intentional states. (If we seem to be attributing less than the minimal degree of rationality, we have, perhaps covertly, become eliminativists of some stripe.) As a result, strictly speaking, we are then not interpreting and we are not addressing the subject matter of the social sciences and intentional psychology. The idea, I suppose, is that the principle of charity can bend somewhat with empirical findings concerning limited irrationality, but ultimately, it sets certain fixed limits on the attribution of intentional states. Another way of expressing these concerns is to insist that charity limits what empirical findings there could be regarding irrationality, and thus it limits what generalizations we might have to explain irrationality in thought and deed. Such limits are thought not to be empirically fluid. So concerns for explicability may tailor charity, but ultimately only minor alterations are possible.

In the fourth chapter, I rebut such arguments. First, I show that they overestimate what appeals to constitutive criteria can accomplish. Ultimately, if philosophically defensible, such appeals have to do with the centrality of certain principles to our present theoretical resources. As a result, they do not give rise to an absolute prohibition on the development of concepts in particular ways. Minimal rationality requirements cannot be more constraining on future developments in psychology than fundamental Newtonian principles (e = $1/2mv^2$, for example) were constraining on the subsequent development of physics. Second, it is significant that contemporary psychological resources may themselves fail to support the claim that beliefs and desires must be *predominantly* rational, depending, of course, on how rationality is itself judged. Finally, the stubbornness of the constitutive criteria supposed to give rise to the rigid minimal rationality requirement is typically understood as the result of a variant of the principle of charity that is perhaps informed to an extent by the principle of explicability, but that is not fully subservient to explicability. Here the considerations adduced in chapters 2 and 3 may be employed to show that this is untenable, for there is simply no good reason for thinking that charity and explicability are ever competing desiderata for social scientific accounts, as they would be if the principle of charity were not freely tailored to explicability.

The second defense of minimal rationality requirements is to insist that the explicability of concern in interpretive contexts is predominantly a matter of explicability in terms of rationality. This is to say that interpretive work must lead us to predominantly rationalizing explanations of those we interpret, perhaps because such is the sort of explanation associated with intentionality. Ultimately, when pressed, such a general position is probably not distinct from that discussed in chapter 4, except as a matter of emphasis. However, in discussions of social scientific explanation in particular, such a position is occasionally put forward with relatively little discussion of charitable constraints on interpretation. In some cases, it is advanced not as a concomitant of intentional interpretation and explanation as such, but as the proper sort of explanation for the social sciences (as distinct from psychology). In this form, it finds an advocate in Jarvie (1964), who insists that such explanations are fundamentally a matter of uncovering "the logic of the situation," and who insists that such a focus is independent of psychological results. Turner's (1980) discussion of sociological explanation as a matter of giving account of the logic of "practices" may also be understood as supportive. The general claim that rationalizing explanation is a preferred form of intentional explanation, and must constitute the clear majority of such explanations, is discussed in chapter 5, where it affords the occasion for making important points about the status of rationalizing explanation.

Rationalizing explanation has proven to be quite limited in some contexts—say the anthropology of religion—leaving much in need of further sorts of explanation. But, while this observation casts doubt on the adequacy of rationalizing explanation as the basis for the human sciences, it is really only a preliminary. The claim that rationalizing explanation must be supplemented (even heavily supplemented) does little to rebut the assumption that rationalizing is a particularly appropriate, fundamental, or pre-ferred sort of intentional explanation. But an adequate account of the nature of rationalizing explanation and psychological expla-nation generally will lead us to repudiate the privileged status often accorded to rationalizing explanations. One particularly sig-nificant complementary alternative sort of explanation is the sort that appeals to cognitive strategies such as are presently the sub-ject of much work in cognitive psychology. These strategies are commonly not optimal, and are sometimes systematically norma-tively inappropriate. When we explain various beliefs or actions by reference to such strategies, we are clearly employing a general-ization-based explanation. We might call such explanations irra-tionalizing explanations. I draw on recent work in the philosophy of mind and psychology to argue that rationalizing explanation and irrationalizing explanations are on a par. Both implicitly or explic-itly posit general cognitive capacities or liabilities characterized in terms of rules of reasoning. The only significant difference between the two is whether or not the rules used to characterize the relevant cognitive dispositions happen to formulate normatively appropriate ways of reasoning.

Together, chapters 5 and 6 present an account of rationalizing explanation that situates such explanations within a general account of the explanation of events. I argue that scientific explanations come in two complementary forms: answers to how-questions and answers to why-questions. Functional analyses provide answers to how-questions by accounting for sophisticated or complex capabil-ities (to maintain homeostasis or to solve a problem, for example) in terms of simpler dispositions (Cummins 1983; Rosenberg 1985a). Dispositions are characterized in terms of particular outputs being keyed to certain inputs. Thus, successful analyses in terms of dis-positions uncover transition laws, nomic generalizations regard-ing a sort of system, which can be used in answering why-questions. Scientific explanations for events, singular causal explanations, are answers to why-questions. They identify causes of an event by picking out what it was about the course of antecedent events that, had things been different in that respect, the explanandum event would (probably) not have obtained. Thus, scientific explanations of events draw on nomic generalizations that allow us to appreciate the causally relevant factors in the course of events. Such a general account of scientific explanation owes much to Salmon (1984) and Humphreys (1989a, 1989b). Now, both rationalizing and irrationalizing explanations, as described in chapter 5, will readily be recognized as cases where a more or less explicit functional analysis has given rise to transition laws regarding human cognitive dispositions that are supportive of causal explanations answering why-questions.

However, some will find that they have a stubborn suspicion that explanations in the human sciences proceed in terms of normative principles, not descriptive generalizations. McDowell (1985) articulates such a view. I argue that this cannot be. Nomic principles *qua* normative principles are irrelevant to answering why-questions, understood as accounting for the occurrence of an event of a particular type. Of course, when statements of such principles are used as representations of basic or acquired cognitive dispositions, they are quite relevant. But this is to transform the principle into a descriptive claim. It is then in this capacity as a descriptive generalization that the principle comes to support answers to why-questions.

My account of both interpretation and explanation in the human sciences requires that there be nomic psychological generalizations—psychological laws. Of course, whether there are such laws has itself been the subject of debate. Recent work in analytic philosophy has led some to the view that there are no nomic generalizations of intentional psychology. This claim has been supported in several ways. Responding to such challenges is the task of chapters 7 and 8.

Alexander Rosenberg has argued that at least certain crucial generalizations of intentional psychology cannot be nomic because they are not empirically refinable, and being so refinable is taken to be characteristic of nomic generalizations. According to Rosenberg, the rudimentary generalizations informing rationalizing explanation are involved in interpretation in a way that precludes their being empirically refined. To be so refinable, it must be in principle possible to obtain cases where the generalizations fail.[1] But, Rosenberg argues, apparent violations of such generalizations must themselves be treated as dubious, due to the way in which these generalizations inform interpretation. Since prima facie counterinstances to the central principles must ultimately be taken as cases of poor interpretation and thus as spurious counterinstances, we could never have empirical grounds for modifying these central principles.

Rosenberg's challenge is taken up in chapter 7. The central difficulty with this argument is that it ignores the range of generalizations that inform interpretation, and, as a result, it ignores the ways in which other portions of this store of generalizations can be used to support interpretations that indicate the need for refinements on those rudimentary generalizations that Rosenberg believes are insulated from test. I develop this point by elaborating an account of bootstrap testing in the human sciences. (My debt to Glymour's (1980) account of bootstrapping will be obvious.) In bootstrap testing, a hypothesis taken from a theory may be tested by using other portions of the same theory to derive instances (or counterinstances) of that hypothesis from what is observed. Confirmation thus is recognized as a triadic relation: evidence confirms a hypothesis with respect to a theory. I am able to show how my account of interpretation allows us to appreciate the range of theory relevant to common psychological experiments and, thus, to appreciate how such experiments can be used in refining even those cherished basic principles informing rationalizing explanation. I illustrate the process by discussing concrete experimental work by Tversky and Kahneman, among others.

Davidson's (1980c, 1980d) discussions of "heteronomic generalizations" and his associated doctrine of the "anomalousness of the mental" pose a second fundamental challenge to the nomic status of generalizations in intentional psychology. Davidson's distinction between heteronomic and homonomic generalizations has to do with what is involved in refining generalizations. We may suppose that rough generalizations are expressed using only vocabulary from a particular level or type of description—physical, biological, or intentional, for example. Generalizations are heteronomic when they cannot be refined into strictly universal, non-ceteris-paribus, generalizations by employing vocabulary of the same basic sort employed in the rough generalizations.[2] Homonomic generalizations can be so refined. Davidson seems to suggest that heteronomic generalizations are all non-nomic; he compares them to Goodman's clearly non-nomic generalization concerning grue emeralds. When one sorts through Davidson's various discussions, one finds that his reservations ultimately suggest that the features mentioned in heteronomic generalizations cannot be real causal factors (even though the events they characterize, including psycholological events, can be causal events). At most, then, heteronomic generalizations reflect there being a range of causal regularities underlying the rough regularity that they describe. According to Davidson, the mental qua mental can only be subject to heteronomic generalizations. It would follow that there can be no nomic psychological generalizations.

Related concerns have been expressed by Malcolm (1968) and Kim (1989a, 1989b). Kim formulates a "principle of explanatory exclusion" holding that "there can be at most one complete and independent explanation" for any given explanandum. With respect to psychology, the issue then becomes: how can a given bit of behavior be explained both by certain neurophysiological antecedents that we all admit cause it and by certain psychological features of the agent as well? If an adequate answer cannot be provided, then it looks as though we may be forced to conclude that psychological features cannot be causally relevant, and that psychological generalizations are, as a result, non-nomic. Kim's own reflections (1989b) lead him to conclude that, if a higher-level feature is to be causally relevant, it must be reducible to causally relevant lower-level features. Such reducibility is thought to render the two explanations not independent, thus bringing them into conformity with the exclusion principle. On this view, if psychological states are to be causally relevant, intentional psychology must be reducible to neurophysiology. Since such a reduction is widely acknowledged to be impossible, psychological states would seem to be causally irrelevant, as was suggested by Davidson.

In chapter 8, I take up Davidson's and Kim's misgivings, arguing that the heteronomic generalizations characteristic of the special sciences can be nomic and deal with causally relevant features, despite the fact that theories in the special sciences are, in an important sense, irreducible to lower-level theories. Thus, generalizations in intentional psychology can be nomic despite the fact they are not reducible to lower-level theories such as neurophysiology. To begin with, I build on Kim's own notion of a "supervenient causal relation." In such relations, certain higher-level features are causally relevant by virtue of "supervening on" and being "realized in" causally relevant features at a lower-level. I argue that this account of the causal relevance of higher-level properties is essentially correct. But, the demand that higher-level theories deal with supervenient causes does not give rise to a significant reductionism. I argue that

Kim's reductionism is either trivial or unacceptable, depending on how reduction is understood.

When the range of points broached in this introductory chapter have been developed and defended, we will have a full and well-integrated account of the human sciences focusing on the pivotal notions of interpretation and explanation. It is my hope that it will then serve as a defense of aspirations some of us hold for a *science* of human psychology and social life, and a defense that honestly answers some of the reservations responsible thinkers have had regarding such a science. In particular, I seek to provide such a defense by acknowledging the importance of interpretive understanding in the human sciences, and by developing an account of such understanding that both reflects interpretive practice and complements an account of a science of human beings. The marriage of interpretation and scientific methodology should be a happy one, I predict, for the parties share the same interest—explanation—and both need the other to pursue this interest.

2

Standard Accounts of Interpretation and the Principle of Charity

2.1: Standard Accounts of Interpretation

It is common to conceive of interpretation as a sui generis activity; this matter of "making sense" out of behaviors and artifacts is often thought to be subject to unique constraints. Indeed, even when interpretation has been viewed as intimately associated with explanation in the human sciences, an association that one would think might turn a writer's thoughts to the sciences and their methodology, interpretation has typically been thought of as dictating the nature of the overall endeavor (Turner 1980; Putnam 1978; Winch 1958). Thus, explanations that are associated with interpretation have often been thought to be of a rather special sort that is fundamentally conditioned by the nature of interpretation. On such a view, one would not think to look to general accounts of scientific explanation to inform our understanding of interpretation, rather, one would look to an understanding of interpretation to inform our understanding of intentional explanation. The unique status of interpretive inquiries is thus reaffirmed.

It should come as no surprise to the reader that I find this general approach to the relations between interpretation and explanation to be fundamentally misguided. Still, writers adopting interpretation-centered accounts of explanation can make significant contributions. For example, Turner's (1980) discussions of interpretive practice are particularly interesting, and I have made use of suggestions found there in my own account of interpretive schemes and theory-based modeling. Further, the concern for interpretation found in such works naturally leads to an issue that is of the utmost importance: What are the constraints on interpretation? What are the adequacy criteria by which interpretations are to be judged? Obviously this issue will be of preeminent importance when, as in the approaches just mentioned, the understanding of some social phenomenon sought by an investigator is thought to be "more like the engineer's understanding of his colleagues' activities than it is like the engineer's understanding of the mechanical systems which he studies" (Winch 1958, p. 88). But it remains a crucial concern in developing my own very different position, for I must show that such constraints are not such as to make interpretation a sui generis endeavor as the methodological separatist supposes. In his *The Very Idea of a Social Science*, Winch chides philosophers and scientists for looking for explanations (in the sense appropriate to the sciences proper) or to statistics when checking interpretive understandings, and he insists that when an interpretation is problematic, "what is needed is a better interpretation, not something different in kind" (1958, p. 113). Granted that a better interpretation would be needed in such a case—but, what makes one interpretation better than another?

In this chapter I will survey what has become the standard account of what makes for adequacy (or degrees of adequacy) in interpretations. I describe how interpretation has been said to be constrained by the principle of charity understood as a fundamental methodological constraint that draws on normative principles, qua normative principles. I also describe commonly recognized refinements on a rudimentary principle of charity. These refinements seem often to draw on descriptive claims. Within the framework of this book, this chapter serves two purposes. First it lays out that separatist view of charitable interpretation that I will argue against. Second, in discussing the refinements on a principle of charity, it provides background for my argument in the next chapter, in which I show that a superior codification of interpretive practice views the principle of charity as a derivative constraint that draws on descriptive information from the start.

Accounts of interpretation (regardless of whether they are produced within the analytic tradition or not) tend to agree in at least two broad respects: first, interpretation is importantly holistic, and second, as a result, interpretation is constrained by a fundamental principle of charity.

2.1.1: The Holism of Interpretation

The claim that interpretation is a holistic endeavor is basically the claim that whatever is interpreted, whether it be an utterance and other action, must be interpreted in light of a set of related interpretations for other utterances or actions, and these interpretations are themselves likewise conditioned. It is helpful here to think of constructing a general scheme to be employed in the interpretation of some group's actions or utterances. We can call such a scheme for the interpretation of their language a *translation scheme*. A translation scheme will map (perhaps with substantial qualifying and elaborating discussion) sentences in some people's language (the source-language) onto sentences in the interpreter's language (the target-language). A scheme for the interpretation of some group's behaviors can be called an *interpretive scheme*. It will allow us to map practices in the group's repertoire onto practices of ours (again, perhaps with substantial discussion). The holism of interpretation can be captured in the claim that interpretive and translation schemes cannot be constructed in a piecemeal way: the interpretation that a scheme can properly assign to some action or utterance is dependent on the interpretations it assigns to a substantial range of other actions or utterances. Obviously this ramifies.

Sometimes rather extreme holist views are entertained in which the ramification of interdependencies of interpretations leads to the conclusion that no interpretation for an utterance, action, or restricted class of such can be judged acceptable until an ideal interpretive scheme is achieved in which all interpretations of individual utterances and actions are clearly acceptable. This extreme view is overdrawn. Holism is intimately associated with the way in which beliefs, desires, and such are interrelated. Accordingly, it should be of most significance where beliefs are closely related, and of less significance where beliefs are from relatively independent domains.

For example, suppose that we are still struggling with interpretations for certain magico-religious utterances and actions. While this should undermine our confidence in interpretations within this general area and in closely associated contexts, it need not undermine our confidence in interpretations for utterances and actions that are not at all closely associated. In the society being studied, kitchen work-practices and instructions might be relatively unaffected by a particular culture's magic (Malinowski [1931] suggests that this characterized the situation in the Trobriand Islands). In such a case, difficulties we are having understanding their magic need not undermine our understanding of utterances such as 'This is chicken soup' or 'This needs more pepper.'

How exactly the holism of interpretation is to be understood so as not to be overdrawn is not my central concern for now. Rather, I am simply noting that there are a range of positions that can properly be called holist with respect to interpretation. When I say that there is wide agreement on the claim that interpretation is holistic, I do not have in mind just the extreme positions.

It is also worth noting that an account of the adequacy of an interpretive scheme will have to include an account of the adequacy of translation schemes, and vice versa. The reasons for this are rooted in a mild form of holism in interpretation. On the one hand, adequate translation schemes will need to be embedded in adequate interpretive schemes. A translation scheme that could not be incorporated in an adequate interpretive scheme would surely be unacceptable. After all, utterances and (other) actions are so intimately associated that if we could not sort out what a people were doing, we should not think that we understood what they were saying. In particular, we should not think that we understood what they were saying that they valued and believed. On the other hand, an adequate interpretive scheme must surely incorporate an adequate translation scheme. For interpretive schemes typically lead us to make fine discriminations with respect to what is wanted and what is believed—that is, fine discriminations with respect to the intentional states accounting for what is done. But such fine discriminations are not generally possible without an interpretation of the agent's language.

Among analytic philosophers of language, Quine, in his discussions of translation, has surely been a particularly influential proponent of holism in interpretation. Indeed, he has argued not just for a holism of interpretation, but for associated, and supporting, holisms of meaning and of scientific theory and testing.

Quine explains the holism of theory and testing as follows. Assent to and dissent from some sentences are keyed relatively directly to impingements at one's sensory surfaces. For some such sentences, there is wide social regularity in assents and dissents that may be elicited in the face of various stimuli. Such "observation sentences" can be thought of as having something like a portion of what the logical empiricists called "cognitive significance" to call their own. (But their connections to further sentences render even this only part of the story.) On the other hand, most sentences of any natural language will not qualify as observation sentences. They simply cannot be associated, one by one, with "a unique range of possible sensory events such that the occurrence of any one of them would add to the likelihood of truth of the statement, and . . . another unique range of possible sensory events whose occurrence would detract from that likelihood" (Quine 1953, p. 41). Quine explains that such nonobservational sentences "face the tribunal of sense experience not individually but only as a corporate body" (p. 41). Together, the sentences of our theory face the tribunal of sensory events by implying (or implying the probability of) observation sentences that are associated relatively directly with stimuli. When the implied sentences are not satisfied, the body of theory is, as a whole, impugned. When the implied sentences are satisfied, the body of theory is to be commended. Thus the holism of theory and testing.

In view of Glymour (1980), it would perhaps be better to recognize that, in practice, Quine's corporate body of scientific theory is itself organized into committees of overlapping membership. As a result, there are significant principles for where blame comes to lie when things do not go well at the observation sentences where the theory must do business. Still, recognizing such principles at most constitutes a moderating refinement on Quine's basic holism with respect to theory and testing: committees of sentences face the tribunal of sense experience.

Insofar as meaning has to do with how our sentences relate to the world, and this has much to do with the ways in which they are connected to observation sentences, meaning must be apportioned to sets of sentences, the committees and the entire corporate body of theory, and not to individual sentences, taken separately. In this way, Quine finds that a holism with respect to meaning follows from a holism with respect to testing.

In keeping with these observations regarding the holistic nature of meaning, and of what can be made of "cognitive significance" in particular, Quine provides a holistic account of translation. According to Quine (1960, pp. 26–68), all the evidence there is for constructing a translation scheme is behavioral evidence: patterns of assents to and dissents from queries of sentences. Now, up to a point, observation sentences need not be treated holistically. The association of source-language observation sentences with particular classes of stimuli affords the basis for finding "equivalents" within the target-language that are associated with the same classes of stimuli. But such results fall quite short of providing a translation (as typically conceived) for observation sentences. For the equivalence relation here must be understood as relating sentences taken "holophrasically": that is, as not telling one anything about the similarity of internal structure and components of the equated sentences or about the referents of whatever components there are.

Further developments will consistently reflect holistic aspects to translation.

To make much headway in dealing with the vast network of source-language sentences and their interrelations, we will need to handle them in a way that reflects the fact that sentences of a natural language are structured representations. We will need to partition the source-language utterances into recurrent parts and to look for ways of equating these "words" or "phrases" with words or phrases in the target-language. This task, which Quine (1960, pp. 68–72) christens the formulation of "analytical hypotheses," is notably holistic. We are to proceed so that the overall result satisfies a certain desideratum:

> [A]s soon as we consider method, we have to recognize that the linguist has no access to native meanings apart from what he can glean from the observed circumstances of utterances. The analytical hypotheses that he contrives are subject to no further check, except that native utterances not conveniently linked to observable circumstances should still turn out on the whole to be plausible messages (Quine 1970, pp. 14–15).

Plausibility here is evidently not just a matter of the plausibility of individual utterances, but also of strings of these: speeches, conversations, and so forth. Obviously, as a consequence of this constraint on admissible analytical hypotheses, how we treat one sentence, and thus its components, will have repercussions for how we treat other sentences and their components. Certain choices in dealing with the components of one set of sentences could easily commit us to a treatment of other sentences (sharing components with the first set) that construes them as expressing implausible messages (either individually or taken together). If such constructions on source-language utterances are to be avoided, so far as possible, then what is done dealing with one sentence will need to condition and be conditioned by what is done in dealing with a rather substantial set of other sentences.

Davidson elaborates on these Quinean themes when he describes the construction of what he terms a "theory of meaning" (for example, 1984a, 1984b, 1984c, 1984d). Such a theory is to provide an account of the "very complex ability . . . to speak and understand a natural language." This is our ability to react to the structure and component parts of sentences in ways that account for our knowing the truth-conditions of an infinite number of sentences.

When we provide such a theory for a given language we also have provided a translation scheme for that language.[1] For Quinean reasons, Davidson believes that we should not suppose that "individual words must have a meaning at all, in any sense that transcends the fact that they have a systematic effect on the meanings of the sentences in which they occur" (1984a, p. 18). But we should capture this aspect of language. Thus, providing a theory of meaning becomes a holistic matter because meaning is holistic:

> If sentences depend for their meaning on their structure, and we understand the meaning of each item in the structure only as an abstraction from the totality of sentences in which it features, then we can give the meaning of any sentence (or word) only by giving the meaning of every sentence (and word) in the language (Davidson 1984a, p. 22).

This is a particularly (and it seems unreasonably) strong holism. The extreme demands here doubtless stem from the fact that Davidson is describing something more than just a translation scheme. A theory of meaning must do more than allow one to understand what the source-language speaker is saying, and it must do more than allow for such understanding by finding structure in the representations that comprise that language. It must also somehow capture the ideal infinitary capacity that would be someone's knowing the full language. Of course, providing for the first two tasks, without addressing the third, obviously gives rise to a similar (if somewhat less rigid) holism. Thus, one expects that Davidson would be willing to accept, as adequate interpretive practice, somewhat less than what is described here.

Davidson's account of theories of meaning elaborates themes already found in Quine's work. However, when we consider the holism of interpretation more generally, Davidson has a somewhat deeper perspective to contribute, a perspective that allows us to appreciate just how much must be sorted out together in interpretation. To begin with, he notes that what we are attempting to get at in translation—the meaning of source-language utterances—is really only one of two factors leading to speakers' verbal responses. What a speaker holds true is a resultant of the two factors: their beliefs and the meaning of their sentences. Thus, from evidence that is the result of the interaction of these two factors, both must be sorted out. "[T]here is no way to test for them independently. . . . we should think of meaning and belief as interrelated constructs of a single theory . . ." (1984c, p. 146). Let us call this the interdependence of belief and meaning.

Davidson's solution to the problem of determining the two unknowns (belief and meaning) on the basis of a single resultant is to impose a structure on the beliefs attributed. In other words, we are to interpret so as to find our subjects' beliefs "structured" or interrelated in a certain characteristic manner. In particular, we are enjoined to attribute beliefs to speakers of the source-language in a way that maximizes, or optimizes, agreement with the structure of epistemic rationality (1984d, p. 169; 1982, pp. 6–7). Of course, what is rational for a person to believe is a function of the range of that person's other beliefs, thus what we can properly attribute to others is a function of what else we attribute to them. The interdependence of belief and meaning thus yields the holism of interpretation.

Davidson has further elaborated on these themes in "Towards a Unified Theory of Meaning and Action" (1980e). The result is a particularly elegant and complete discussion of holism in interpretation.[2] Davidson begins by observing that actions, and the choices made by agents, are also the resultant of two factors: degrees of belief and strength of desire. How these interact to produce choices is supposedly the subject of decision theory. But here, parallel to what was observed in connection with the interdependence of belief and meaning, the resultant of these interactions, choices, are what is most accessible to observation. *Assuming that we can understand an agent's language*, his or her choices are relatively accessible. But, on this basis we need to sort out both the factors. Thus, again we find two unknowns and (at best) only one known— an interdependence of belief and desire results.

As before, the way to undertake sorting out beliefs and desires is to impose a structure: interpretation will involve making attributions regarding the two factors in such a way that they are found to conform to a certain pattern. Again, attributions regarding the two factors will be mutually constraining and committing. Thus, we again encounter the holism of interpretation.

But, the resultants that are to serve as evidence in this case— the choices—are only accessible given that we can understand the agent's language. If we do not assume this, and to fully comprehend the extent of the holism of interpretation we should not assume this, then we find that the holism of interpretation is ultimately a result of needing to sort out together three matters: meanings of utterances, degrees of belief, and strengths of desires. This is the result of compounding the holism of interpretation resulting from the interdependence of belief and meaning and the holism of interpretation resulting from the interdependence of belief and desire. (Of course, these last remarks allow us to again appreciate why interpretation schemes include translation schemes, and adequate translation schemes must have a supporting interpretation scheme.)

Ultimately, Davidson is able to articulate the holism of interpretation more fully than Quine because Quine's initial and principal concern with interpretation and what can be made of meaning stems from an interest in the import of translation for notions such as the logical positivist's "cognitive significance." The factors he considers are conditioned by what might be directly relevant to such notions. Evidence, for Quine, is assents to and dissents from queries. Translation is to give one access to theories. In contrast, Davidson is concerned with a more complete set of interpretive issues. We want to understand more than source-language theories; we also want to understand others' desires and actions.[3] As a result, the range of recognized evidence is expanded so as to also include utterances of (and reactions to) various nonstatements, and behaviors such as manipulations of one's environment and nonverbal expressions. While the range of recognized evidence undergoes an expansion in Davidson's writings, so also does the range of matters to be sorted out together. As a result, more (and compound) sources of holism come to our attention.

I do believe that Quine and Davidson have been particularly clear in articulating holistic aspects of translation and interpretation. They have sought to specify what sorts of evidence there are for settling particular issues, and have thereby led us to appreciate the need to impose a structure on what is attributed in interpretation. This need, together with the associated interdependent character of attributions in individual cases, leads directly to holism. Davidson has managed to articulate the holism of interpretation with a particular and helpful thoroughness, and his discussion has deservedly been focused on here. However, Quine and Davidson, and analytic philosophers strongly influenced by them, are certainly not alone in recognizing holistic aspects of interpretation.

Writers who have been much influenced by the later Wittgenstein have typically also recognized the holism of interpretation. In this, they have traced out the implications of Wittgenstein's own holistic views on meaning.

Insofar as Wittgenstein provides a theory of meaning, its central tenet is that the meaning of a word or expression can be understood in terms of its use within the language-game that is its ordinary-language home (Wittgenstein 1958, sects. 10, 20, 40–43). More fully, on the level of sentences, Wittgenstein replaces the notion of meaning as truth-conditions with a notion that leads us to consider two questions in ascertaining the significance of a sentence: (1) "Under what conditions can the sentence be correctly uttered?"; (2) "What is the use or function of such utterances?" (Kripke 1982, p. 73). Of course, both the conditions for, and the functions of, correct utterances typically involve interrelations between utterances of that sentence and other utterances and actions. Thus, in ascertaining the significance of a sentence, we are to understand how utterances of that sentence are related to a range of other sentences and actions, which must themselves presumably be understood.

The holistic dimension of Wittgenstein's thought here can be appreciated by reflecting on his notion of a language-game as a unit of holistic attention in interpretation. In effect, in interpretation we must come to understand the conditions for, and functions of, correct usage in contexts, and the relevant contexts are language-games. Now, Wittgenstein's usage of the term 'language-game' is varied (Black 1979). Sometimes he uses this term to refer to simple, artificial cases, which he contrives in order to illustrate some aspect of the way in which languages work. But, this usage is not central to our concerns. At other times, he seems to use the term to refer to pretty much any constellation or pattern of interrelated ordinary-language use as a language-game (Churchill 1983, pp. 250–55). So used, the term does not denote a particular sort of unit within a systematic taxonomy of the components of language. Such language-games may have other language-games as component parts, and overlap with many other language-games. A language is composed of many overlapping language-games. And, in the limit case, a language can itself be considered one big language-game (Wittgenstein 1958, sects. 7, 18). This flexible usage is the one most significant for our concerns, for each such language-game would seem to be a focus of holistic meaning, and thus, interpretation.

Wittgenstein repeatedly stresses that language-games are "processes of using words," and, as such, include not just a set of utterances, but also the "actions into which it is interwoven" (Wittgenstein 1958, sect. 7). Thus, a length-measuring language-game would include the various manipulations of the measuring instruments (rulers, etc.), just as his artificial slab-fetching language-games involve the systematic fetching that he describes

(Wittgenstein 1958, sects. 2–6, 19, 50). One way in which Wittgenstein expresses these connections is to say that language-games are connected with forms of life in such a way that "to imagine a language means to imagine a form of life" (Wittgenstein 1958, sect. 19). The rules that characterize a language-game will, thus, involve reference to the set of activities that comprises an associated form of life. These remarks suggest the intimate connections between translation and interpretation; the set of associated utterances and activities that comprise a language-game-cum-form-of-life must be interpreted/translated together.

On Wittgenstein's view, utterances (and associated actions) within a language-game must be interpreted together. For, as mentioned above, an utterance has meaning only within the context of a language-game. Words do not have meaning outside of sentences, for it is with sentences that moves are made in a language-game (Wittgenstein 1958, sect. 49). And sentences have meaning as parts of language-games, as parts of complex sets of verbal and nonverbal practices having characteristic points or functions. Thus, to understand a sentence is to understand its use within such a context. This will obviously involve understanding the uses of many other sentences and acts within the same context or language-game. And ultimately, understanding these, like understanding moves in a game, will involve understanding the entire constellation of activities.

The suggestion that each such language-game-cum-form-of-life would serve as a context demanding holistic treatment is borne out in the neo-Wittgensteinian positions developed by writers such as Peter Winch and Stephen Turner.

In discussing Winch's views on interpretation, it is useful to make a terminological distinction between "ways of life" and "forms of life." I will use 'ways of life' to refer to the particular social contexts, for example, religion in a given society and science in a given society. Particular ways of life are instances of types of social contexts such as religion and science. These latter will be called 'forms of life.' (This distinction follows a tendency in Winch's own usage, but it is not explicit in his writings.)

According to Winch, actions and utterance within a form of life serve certain "considerations," or "points," or purposes that are characteristic of the form of life of which it is an instance (Winch 1958, 100–101). The justification for calling some such points "the points of," or "the characteristic considerations of," a particular form of life is that these points are characteristic of actions performed within that form of life. As prominent examples of forms of life, science, religion, magic, business, and art each are thought to have certain characteristic considerations.

Winch insists that the proper approach to understanding a way of life will lead us "to see the *point* of the rules and conventions followed in [the] alien form of life" (1964, p. 181). Or again, "'Understanding', . . . , is grasping the *point* or *meaning* of what is done or said" (1958, p. 115). To accomplish this, the range of actions in the way of life, including the various moves in the associated language-game, must be found generally informed by a certain set of characteristic considerations which make sense of the range of what is observed. To see one such action as having a certain point is then somewhat committing with respect to the interpretation of the other actions within that way of life. Thus, we find a certain holism of interpretation—how one action or utterance is interpreted conditions, and is conditioned by, how other related utterances are interpreted. The task then, for the Winchian investigator, is to sort out together the interpretation of the various actions within a way of life (including utterances in the associated language-game) and the points informing and unifying that way of life generally. This will determine which form of life the way of life instances. (For a discussion of Winch's neo-Wittgensteinian holism, and associated principle of charity, and illustrative applications, see Henderson 1987c.)

Stephen Turner provides a related, but more concrete and developed neo-Wittgensteinian account. According to Turner, interpretation generally can be understood on the model of translation (when the latter is properly understood). In both cases, what is understood is properly understood in terms of uses or points. Thus, in constructing a translation scheme, one formulates a set of "translation hypotheses" of the form 'Where they say X, we say Y' (Turner 1979, p. 409). Such translation hypotheses draw analogies between the uses of utterances in the two languages. *Sets* of translation hypotheses have implications that may or may not be borne out upon further investigations (p. 410). These implications are determined by the relations between utterances, and between utterances and actions, in the target-language.[4] The interrelated uses of utterances in the source-language is to be modeled within the target-language by setting out the relevant set of analogies. But, individual translation hypotheses obviously cannot be judged singly. Rather, the unit of evaluation is the translation scheme, the set of such hypotheses, for it is this set that models source-language practice by drawing on a set of analogies with the uses of utterances in our own language-games.

Similarly, in the more general matter of interpretation, Turner recommends using "same-practice hypotheses" of the form, 'Where we would follow such and such a rule or practice, or act in such and such a way given some reason, they would do the same' (1980, p. 56). By so matching practices (and reasons), much as he would have us match utterances in translation, the successful Turnerian social scientist will be able to model the behavior that obtains in the society under study. Again, it is the complete set of hypotheses that is a candidate for being adequate.

Finally, it should be noted that the holism of interpretation is clearly reflected in discussions of interpretation within the continental tradition. Ricoeur's (1981) short history of hermeneutics captures this in the following characterization of Dilthey's influential work. Dilthey is said to transform the hermeneutical problem from that of "understanding, defined primarily in terms of the capacity to transpose oneself into another" into the more sophisticated task of "interpretation, in the precise sense of understanding the expressions of life" (Ricoeur 1981, p. 50). Significantly, such expressions are essentially interconnected—"life produces forms, externalizes itself in stable configurations; feelings, evaluations and volitions tend to sediment themselves in a *structured acquisition [aquis]* which is offered to others for deciphering" (p. 50) Of course, deciphering such a structured set of expressions will be a holistic matter of appropriately modeling the structure. Thus:

> [H]ermeneutics comprises something specific; it seeks to reproduce an interconnection, a structured totality, by drawing support from a category of signs which have been fixed by writing or by any other process of inscription equivalent to writing. So it is no longer possible to grasp the mental life of others in its immediate expressions; rather it is necessary to reproduce it, to reconstruct it, by interpreting objectified signs (p. 51).

One can justifiably see Dilthey's recommended reconstruction of the structured set of expressions of life as analogous to the sort of interpretation as modeling that Turner discusses in neo-Wittgensteinian terms. Here we are to come to understand a structured set of states by holistically reconstructing them to account for structured expressions.

The holistic aspects of interpretation have been used to justify the claim that interpretation (and translation) must conform to a rather special constraint: the principle of charity. The most important arguments to this effect must now be rehearsed.

2.1.2: A Fundamental Principle of Charity

The central arguments for a principle of charity in interpretation are codificational: they begin with a recognition of a need for standards that will allow us to settle on some interpretive scheme in the face of the holism described above, and they proceed to suggest that charity in interpretation is the only plausible candidate principle for this role. Charity would turn the trick of allowing us to settle on an interpretive scheme, and it is thought to characterize our interpretive practice. While this view is implicit, if not explicit, in the works of many writers, for example Winch,[5] Davidson's very influential arguments for the view are particularly clear and instructive.

To begin with, consider Davidson's account of constructing a theory of meaning. (Here the influence of Quine is marked.) Davidson believes that the need for a general principle of charity becomes evident when one considers, how, in the face of holism, one can construct a finite theory of meaning that accounts for the ability of source-language speakers to understand an infinite number of sentences. All we could have to go on is assent to and dissent from sentences. If, on that basis, source-language and target-language sentences alike in truth-conditions could be matched, then the results might provide the basis for isolating recurrent parts of the source-language and assigning to them systematic contributions to the truth-conditions of the sentences containing them. Such assignments would result in the ability to frame further new source-language sentences that could be paired with target-language sentences taken to have the same truth-conditions. These results could then be checked by the same methods that yielded the initial equivalences. After numerous such sequences, we should have arrived at a theory of the desired sort. The trick here is to match sentences alike in truth-conditions on the basis of patterns of assent and dissent. If we could do this, the rest can be taken care of with careful work.

Of course, the principle of charity is to provide the needed standard for matching sentences as presumably alike in truth-conditions. Davidson explains that we must begin matching sentences having like truth-conditions by assuming that the speakers of the source-language are correct most of the time, and thus, that their assents and dissents reflect the truth-values of their sentences. We find that some sentences vary in truth-value from one utterance to another (situationally), and yet with regard to any one situation, there is wide agreement within the source-language community. Under the charitable assumption, we can correlate the variations in truth-value (as indicated by assent and dissent) with variations in the truth-values of sentences in the interpreter's language. This provides an important beginning to constructing a translation scheme: it allows us to identify pairs of putatively equivalent observation sentences, and this provides a basis for beginning to find possible equivalent components. On this basis, the investigator "will attempt to construct a [theory] which yields, so far as possible, a mapping of sentences held true (or false) by the native on to sentences held true (or false) by the linguist" (1984a, p. 27). In addition to accommodating the relatively observational sorts of sentences, this mapping is to pair the full range sentences in the interpreted language with sentences in the linguist's language on the basis of their component parts. Success at providing a generally charitable mapping comes to be the test for adequacy of the resulting theory of meaning. After all, at this point, the investigator is still thought to be dependent on assent and dissent as indicators of truth-value, and agreement then serves as a test of the theory.

Davidson takes this line of thought to support a *general* application of the principle of charity. The "meanings" of the components of sentences are their contributions to the truth-conditions of the full range of sentences in which they occur. So the linguist's theory must be tested against the truth-conditions of the full range of source-language sentences. Accordingly, in judging the adequacy of the interpretive scheme, the linguist is supposedly obligated to charitably read truth-conditions off from verbal dispositions towards the full range of such sentences.

Initially, Davidson (1984a, p. 27) formulated the charitable procedure in the maxim, 'Maximize agreement.' However, he has refined the charitable standard by weighting the *importance* of agreement found on various sorts of sentences. He now writes of "optimizing agreement" (Davidson 1984d, p. 169; 1984b, p. 136). However, he makes it quite clear that the modifications do not cumulatively overturn the general policy of finding agreement when dealing with the full range of sentences: "I advocate adoption of the principle of charity on an across-the-board basis" (Davidson 1984c, p. 153). That is, Davidson never comes to restrict charity in translation to constraining only the translation of a limited subset of the source-language sentences, although he does come to weight it differently in different cases. (We will return to such modifications and their bases, for this is important for understanding what I will argue is the ultimately derivative status of charity.)

Ignoring my substantive misgivings for now, we see that Davidson is proffering an abstract reconstruction of what seems to be good interpretive practice. He identifies a methodological problem faced in the daunting task of interpreting a language: the need to have some access to the truth-conditions of source-language sentences. He then makes a plausible case for this need actually being satisfied (at least in part) by a general charitable procedure in constructing a theory of meaning.

This initial codificational argument for a principle of charity is focused on something rather like translation—the construction of a theory of meaning. However, to escape its somewhat narrow focus on language, it can be recast to explicitly deal with beliefs as well as sentences and their truth-conditions. We can begin to do this by recalling the interdependence of belief and meaning. From the point of view of interpretation, these are two unknowns that conspire together to produce what may be taken as relatively knowable—what sentences a speaker holds true. As noted earlier, Davidson believes that we can only deal with this problem of determining two unknowns on the basis of the one known by imposing a structure on the unknowns. The principle of charity does just this: it "is intended to solve the problem of the interdependence of belief and meaning by holding belief constant as far as possible while solving for meaning" (1984c, p. 137).

On this codificational line of thought, the principle of charity is to restrict attributions of belief in two ways. First, Davidson (1984d, p. 168) says that we must interpret people so as to find most of their beliefs about any one thing to be true. Second, he insists that their beliefs must be found to be preponderantly rational (1984d, p. 159; 1980e, pp. 6–7). Again, such a principle of charity is taken to meet our methodological need in what is apparently the only plausible manner. Further, although little real attention is devoted to this point, Davidson, like most writers, believes that this plausible procedure obviously reflects interpretive practice.

These last suppositions harbor what are ultimately the real weakness of Davidson's codificational arguments for a fundamental principle of charity. For I will soon argue that there is another principle that can subsume the principle of charity as a derivative rule of thumb where charity is compelling, and that does more justice to the full range of interpretive practice and concerns. But, for now we need to focus further on Davidson's argument in order to fully appreciate how it envisions imposing rationality in interpretation, and to understand how it treats such charity as a fundamental, not derivative, constraint.

As Davidson says, in sorting out belief and meaning on the basis of what is held true, we must impose a structure on the beliefs attributed to those interpreted. This much is clear. But crucial issues remain: what structure is properly employed here, and what is the status of its use here? Davidson (1980e, p. 6) talks of "stipulating" a structure. This suggests a rather special a priori status to what we employ here. If a structure, principle, or desiderata is simply stipulated, then it is not derivative on further desiderata. It is basic or *fundamental*. Further, Davidson (p. 6) insists that the structure imposed in interpreting others "must derive . . . from normative considerations." The implication is that in interpretation we are bound by a *basic methodological constraint to find people's beliefs to be interrelated in ways that are normatively appropriate*, which is to say, *rational*. In this vein, Davidson (1984d, p. 159) writes of "the *methodological presumption* of rationality" and concludes that "*the basic methodological precept* is, therefore, that a good theory of interpretation maximizes agreement [where this involves finding others rational and believers of truths]" (1984d, p. 169, emphasis mine).

Now, were such a basic methodological presumption necessary or ineliminable in interpretation, as Davidson suggests, then, as the sort of thing gotten at in interpretation, intentional states would be by their nature rational. Various extended passages assure us that this is indeed how Davidson understands interpretation and intentional states. For example, in the following extended passage, Davidson moves from the supposed necessary imposition of a normatively derived structure in interpretation to the claim that beliefs must be basically rational (and then back to the purported need to impose our logic in interpretation):

> If we are to derive meaning and belief from evidence concerning what causes someone to hold sentences true, it can only be (as in decision theory) because we *stipulate a structure*. . . .

> But the *guiding principles* [regarding the structure to impose on beliefs] *must derive* here, as in the cases of decision theory or the theory of truth, *from normative considerations*. We individuate and identify beliefs, as we do desires, intentions and meanings, in a

great number of ways. But the relations between beliefs play a decisive *constitutive* role; we *cannot* accept great or obvious deviations from *rationality* without threatening the intelligibility of our attributions. If we are going to understand the speech or actions of another person, we *must* suppose that their beliefs are incorporated in a pattern that is in essential respects like the pattern of our beliefs. First, then, *we have no choice but to project our own logic* on to the beliefs of another (1980e, pp. 6–7, emphasis mine).[6]

Other passages point in the same direction (for example, Davidson 1980c, p. 221; 1980d, pp. 236–37; 1982, pp. 6–7).

It is crucial not to lose sight of the twin claims uncovered just now. The first is the claim that the principle of charity in interpretation is a response to the methodological situation of interpreters that is not subject to deeper justification.

> *The Fundamental Methodological Constraint (FMC)* view of charity in interpretation: It is a "stipulative" or a "basic methodological" constraint on interpretation that we impose a charitable construction on others. We simply cannot but so proceed.

The second claim has to do with the nature, or the source, of the structure to be imposed in interpretation.

> *The Normatively Derived Structure (NDS)* view of charity in interpretation: The structure we must impose in interpretation is derived from normative principles, *qua normative* principles.

NDS and FMC comprise the central components of the view to be repudiated in the next chapter.

The NDS claim stands in need of further clarification at this point. What does it mean to claim that the constraints on interpretation derive from normative principles, not from descriptive generalizations? This much is clearly indicated: when we charitably impose a structure in interpretation, this is emphatically not a matter of seeking to find people reasoning in the sort of ways we expect of people. That would be to so interpret as to find the rationality we expect, and (presumably also) the irrationality that we expect. And that would be to impose a structure in light of descriptive generalizations.

The contrast between imposing a normatively derived structure and imposing a descriptively derived structure is crucial. Normative principles of reasoning express how people ought to reason. They often can be expressed using schematic or formal rules representing desirable transformations in a store of beliefs.[7] Sometimes people are disposed to reason in the ways represented by a given rule formulating some normative principle. Such dispositions can obtain either by virtue of rudimentary human reasoning capacities or by virtue of special training. In either case, when people are so disposed, one can use the rule formulating the relevant normative principle within a descriptive generalization. This does not make the resulting descriptive generalization normative. The distinction is elementary. It is the distinction between a normative principle to the effect that one ought to reason in such-and-such a way, and the corresponding descriptive generalization that people (or these people) tend to reason in such-and-such a way. Now we can readily envision interpreting so as to impose a structure derived from such descriptive generalizations; in fact, I will soon argue that this understanding would provide the best codification of our interpretive practice. Insofar as descriptive generalizations often borrow and "transmute" normative generalizations into descriptive principles, such an interpretive approach will, on the face of it, resemble interpretation as understood in terms of FMC and NDS. However, on the NDS view of the principle of charity, this fundamental aspect of the methodology of interpretation draws directly on principles of the normative sort, not on descriptive generalizations at all. That is, on the NDS view, we are methodologically obligated to (so far as possible) find people reasoning according to normative principles, without regard to whether or not we have generally found people to reason in this way.[8] We are supposedly to draw on normative principles without regard to whether any particular normative principle can be put to work within descriptive principles of an empirically adequate psychology.

Of course, the twin claims (FMC and NDS) are intimately related, and make a conceptually nice package. Any view of the constraints on interpretation that directs us to impose patterns of reasoning that are in keeping with descriptive expectations is unlikely to see charitable interpretation as a *fundamental methodological* constraint. Also, the insistence that we impose a pattern drawing on normative principles, qua normative principles, must, it seems, rest on a fundamental methodological injunction. What else would lead to such a demand?[9]

Returning now to consider Davidson's view in particular, it is interesting to note that his holding the NDS view explains an otherwise curious aspect of one of his attempts to refine a rudimentary principle of charity.[10] He clearly recognizes that in any actual interpretation some residual error will be attributed to those interpreted. Thus, the issue arises: how do we decide where it is best (or the least undermining of interpretation) to attribute error, and where is it best to most avoid attributing error. It seems to me that in making the needed refinements in a rudimentary principle of charity, one would most naturally draw on descriptive information about human psychology. That is, one would quite naturally draw on information concerning the relative likelihood of mistakes. This turns out to be a matter of wide agreement; even Davidson eventually seems to concur on using empirical information to refine the principle of charity in this way. But, curiously, in several passages where he addresses the question of what agreement (including rationality) we most need to impose in interpretation, Davidson makes this a matter to be decided by clarifying and then imposing our own normative standards for how beliefs should be interrelated:

> It is impossible to simplify the considerations that are relevant, for everything we know or believe about the way evidence supports belief can be put to work in deciding where the theory [of meaning] can best allow error, and what errors are the least destructive of understanding. The methodology of interpretation is, in this respect, nothing but epistemology seen in the mirror of meaning (1984d, p. 169).

Or, again: "It is uncertain to what extent these principles can be made definite—it is the problem of rationalizing and codifying our epistemology" (1980e, p. 7). Thus, Davidson apparently would have us first determine what are the most and least important or central principles of rationality. Then we are to seek to avoid attributions of breeches of the most central principles, and to seek to minimize the seriousness of the irrationality attributed. (As we will see, not everything Davidson says can be understood as agreeing with this suggested basis for modifying a rudimentary principle of charity, but, the fact that the suggestion was even entertained at all reflects the hold that the NDS has on him and other writers.)

The twin suggestions that charity is a fundamental methodological constraint on interpretation (FMC) and that the structure thereby imposed in interpretation is informed by normative principles qua normative principles (NDS) have been recognized and approved by some commentators on Davidson's work. For example:

The norms or principles that guide interpretation are the norms of rationality. The thoughts that the interpreter attributes to the agent to explain her actions *must* rationalize them. They *must* make the action a reasonable one for the agent to have performed. Minds are, for the most part, rational because *we cannot but understand them as so* (Root 1986, pp. 227–38).

And when McDowell (1985, p. 389) urges us to follow Davidson in recognizing "the ideal status of the constitutive concept [of rationality]" in connection with "the concepts of the propositional attitudes" his formulation reflects the twin claims. The NDS view is particularly in evidence when he writes of accounts "in which things are made intelligible by being revealed to be, or to approximate to being, as they rationally ought to be," and contrasts this with accounts "in which one makes things intelligible by representing their coming into being as a particular instance of how things generally tend to happen" (McDowell 1985, p. 389). He goes on to criticize Loar's (1981) functionalist philosophy of mind for selectively employing normative structures.

The twin claims (FMC and NDS) together constitute what has come to be the most common understanding of the constraints on interpretation. This "Standard Conception" of charity in interpretation can be summarized:

The Standard Conception of charity in interpretation: we are bound by a fundamental methodological constraint to find people rational.

This view is held, with varying qualifications, by writers such as Føllesdal (1982), Rosenberg (1985b), Loar (1981), Hollis (1970a, 1970b, 1982), McDowell (1985), Root (1986), Roth (1985), to name a few.[11] At the very least, Habermas (1984, pp. 102–41) seems to hold to a closely related position. He argues that social scientific interpretation requires us to come to find and appreciate validity claims in the word and deed of those we study, and that this requires us to uncover one, or rather a combination, of three normative structures (formal commonalities) in the ways of those interpreted (for example, Habermas 1984, pp. 136–37).

The point of the following chapter is to rebut the Standard Conception by presenting and arguing for a superior codification of interpretive practice. Preparatory to doing this, I will need to say a good deal more about interpretive practice and some of the common refinements in principles of charity that have been advanced to accommodate such practice. Providing the needed information will be the task of the next section.

However, before moving on, I should note one simplification effected in my discussion in this section. I have sketched the codificational sort of argument for a principle of charity in interpretation by considering Davidson's influential version. In particular, I have concentrated on a variant of that argument that responds to the holism of interpretation resulting from the interdependence of meaning and belief. Such an argument leads us to think of charity as the imposition of a structure on the beliefs attributed in interpretation. However, it will be remembered that another facet of holism in interpretation also results from the interdependence of belief and desire. This provides a basis for conceiving of charity in interpretation as more than a matter of imposing a structure on beliefs. It must be understood as a matter of imposing a structure on beliefs, desires, and actions. The rationality that comes to be of interest in interpretation thus comes to include more than narrowly epistemic rationality. This complication does not, however, seem to add anything fundamental to the issue focused on here—the issue of the nature and status of structure imposed in interpretation. Many writers would see the structure—now incorporating more than epistemic rationality—in terms of FMC and NDS.

2.2: Common Refinements in the Principle of Charity

The principle of charity is advanced as an adequacy criterion for interpretation. However, as this proposed adequacy criterion has been developed to this point, it seems to lead to a result that even strong partisans find disconcerting: Since, as a matter of fact, no interpretive scheme ever makes people out to be fully rational believers of only true things, no interpretive scheme is ever really adequate. Consider, for example, the claim that we are bound by a methodological maxim to "maximize agreement," where this includes maximizing the rationality attributed to others. Taken at face value, this formulation suggests an untenable view of interpretation: either we will find ourselves attributing perfect rationality or we will be continually frustrated by apparent inadequacy and led to make endless refinements in our interpretive scheme. For, as should be clear, any one set of attributions of inconsistency and rationality can be dispensed with by making sufficiently special adjustments in the interpretive scheme that led to that attribution. Thus, if we really were methodologically bound to maximize the rationality attributed in interpretation, this *could* be pursued in the direction of eliminating attributions of irrationality altogether, provided we are willing to make adjustments without end. But, it is universally recognized that any such policy of eradicating attributions of error altogether is no part of good interpretive practice. In Quine's words: "Eventually, of course, the linguist drops his initial assumption that natives tell the truth. He does not go on forever modifying his growing theory of the native language so as to accommodate each succeeding affirmation as true . . ." (1970, p. 17). If we are to codify interpretive practice, then we will need to provide an account of what limits there are in applying the rudimentary principle described to this point.

One particularly obvious suggestion will doubtless be that the principle of charity is only one constraint on interpretation. Supposedly there are others. These further constraints might, in certain cases, compete with the principle of charity, limiting the lengths to which we ought to go in satisfying it. Davidson, for example, notes that, "No simple theory can put a speaker and interpreter in perfect agreement, and so a workable theory must from time to time assume error on the part of one or the other" (1984d, p. 169). This suggests that the theoretical virtue of simplicity can serve the moderating role.

However, further reflection should convince us that modifications in the rudimentary principle of charity itself are appropriate. Again, this is reflected in Davidson's discussions:

> Not all the evidence can be expected to point the same way. There will be differences from speaker to speaker, and from time to time for the same speaker, with respect to the circumstances under which a sentence is held true. The general policy, however, is to choose truth conditions that do as well as possible in making speakers hold sentences true when (according to the theory and the theory builder's view of the facts) those sentences are true. That is the general policy, to be modified in a host of obvious ways. Speakers can be allowed to differ more often and more radically with respect to some sentences than others, and there is no reason not to take into account the observed or inferred individual differences that may be thought to have caused anomalies (as seen by the theory) (1984c, p. 152).

This nicely reflects a point of general consensus: the basic principle of charity must be refined so as to provide for, and even to guide (as the need arises), attributions of error. After all, "once the theory begins to take shape it makes sense to accept intelligible error and to make allowance for the relative likelihood of various kinds of mistake" (Davidson 1984b, p. 136)[12] and interpretive schemes of about the same simplicity might yet differ on how well they do on the score of attributing "intelligible error" or error of sorts that are relatively likely.

Common modifications in the basic principle of charity fall into two interrelated classes. First, there are modifications that reflect the differences in an investigator's epistemic situation in earlier and later stages of interpretation. Second, the principle of charity comes to be weighted so as to be differently constraining when dealing with different types of errors.

2.2.1: Modifications Related to Stages of Interpretation

Suppose we have set for ourselves the daunting task of understanding the language and actions of a people that are, at present, completely foreign to us. Suppose also that we cannot rely on bilingual informants to initiate us into the source-language, and that we cannot rely on knowledge of languages closely related to the source-language for clues. This is the project of "radical translation" or "radical interpretation." The point of considering such an imposing task is to help us to appreciate constraints on interpretation that may be too easily taken for granted.

The principle of charity is at its most compelling when we consider how we might begin this task. We are faced with a range of coordinated activities. Verbal productions obviously play some role in the coordination. Supposedly, they communicate information and express concerns, and do other sorts of things familiar to us. We must find a way of breaking into the language and activities of those we seek to understand. The only plausible ways to begin may be aptly described as charitable.

To begin with, we must look for particularly accessible and yet somehow significant patterns in the verbal (and other) behavior of those we are attempting to understand. These are needed to provide us something of an entering wedge into the language and actions of those who we seek to understand. The patterns might be in their willingness to utter or assent to various sentences given their willingness to utter or assent to certain other sentences (patterns within the language, we might say), or in their willingness to utter or assent to sentences in varying circumstances (patterns between language and environment).[13] In either case, the patterns must be accessible enough that we could reasonably hope to recognize them without some incredible stroke of luck. And, they need to be "significant" in the sense that we have a fair idea of what to make of them when found. Patterns fitting the bill are, of course, associated with simple cases of logical reasoning and with what Quine has called "observation sentences." We would then do well to attempt, in the early going, to identify and give a partial interpretive treatment to the relevant bits of the source-language. Plausible treatments of the source-language in these cases are charitable.

Martin Hollis provides a nice discussion of these early interpretive contexts; his discussion reflects interpretive practice. According to Hollis, we must begin constructing the translation component of an interpretive scheme by focusing a fair amount of our attention on the relations between the world and a particular set of utterances: "utterances whose situations of use [the anthropologist] can specify" (1970a, p. 214). And more precisely, the anthropologist is to begin by dealing with those sentences to which assent depends on "simple perceptual situations" (1982, p. 74). Hollis does not provide a systematic characterization of the simplicity of perceptual situations. However, his discussion (p. 73) does suggest that in such situations we can identify some "external determinant" of belief. Presumably, then, part of what is characteristic of such situations is the presence of some salient stimulus. Further, Hollis suggests that in a simple perceptual situation, we can expect that our informant holds true beliefs (and should translate accordingly). At one point, he alludes to these expectations by writing of what it is "likely" that the informant believes. Putting these suggestions together, the following view emerges: we seek to find agreement on sentences uttered in situations where we have reason to believe that there are salient stimuli of an unproblematic sort that tend to induce correct everyday beliefs.

In the early going then, we focus on sentences whose situations of use are typically such simple perceptual situations. By specifying the perceptual situations where such sentences are used or assented to, the anthropologist provides the grounds for translations into target-language sentences similarly related to the world. For example, after noticing that source-language users utter or assent to some sentence, p, just when they are in a position to perceive that there is a cow in the corn field, the anthropologist has grounds for translating p as 'The cow is in the corn' or 'There is a cow in the corn.' (Of course, there is room for some variation here.)[14] The concern to provide for such rough translations, which is characteristic of the early stages of interpretation, is also reflected in Davidson's account of constructing a theory of meaning and Quine's discussion of the evidence for translation.

Obviously, this method of relating the utterances of the source-language users to the world leads us to charitably find general agreement between the subject and the anthropologist with respect to many perceptual judgments.

There is, of course, much more to the early stages of constructing a translation scheme than providing for the translation of observation sentences. An anthropologist will also concentrate on isolating telling, simple, relations among utterances of source-language speakers. According to Hollis (1970b, pp. 231–33), the relations that must be discerned include some that show that the natives share and honor our notion of deductive validity and our broader notion of "having a good reason for a belief." In this respect, one important task facing the translator is the identification of the source-language signs for truth-functions, for these are associated with simple patterns that are particularly accessible in the early going. As Hollis, following Quine, argues, this is done by matching certain source-language particles and associated patterns of assent and dissent (with respect to sentences featuring these particles) with target-language truth-functions and the truth-conditions for sentences featuring them. To take a simple example, we identify a particle as negation just in case source-language speakers (typically) will assent to the result of combining it with a sentence they would dissent from, and dissent from the combination of it with a sentence they would assent to. Proceeding in this way, basic logical truths and notions (such as the notions of contradiction and validity, and basic truths such as the law of noncontradiction) will be found shared by all language users. Proceeding in this way, speakers of the source-language must then be found to reason in truth-functionally valid ways most of the time. If they do not appear to do so when we use our translation scheme, this is evidence that the native constructions treated there as truth-functions are not appropriately so treated.

Truth-functions are presumably just the simplest and most tractable of logical particles. While they thus become an important focus in the early stages of translation, other logical particles will also come in for attention there, at least to the extent that they give rise to easily detectible simple patterns of usage in the source-language.

Of course, the proper role of charity in translation is not exhausted by the generally charitable treatment of logical vocabulary and utterances in simple perceptual situations. However, Hollis argues that the application of the principle of charity to these matters provides a uniquely important set of rough equivalences that serves as a necessary "bridgehead" upon which all subsequent development of a translation scheme (and associated interpretive scheme) depends. This notion of a "bridgehead" is useful. Whatever its exact extension, a bridgehead for translation is comprised of the set of utterances in the source-language whose translations are supposedly constrained by the principle of charity in the following strong sense: the charitable translation of these sentences is largely unchecked by competing considerations, and serves as a basis for further work, in which there is the strong presumption that the bulk of the initial interpretations are correct. The considerations related above are intended by Hollis to show not just that there is such a bridgehead to be established early on, but also that it includes utterances having to do with a particular sort of matter: "The set consists of what a rational man cannot fail to believe in simple perceptual situations, organized by rules of coherent judgments, which a rational man cannot fail to subscribe to" (Hollis 1982, p. 74).[15] It is possible to hold that there is such a bridgehead while being more flexible than Hollis regarding its contents (Lukes 1982, Stich 1990, Henderson 1990a).

It is an integral part of the notion of a "bridgehead" that the translations that are so strongly constrained by the principle of charity serve as an anchor in the subsequent development of a translation scheme: "The force of calling a set of utterances a bridgehead is that it serves to define standard meanings of native terms and so to make it possible to understand utterances used in more ambiguous situations" (Hollis 1970a, p. 215). Without this bridgehead, there is no way into the "maze" that is the native's language (Hollis 1970b, p. 222). For Hollis to call the set of utterances for which the rudimentary translation scheme is constructed a bridgehead, and the way into the maze, is to emphasize the extent to which the strong charitable assumptions he describes deal with the earliest stages of constructing a translation scheme. This association of strong constraint from the principle of charity with the early stages of interpretation is a point worth developing and refining further.

The picture of practice that one finds suggested by talk of a bridgehead has the virtue of reflecting practice: first, a rudimentary translation scheme is constructed that is adequate to much "everyday usage." An important component of everyday usage will be the sorts of utterances that Hollis includes in his bridgehead. At this stage of inquiry the principle of charity is, in practice and in principle, particularly compelling. Here we get translations for source-language constructions as, for example, 'bird', 'macaw', 'red', 'sun', 'brother', truth-functions and the quantifiers. Such a translation scheme will have a wide, if tentative, application. Thus, in these earlier stages of translation we are to charitably provide a rudimentary translation scheme from which subsequent work will proceed. I will refer to such a translation scheme as a "first-approximation translation scheme"; and I refer to the results of the application of such a scheme as a "first-approximation translation."

As a first-approximation translation scheme is used in the investigation of the society studied, we may be led to attribute apparently awkward sets of beliefs or even apparent inconsistencies to the source-language speakers. We might, for example find ourselves attributing to them beliefs expressed using indicative sentences such as 'Twins are birds' (Evans-Pritchard 1956), or 'We are red macaws' (Crocker 1977). These expressions, taken literally, seem too extravagantly false to credit—we wonder what is really being said. Or we might find ourselves attributing to them some surprisingly false beliefs about relatively accessible empirical matters such as the connection between human intercourse and human pregnancy (Roth 1903). Or, we might find them apparently claiming that witchcraft is hereditary, implying that some clans ought to be comprised of mostly witches, while denying what is implied (Evans-Pritchard 1937). When the first-approximation translation scheme leads to such attributions, alternative suggestions for modifying, or refining, the scheme are often advanced. I will refer to the results of such fiddling to "fine tune" a first-approximation translation scheme as a "refined translation scheme." I will later provide a more sophisticated characterization of first-approximation and refined translation schemes. For now, however, the important point is that first-approximation schemes are arrived at by charitably providing for a range of everyday utterances in the early stages of translation and interpretation. With respect to any problematic case in interpretation or translation, there will be a first-approximation scheme that at least does this (and may have been refined somewhat itself).

Now, almost all writers on these matters recognize that the

principle of charity is not as constraining in judgments regarding the merits of alternative refined translation schemes as it was in the construction of the relevant first-approximation scheme. In other words, a common refinement on the rudimentary principle of charity is the recognition that the principle is a less powerful constraint on the later stages of translation than it is in the earlier stages. For example, the following discussion by Quine (1970, p. 17) suggests that (at least to some extent) charitable constraints give way to concerns for explanation in later interpretive contexts:

> Eventually, of course, the linguist drops his initial assumption that natives tell the truth. He does not go on forever modifying his growing theory of the native language so as to accommodate each succeeding affirmation as true . . .
>
> How do we decide whether to change our theory of a man's language or to impute falsity to his statements? . . . What we ordinarily base such a decision on is a swift and unpretentious speculation in the psychology of learning. . . .
>
> The same, surely, is true of the linguist. Whether he should change his mind about the native language in the face of unexpected native testimony on some topic, or should rather just count the testimony factually false, is a question to be settled by weighing of probabilities regarding native psychology.

The suggestion then is that the early stages of translation or interpretation may be strongly constrained by a principle of charity, but this is a somewhat *preparatory* period in which we lay the basis for a less charitably constrained investigation of native beliefs and practices, some of which we might, without stigma, judge seriously mistaken or in error. This is not unlike Habermas's claim that interpretive understanding must allow us to understand the validity claims of those who we interpret, and thus, ultimately, to criticize, as well as learn from, them (1984, pp. 102–41).

A similar suggestion is found in Davidson's (1984e, p. 196) summary of the place of charitable constraints on the course of interpretation:

> We get a first approximation to a finished theory by assigning to sentences of a speaker conditions of truth that actually obtain (in our opinion) just when the speaker holds those sentences true. The guiding policy is to do this as far as possible, subject to considerations of simplicity, hunches about the effects of social con-

ditioning, and of course our common-sense, or scientific, knowledge of explicable error.

The method is not designed to eliminate agreement, nor can it; its purpose is to make meaningful disagreement possible, and this depends entirely on a foundation—some foundation—in agreement.

Here again the suggestion is that charity in interpretation is most important in the early going, where we will generate a foundation of agreement serving as the basis for further inquiry. (This early-achieved foundation of agreement is well characterized as a first-approximation. However, if we have managed to attribute error, so far as possible, subject to scientific knowledge of explicable error, we would seem to have progressed beyond the early stages of interpretation, to a more advanced stage of interpretation. Further, if the scientific theory we have employed is adequate, we would seem to have more than a "first-approximation," we have a relatively polished, finished, product.)

For now, we need only note that a common refinement on a basic principle of charity is to recognize that it should be less constraining in the later stages of translation or interpretation. In chapter 3, I will argue that this variable strength of the principle of charity across stages of interpretation is itself fully accounted for by viewing the principle of charity as a derivative constraint (in contradiction to the FMC view). Before making this case, I need to discuss a second family of common refinements on the basic principle of charity in interpretation.

2.2.2: Modifications Related to Types of Error

As Davidson observes, "No simple theory can put a speaker and interpreter in perfect agreement, and so a workable theory must from time to time assume error on the part of one or the other" (1984d, p. 169). Deciding where to attribute error to those we study, and where to avoid it, thus becomes a significant problem. For two reasons, this problem is not adequately dealt with simply by noting the differences between early and later stages of interpretation.

First, the problem can be recognized as significant in various stages of interpretation. A full appreciation of the form the problem takes in different stages of interpretation cannot be had until we have progressed further in our examination of the principles of charity and explicability. (The more sophisticated treatment is found in section 3.3.2.) For now, we will have to focus on the need for a weighting of attributions of error in the earlier, more charitable, stages. While the principle of charity may not be particularly constraining in the later stages of interpretation, acceptable work in those stages depends on our being able to employ a workable first-approximation interpretive scheme to acquire tentative information regarding the society studied. The first-approximation scheme is to provide us with a rough understanding from which to work. Now, because "some disagreements are more destructive of understanding than others, and a sophisticated theory must naturally take this into account" (Davidson 1984d, p. 169), the best basis from which to work will be one that attributes errors that are, on the whole, not particularly destructive of understanding. This can be viewed as a matter of weighting the principle of charity according to types of errors. We might then see the earlier stages of interpretation to be a matter of minimizing the attribution-of-error costs, judged in terms of a weighted sum of attributions of error.

Second, even the distinction between the earlier and later stages of interpretation implicitly makes some use of this weighting of the principle of charity. It will be remembered that in the earliest stages one would seek to find and deal with behavioral patterns which are accessible enough that we could reasonably hope to recognize them without some incredible stroke of luck, and yet, "significant" in the sense that we have a fair idea of what to make of them when found. Patterns fitting the bill were associated with simple cases of logical reasoning and with what Quine calls "observation sentences." But, we know what to do with these cases in large measure because they are cases where the principle of charity is especially compelling. Thus, in the early stages of translation, charity seems particularly compelling, in part because of the sorts of cases we properly focus on there.

I believe that there is wide agreement on the conclusion that we need to weight the principle of charity to reflect the varying destructiveness of attributions of different types of error. The crucial issue then becomes one of how to so weight the principle. What is to inform our weighting?

Quine provides a particularly clear formulation of what seems to be the common and, I think, correct approach here: the weighting of the principle of charity is to be informed by psychological theory regarding the relative likelihood of various types of error. The destructiveness of disagreements is to be proportionate to the relative improbability of the errors attributed. To appreciate how this approach emerges in Quine's influential writings, it will help to return once more to the now familiar matter of the charitable treatment of certain sorts of sentences in the earliest stages of interpretation.

According to Quine, in the earliest stages we will look to patterns of assent and dissent to settle the rough translation for "observation sentences" and simple logical particles (particularly the truth-functions). Quine strongly weights the principle of charity when dealing with observation sentences by insisting that we pair observation sentences across the two languages according to sameness of "stimulus meaning," according to the ranges of stimuli which will provoke assent to and dissent from the sentences. Insofar as we are typically correct in our use of observation sentences, the speakers of the source-language must be found to be correct in their use of observation sentences. Quine also strongly weights the principle of charity in dealing with logical truths and inferences. This is clearest when he discusses truth-functions. We are to find patterns of assent and dissent in the source-language that mirror (subject to certain gaps) the semantics for truth-functions (Quine 1974, pp. 75–78). In this way we "build our logic into our manual of translation" (Quine 1986, p. 82).

These foci of strongly charitable interpretation are already familiar from my discussion of Hollis's account of the bridgehead of translation, which itself draws on Quine's work. However, Quine does not simply recommend or stipulate such a weighting of the principle of charity. Rather, he articulates a general account of what makes such a weighting compelling. He explains that this strongly charitable treatment of observation sentences and basic logic is prescribed by the implicit maxim: 'Save the obvious':

> Now this canon—'Save the obvious'—is sufficient to settle, in point of truth-value anyway, our translations of *some* of the sentences in just about every little branch of discourse: for some of them are pretty obvious outright (like '1 + 1 = 2') or obvious in particular circumstances (like 'It is raining') (Quine 1986, p. 82).

It is significant that Quine here uses 'obvious' in a behavioral sense: a sentence is obvious to a community just in case nearly everyone in the community will assent to it. Thus, Quine states in behavioral terms the principled basis for heavily weighting the principle of charity in these central cases. (This indicates that he, who is suspicious of what cannot be behaviorally grounded, conceives of this weighting as resting on substantive, empirical, matters.)

So stated, the principle of "saving the obvious" is amenable to empirical justification. Why should we equate sentences to which almost everyone in one community assents under certain circumstances with sentences to which almost everyone in another community assents under similar circumstances? Why should we construct translation schemes so that sentences commanding almost universal assent regardless of the circumstances in one community are equated with sentences commanding almost universal assent regardless of the circumstances in the other speech community? Quine remarks, "The common sense behind the maxim [that assertions startlingly false on the face of them are likely to turn on hidden differences of language] is that one's interlocutor's silliness beyond a certain point, is less *likely* than bad translation" (1960, p. 59). What is likely is, of course, an empirical matter. Thus, at least this aspect of the weighting is indicated by empirical psychology; as a general rule, subject to exceptions in special cases, significant error in simple logical reasoning and in assent to observation sentences is unlikely, and attributions of what is unlikely are implausible and to be avoided. (In chapters 3 and 4, we will need to return to the issue of how this can be an empirical matter.)

Quine's formulation and justification of this aspect of the weighting in behavioral terms indicates that he does not understand it as a matter settled by stipulation. Quine certainly recognizes that some principles informing the construction of translation schemes are not founded in "an objective trend in linguistic behavior" (1970, p. 14–15). Such principles may make for massive gains in the convenience of the resulting manual, but he recognizes that the results concern matters on which there is nothing to be right and wrong about (Quine 1960, pp. 68–79). Still, to the extent that a weighted principle can be stated and justified in behavioral terms, it is not, for Quine, to be understood as such a merely methodological matter.

Quine's concern for what is likely in connection with weighting the principle of charity should not be dismissed as a slip of the pen. It is a consistent concern. It carries over from his discussions of the cases where we must be strongly charitable in the early going to his discussions of how to proceed in the later stages. Quine would look to empirical psychology when deciding on the what error is attributable in the later stages of translation. When moving beyond simple rough equivalences gotten in the very earliest stages of translation, Quine counsels us to adhere to a more weakly and flexibly charitable approach:

[A]s soon as we consider method, we have to recognize that the linguist has no access to native meanings apart from what he can
glean from the observed circumstances of utterances. The analytical hypotheses that he contrives are subject to no further check,
except that native utterances not conveniently linked to observable
circumstances should still turn out on the whole to be plausible
messages (1970, pp. 14–15).

While such constraints are recognizable as among those Quine elsewhere (1960, p. 69) discusses as a matter of charity in translation,
it is important to notice that Quine says here that we are to find
source-language utterances to express on the whole *"plausible* messages"; he does not say "true messages." His discussion makes it
clear that plausibility is a matter of "plausibility-for-the-subjects,"
not a matter of "plausibility-for-us." This is to appeal to the distinction between their predicament and ours, and not, as some writers have done, to a distinction between their standards of rationality
and ours. Plausibility-for-the-subject is a psychological matter:
given our best psychological theories, and what the subjects apparently have to go on, what could they be expected to believe or say.

The psychological nature of the information informing the
weighting of charity by plausibility is most clearly reflected in
Quine's discussion of how we provide for the translation of religious utterances in the later stages of translation:

If we master religious vocabulary sufficiently to join substantive
issue with religious speakers, we do so not just by taking their statements as true, but by reconstructing in some measure the psychology of their belief. There need be nothing unbehavioristic about
their psychology or our reconstruction of it, and therefore nothing
unbehavioristic about our approach to meaning (1970, p. 18).

Quine's insistence that behavioral psychology informs choices in
these contexts may be taken to reflect his insistence that the
strength of charitable assumptions is to be informed by substantive
empirical psychology.

I believe that remarks such as those just canvassed actually
indicate that Quine ultimately adopts a view of the principle of
charity in translation that repudiates both FMC and NDS; for they
indicate not just that the principle of charity is to be weighted
according to the results empirical psychology, but that the motivation for that principle itself rests on such grounds (Henderson
1990a). Thus Quine can say:

> The translator will depend early and late on psychological conjectures as to what the native is likely to believe. This policy already governed his translation of observation sentences. It will continue to operate beyond the observational level, deterring him from translating the native assertion into too glaring a falsehood. ... Practical psychology is what sustains our translator all along the way (1987, p. 7).

I will soon argue that the suggested understanding of the principle of charity provides a superior codification of the constraints on translation and interpretation. For purposes of this section, however, we must concentrate on the more limited claim evinced in Quine's writings: the claim that the principle of charity is to be weighted according to the results of empirical psychology.

Quine is certainly not alone in suggesting such empirical refinements on the principle of charity. The point is generally appreciated. Even Davidson sometimes describes the construction of a theory of meaning as subject to such an empirically informed constraint:

> The guiding policy is to do this as far as possible, subject to considerations of simplicity, hunches about the effects of social conditioning, and of course our common sense, or scientific, knowledge of explicable error (1984e, p. 196).

Put simply, the refinements in the basic principle of charity are needed because "it makes sense to accept intelligible error and to make allowance for the relative likelihood of various kinds of mistakes" (Davidson 1984b, p. 136), and likelihood is an empirical matter.[16]

Similarly, David Lewis (1974, p. 336) observes:

> A crude version of the Principle of Charity might just require that, so far as other constraints allow it, the beliefs and desires ascribed to [our subjects] by [our interpretive scheme] should be the same as our beliefs and desires [which is to find them correct, by our lights]. ... But it would be more charitable to make allowances for the likelihood that [our subjects'] circumstances—his life history of evidence and training, recounted in physical terms from our data base P—may have led him understandably into error.

And this point is echoed by a range of other writers. Steven Lukes (1982), for example, provides a particularly interesting development on this line of thought. Lukes is concerned with refining Hollis's account of a "bridgehead" for interpretation. He acknowledges that there is a set of utterances the interpretations for which are particularly strongly constrained by the principle of charity and which must be dealt with early in the construction of an interpretive scheme. However, while Hollis believes that this bridgehead can be specified a priori, Lukes insists that only the fact that there must be some common core of agreement is a priori; Lukes argues that the contents of the bridgehead are an empirical matter. Because the issue of the contents of the bridgehead reduces in good measure to the issue of how the principle of charity is to be weighted, Lukes's claim amounts to the claim that the proper weighting of the principle of charity is an empirical matter.

As I understand Lukes's account, we begin with (perhaps theoretically informed) "assumptions" regarding what sorts of agreement we are to find in translation. These assumptions are, in effect, tested for fruitfulness: if an assumption leads to explanatory accounts (as translation and interpretive schemes using it are developed and applied), then the assumption is supported. If following an assumption fails to lead us to explanatory accounts, then the assumption will and should be dropped. Thus:

> What we assume to be in the common core will be subject to endless correction by the consequences of making such assumptions: evidence for any given assumption comes from whether the translations that result make better sense of what they say and do than translations flowing from alternative assumptions (Lukes 1982, p. 273).

Success as an invariant component of translations associated with explanatory accounts thus provides an empirical basis for including an assumption of agreement on a certain sort of sentence in the bridgehead. Importantly, Lukes also insists that what "makes better sense" of what is observed is not to be settled a priori either. He envisions a competition between (purportedly) explanatory theories, and a corresponding development in what is taken to be explanatory. On the whole, this account has what I take to be the proper concern for empirical results informing interpretation. In the next chapter I take my cue from this sort of approach to the weighting of the principle of charity, and develop Quine's ill-appreciated suggestion that charity in interpretation is from the first informed by empirical psychology.

The central task of this chapter has been twofold. First, I have sought to explain how a codificational line of thought has led many writers to view the principle of charity as a fundamental methodological response to the holistic nature of interpretive tasks. Interpreters are thought to be bound by a *fundamental methodological constraint* to find peoples' beliefs, desires, and actions to be interrelated in ways that are *normatively appropriate*, which is to say, *rational*. I have explained what it is to see a principle as a fundamental methodological constraint, and what it is to say that such a constraint involves imposing a normatively derived structure. And I have described how such a principle of charity is taken to meet our methodological need in the only plausible manner. Although little real attention is devoted to this point, most writers believe that this plausible procedure obviously reflects interpretive practice. I will soon show that these last suppositions harbor what is ultimately the real weakness of the codificational arguments for a fundamental principle of charity. For, I will next argue that there is another principle that can subsume the principle of charity as a derivative rule of thumb where charity is compelling, and that does more justice to the full range of interpretive practice and concerns. Second, I have described two common modifications proposed in a rudimentary principle of charity. I believe that both modifications are important and well motivated. I have shown how such modification is informed by empirical information regarding human psychology. The nature of such modification serves to buttress the claims made in the next chapter for the superiority of my alternative codification of the constraints on interpretation. The account that I propose will allow us to understand the common modifications in the principle of charity as motivated by the deeper reason for the principle of charity itself, and not as secondary elaborations on a methodological constraint to which they are foreign.

3

A Better Codification of the Constraints on Interpretation

3.1: The Primacy of the Principle of Explicability: The Central Argument

In the preceding chapter, I described how the principle of charity is most constraining in the early stages of interpretation, and how one there focuses on the sort of cases where the principle of charity is relatively heavily weighted in view of the empirical likelihood of error. The constraint of the principle of charity then grades off as one moves into the later stages of interpretation, where debates over refinements in an interpretive scheme center on the explicability of what is attributed to the people in question. These points strongly suggest that, where the principle of charity is significantly constraining in interpretation, namely in the earlier going, it plays a largely preparatory role. This suggestion is reflected in Davidson's (1984e, pp. 196–97) remark: "The method is not designed to eliminate disagreement, nor can it; its purpose is to make meaningful disagreement possible, and this depends entirely on a foundation—*some* foundation—in agreement." The role of the principle of charity is to prepare the ground for our engaging in the central social scientific endeavor: studying and explaining similarities and variations in beliefs and practices. To this end, the principle of charity allows us to develop provisional interpretive schemes that can serve as the basis for further inquiry, although not necessarily further charitable work. To appreciate the preparatory role of the principle of charity, this provisional role of what I have called first-approximation interpretive schemes must be carefully attended to. Once we have examined these matters, we will be in a position to see how the principle of explicability provides a fundamental constraint on interpretation, whereas the principle of charity is a derivative or subservient matter. So, let us now examine further the distinction between first-approximation and refined interpretive schemes.

At any stage in the interpretive endeavor, we will find ourselves attributing to others some more or less extreme errors. Obviously, then, first approximation schemes are not (and, in practice, could not be) arrived at by invariably satisfying the principle of charity. They are arrived at by generally satisfying our weighted principle of charity. In particular, they are *schemes that have been developed, according to a weighted principle of charity, to a point where attributions of particular errors can be taken seriously.* At some point, our partial success in the charitable tasks described in the previous chapter will result in an interpretive scheme that provides for a (more or less) charitable interpretation of a wide range of utterances (and actions). Crucially, *it is only against the background of such schemes that attributions of egregious error or obvious inconsistency can be troubling, or warrant further investigation.* There are two important reasons for this: (1) *only by using such a scheme can the identification of putative error be made sufficiently precise and well-grounded to warrant investigation,* and (2) *well-grounded information needed for the investigation of such attributions of error for explicability is accessible only through the use of such a scheme.* The preparatory role of the principle of charity and the provisional nature of first-approximation interpretive schemes are understood only when these two points are appreciated.

Attributions of error can raise questions about the adequacy of the interpretive scheme on which they are based, but these are questions that can be answered without ultimately undermining in any degree our confidence in the interpretive scheme. Such attributions can raise questions about the sponsoring interpretive scheme because they can be what I will call *initially anomalous.* Certain sorts of beliefs or actions may be initially surprising in that they seem *generally at odds with our best theories,* although *upon further examination* it *may* turn out that they are *explicable under the circumstances.* Such *initially anomalous* beliefs (or actions) call for further investigation in order to determine whether they are ultimately explicable or not. Attributions of *surprising* error comprise one common type of anomaly, and particularly egregious and seemingly obvious errors are not generally expected. Attributions of surprising correct beliefs comprise another set of anomalies. Thus, attributions of correct beliefs regarding parts of atomic physics to a people without the seemingly requisite technological base would be anomalous. The question faced in the later stages of interpretation is whether initial anomalies will, upon investigation, turn out to be recalcitrant anomalies or turn out to be explicable. Recalcitrant anomalies, of course, are what induce modifications in first-approximation interpretive schemes.

Strictly speaking, *it is with respect to a particular attribution of initially anomalous beliefs (or actions) that interpretive schemes become first-approximation schemes.* To designate an interpretive scheme a "first-approximation" does not indicate that it will subsequently be modified in the face of attributions of surprising error or other anomaly. It indicates that the interpretive scheme provides the context within which such anomalous belief or action can be examined.

There does not seem to be any precise way to specify how much or just where agreement must be provided under interpretation before an interpretive scheme can serve as a first-approximation. This is understandable. For the needed basis should vary relative to the attributed beliefs (or actions) to be explained and the sorts of information necessary to provide an explanatory account of them (or to determine that they are not ultimately explicable). Further, it would be misleading to suggest that only agreement can serve as the basis for further investigation. Rather, what is needed is a basis in (at least now) non-anomalous attributions.

Still, it is clear that first-approximation interpretive schemes typically must be sufficiently developed to provide for the generally charitable interpretation of a wide range of native utterances and actions. This is because the attributions of error that prompt significant further investigation typically involve us in the holistic aspects of interpretation. Consider, for example, the case of apparently obviously false beliefs. Most interesting cases will involve the translation of source-language utterances beyond observation sentences and truth-functions. As we have seen, this is a holistic task: the results must lead us to find plausible messages and must agree with the generally charitable treatment of the behavioral evidence (as in the pairing of observation sentences by stimulus meaning and the identification of truth-functions by patterns of assent and dissent). Thus, confidence that a translation scheme provides for the translation of sentences "not conveniently linked to observable circumstances" turns upon general success in construing the source-language speakers as expressing "plausible messages." Without such confidence in the translation scheme and associated interpretive scheme, when the putative error involves such sentences and associated actions, the investigator will justifiably decide that there is not 'probable cause' to believe that egregious error has been committed, and will not embark on further investigation. This is the respect in which a generally charitable first-approximation interpretive scheme is needed as a provisional basis allowing us to take seriously attributions of even surprising error (and initially anomalous beliefs and actions generally).

The importance of having a well-founded first-approximation scheme is not simply that it provides us a reason for taking seriously, and investigating, putative error. For, typically, only by using the first-approximation interpretive scheme can we acquire much of the evidence in terms of which the ensuing investigation will proceed. This essential role of first-approximation interpretive schemes is nicely illustrated in what has become a classic debate over an attribution of surprising error: anthropologists Melford Spiro and Edmund Leach's quarrel over a particular attribution of ignorance regarding the simple biological antecedents of human pregnancy.

Natives in the Tully River area of Australia were originally reported to be ignorant in these matters (Roth 1903). They were said to hold that there were four antecedents to human pregnancy. However, they apparently did not so much as mention copulation in this connection. Instead, they spoke of things like women catching bullfrogs and standing close to certain roasting fish. Leach (1961, p. 376) argues that the relevant source-language utterances are best treated as symbolic utterances expressing the importance of social as opposed to biological relations:

> The modern interpretation of the ritual described would be that in this society the relationship between the woman's child and the clansmen of the woman's husband stems from the public recognition of the bonds of marriage, rather than from the facts of cohabitation, which is a very normal state of affairs.

Spiro (1966) defends the attribution of ignorance. The pivotal issue quickly comes to be that of the explicability of the natives under the respective accounts.

Leach (1969, p. 93) objects to this attribution of ignorance, saying: "I find it highly improbable on common-sense grounds that genuine 'ignorance' of the basic facts of physiological paternity should anywhere be a cultural fact." In support of this appraisal, Leach notes that humans display an almost obsessive interest in sex, that humans generally evidence a high collective problem-solving intelligence, that the Tully River natives evince this general capacity in

other matters, that they interact with peoples who are not ignorant of physiological paternity, and that they also have knowledge
of the antecedent of pregnancy in animals. And, so, Leach is led to
object to the attribution of *inexplicable* ignorance, not simply to
the attribution of ignorance.

Spiro recognizes the force of this objection. His response is
to defend his position by attempting to explain what Leach finds puzzling, and he offers two possible explanations in an attempt to show
that his attribution of ignorance is "consistent with what we know
about human society and personality" (1968, pp. 253–58).

For our purposes here, it is most important to notice that
such a debate concerning whether to modify the interpretive
scheme, and concerning the merits of various refined interpretive
schemes, turns on information available only by relying on the
first-approximation interpretive scheme at points. By relying on
many of the same sources, Spiro and Leach in effect rely on much
the same first-approximation interpretive scheme for information
bearing on the explicability of the apparent error. Only by relying
on such a scheme is it possible to have reasonably settled, as data
for any account, such facts as that the Tully River natives literally say that hunting bullfrogs is one possible antecedent to human
pregnancy, or that the natives also attribute pregnancy in animals
to copulation, or that the natives cite these differences as indications
of the special status of human beings, or that there are groups with
whom they interact whose members cite copulation as the cause
of human pregnancy. Thus, not only the puzzling apparent beliefs,
but also much of the data from which an explanatory account for the
puzzle is to be constructed, come by way of a commonly accepted
first-approximation interpretive scheme. In short, refined interpretation depends on such a basis.

Thus, we see how charity in interpretation is preparatory.
Given a first-approximation interpretive scheme that leads to attributions of apparently irrational belief (or action) and provides
information for explaining them (if they are in context something
that can be explained), the investigator no longer requires the
principle of charity. In these later stages of constructing the interpretive scheme—in deciding on a refined interpretive scheme—
construing our subjects as correct is beside the point. With access
to generally correct information regarding the beliefs of source-
language speakers, the time has come to get on with the central
social-scientific business: explanation. Accordingly, the constraints
of the principle of charity grade off and eventually dissipate entirely

in the later stages of interpretation. Taking our cue from the way issues are framed in the Spiro-Leach controversy (and many other cases), we recognize that the principle of explicability—so translate as to maximize the explicability of beliefs and actions attributed to the speakers of the source-language—guides the investigator in the later going. This primary concern for explanation is justifiable, while a continued concern for charity in interpretation as a constraint on interpretation that would rule out, or undermine, otherwise explanatory accounts is unjustified. To continue to pursue charitable interpretation in the later stages of interpretation would be to forget the preparatory role of charity in developing first-approximation schemes as provisional bases from which to construct refined interpretive schemes. When engaged in the later task, the concern is with explanation.

To say that the principle of charity is preparatory to the business of the later stages of interpretation is already to view it as ultimately subserviant to concerns for explanation. But, this point can be made even more forcefully, for we are now in a position to subsume the principle of charity under the principle of explicability. Of course, interpreting charitably, understood as an unqualified matter of maximizing agreement, is not the same as interpreting so as to construe our subjects as explicable. But I have no desire to subsume such simple (and simpleminded) charity under the principle of explicability. For, it is not in this form that we find charitable constraints operative in the construction of first-approximation interpretive schemes. Descriptively and normatively, a weighted principle of charity such as described earlier is what is followed there. I subsume only the weighted principle of charity, employed in the preparatory ways just discussed, under the principle of explicability.

The following results are central to the subsumption: if the empirical knowledge (regarding the likelihood of sorts of errors) on which the weighting of attributions of error (and thus the first-approximation scheme) is based is sufficient to support explanations, then the errors attributed to our subjects will often be explicable in terms of that knowledge. For, then, the interpretive scheme that is constructed will lead us to attribute error primarily where it is expected according to an explanatory theory. The actual explanation of attributed error may need to wait on the acquisition of further information, regarding particular antecedent conditions. But, the errors attributed to subjects will primarily be of sorts that we can explain in terms of the theories used in weighting attributions of error.

If, however, the empirical basis for weighting attributions of error is of a less developed sort that supports at best rough and very sketchy explanations, but is nevertheless generally correct, then the errors attributed to those we interpret and study will often be more satisfactorily explicable in terms of some successor theory. In this kind of case, by applying such a weighted principle of charity, if we do not so interpret that we attribute (satisfactorily) explicable beliefs (and actions) to our subjects, we at least so interpret that the attributed beliefs (and actions) will relatively often prove satisfactorily explicable on further investigation and theory development.

It may be that, in addition to being too ill-developed to be satisfactorily explanatory, our best present theories are no more likely correct than mistaken, but only more likely correct than any alternative theories we can presently formulate. Still, in following such theories in weighting the principle of charity, we are maximizing our chances of using a theory that is "correct so far as it goes," and, indirectly then, of attributing ultimately explicable beliefs to the speakers of the source-language.

Generally, then, the principle of charity weighted according to our best information regarding the likelihood of various sorts of errors leads us to construct interpretive schemes that construe our subjects in ways that are most likely to prove explicable. We are maximizing our chances of finding them explicably right and explicably wrong. This, it seems, is just what the principle of explicability demands in each of the cases surveyed just now.

Notice that the beliefs and actions attributed to those interpreted using a first-approximation interpretive scheme complying with the weighted principle of charity may be only *prospectively* explicable. This may happen for either of two different reasons. One has to do with limitations in our best present theories, the other with limitations in the information available to the investigator at a given point in the investigation.

First, certain attributed beliefs may be only prospectively explicable because our best theory of such beliefs is too ill-developed to lead us to satisfactory explanations, although we believe it to be correct as far as it goes, or believe it to be more likely correct than any other presently constructible alternative theory. To seek to attribute explicable errors, and to settle for attributing errors that are only prospectively explicable due to the limits of our present theories, is to work within our best present theories. As noted above, in following such theories, we are maximizing our chances (given our present resources) of attributing ultimately explicable beliefs to those who we are studying. Translating so as to attribute such prospectively explicable beliefs is appropriate in all stages of constructing an interpretive scheme.

Consider the following example of a prospectively explicable error. We may have noted that, instead of multiplying probabilities, people seemingly tend to average probabilities, unless trained to do otherwise. This observation itself constitutes an ill-developed theory, but, by itself, it hardly gives rise to particularly satisfying explanations. Still, if it is the best information that we have, we do well to use it in weighting the principle of charity. Using the resulting principle, an interpretive scheme might be constructed that would readily attribute such inductive errors to some group. Suppose then that we are led by this scheme to attribute the following error to our informants: an individual judged very likely to be a Republican but rather unlikely to be a lawyer is judged moderately likely to be a Republican lawyer. Were the rough generalization all we had, then we would only prospectively have a satisfactory explanation for the attributed inferential error. However, recent work in cognitive psychology suggests a somewhat more developed account of such errors. Nisbett and Ross (1980) argue that such errors (and many other inferential errors) can be explained in terms of the overuse of certain useful "heuristics." If, as their theory is developed, it holds up under testing, then what was once only a prospectively explicable error will have become an explicable error.

Second, certain beliefs may be only prospectively explicable because not explicable without the help of information that is not available until the first-approximation interpretive scheme is further developed and applied. Of course, this is particularly characteristic of the early stages of constructing an interpretive scheme. Here, regardless of the explanatory power of our present theories, we often lack the information needed to apply them.

For example, we have various ill-developed theories—crude generalizations really—in which we account for some inferential errors in terms of strong motivational structures such as vested interests and emotional needs or desires. However, information regarding interests and desires often requires substantial translation or interpretation. Accordingly, in the early stages of constructing an interpretive scheme, we will frequently be unable to bring such theories fully into play. If these ill-developed theories give rise to explanatory successor theories, these will probably also prove, on the whole, to have limited direct application in the early stages.

The weighted principle of charity, then, leads us to construe our subjects as holding beliefs and doing actions that are either explicable or relatively likely to prove explicable. This is the basis for the general subsumption of charity in interpretation under the principle of explicability. Charitably to construct an interpretive scheme is just what the principle of explicability requires in the early stages of interpretation. In such contexts, the investigator often lacks sufficient information to provide much in the way of explanation for a judgment, correct or erroneous. Accordingly, the principle of explicability directs the investigator to interpret in such contexts in a way that holds the greatest prospect of leading to explanations. To do this, the investigator begins with broad sorts of sentences, such as observation sentences, where there are good reasons to believe that people are generally correct. In such basic cases, where error is likely to prove inexplicable and correct judgment explicable, the investigator strives to attribute correct beliefs. The result is also to concentrate attributions of error in sorts of cases where we have found error most readily explicable, where we expect relatively more error. Thus, the weighted principle of charity expresses one dimension of the principle of explicability.

We can now appreciate just how fine a codification the principle of explicability provides for interpretive practice. To begin with, the above subsumption of the principle of charity to the principle of explicability allows the latter principle to claim every advantage as a codification that is enjoyed by the principle of charity. Thus, in proceeding according to the principle of explicability, we meet the challenges posed by holism by seeking to impose a pattern on the beliefs, desires, and actions attributed to those we come to understand. In the early going, the pattern can be thought of as that dictated by a principle of charity weighted according to empirical information regarding the relative likelihood of various sorts of errors and various sorts of correct judgments. But, as we have seen, this is just what is dictated by a principle of explicability applied in the epistemic context of the early stages of interpretation. In addition, the principle of explicability also accounts for the way in which, in the later stages of interpretation, discussions of troubling cases come to center on the explicability of the beliefs and actions attributed to those we seek to understand. This focus, illustrated in the case of the Spiro-Leach controversy, is characteristic of the later stages of interpretation. Thus, the force of a codificational argument for the principle of explicability: it provides powerful, unifying, codification by accommodating all the cases handled by a refined and weighted principle of charity, plus additional cases that are more typical of the later stages of interpretation where charity is not compelling.

The principle of explicability manages this scope with particular elegance; for whereas the proponents of a principle of charity, understood as a fundamental constraint, need to appeal to competing desiderata such as the principle of explicability to account for cases in which one happily acquiesces in attributions of explicable error, the proponent of a principle of explicability needs few, if any, competing principles. The elegance of the principle of explicability is also seen when we reflect on the motivation for weighting the principle of charity. From the viewpoint of a fundamental principle of charity (fundamental methodological constraint [FMC] and normatively derived structure [NDS]) the weighting of the principle must look like some alien graft onto an a priori constraint. However, from the viewpoint of the principle of explicability, the weighted principle of charity is very natural, as seen above.

On the basis of these considerations, I am led to repudiate the standard conception of the principle of charity, as described in the second chapter. The principle of charity is a derivative principle, not a fundamental methodological constraint. Further, interpretation is not a matter of imposing a normatively derived structure on those interpreted, rather, it is a matter of theory-laden description of cognitive and social phenomena.

3.2: Two Concrete Illustrations

The force of the above subsumption of the principle of charity to the principle of explicability, and, in particular, the way in which a weighted principle of charity "sets the table" for explanation, can be fleshed out somewhat by considering two classic foci of charitable treatment in the early stages of interpretation: observation sentences and truth-functions.

3.2.1: The Treatment of Observation Sentences

In reflecting on the charitable treatment of observation sentences, it is particularly important to appreciate the complexity and epistemic richness of this treatment hidden behind an apparent simplicity of useful characterizations. To this end, we may begin with Quine's classic formulation of the charitable procedure: we are to pair observation sentences by matching sentences that have the same stimulus meaning. Properly understood, this is a fair characterization. In the earliest stages of constructing a translation scheme, this is what is and should be done (subject to qualifications to be discussed below). The procedure is, in its effects, charitable, but it is not fundamentally charitable.

When we consider how observation sentences are paired according to their stimulus-meanings, we find that this is not the fully mechanical process it might at first appear to be. It involves a good amount of extrapolation from limited samples on the basis of psychological considerations. Several important points should be noted now, and developed below. First, in pairing observation sentences according to the ranges of stimuli that dispose the speakers of the languages to assent to them and to dissent from them, the translator relies on a very limited sample of the speech dispositions. Secondly, within the sample there may be mistakes by speakers of the source-language.[1] Third, the stimulus meaning of both target-language and source-language observation sentences include stimuli that would induce mistaken assent and stimuli that would induce mistaken dissent. Fourth, we often are able, sometimes in commonsense terms, sometimes in more sophisticated psychological terms, to account for such mistakes as perceptual illusions, the results of inattention, and so on.

In order to pair observation sentences by matching similar stimulus meanings, the translator must work from reconstructions of the stimulus meanings of the relevant sentences. The needed reconstructions are provided only with the help of more or less explicit knowledge of perceptual error and success. Using a theory of perception and beginning with the sample of verbal behavior, the investigator must arrive at both a reconstruction of stimulus meaning and an associated pairing of observation sentences. This will involve tentatively pairing sentences and testing these pairings in terms of expected (correct and incorrect) utterances, given our theories of perception.

Because the stimulus meaning of observation sentences includes "deceptive" stimuli that provoke mistaken assent or dissent, the investigator who pairs observation sentences according to stimulus meaning will provide for the translation of the speakers of the source-language as mistaken in roughly those cases where the speakers of the source-language would be mistaken. Now, it is crucial to notice that the error so provided for will generally be presently or prospectively explicable. Basically, this is so because stimulus meanings for paired sentences are reconstructed from behavioral samples using (naive or sophisticated) psychological theory. More fully, deceptive stimuli are included in the stimulus meaning of the source-language utterances in part on the basis of the translator's sample of speech behavior and in part on the basis of our knowledge of perceptual error. If this knowledge of perceptual error is adequate for accurately reconstructing stimulus meanings from samples of behavior, then the source-language speakers will be disposed to just those utterances we expect, and their errors will be just those we expect, given our knowledge of perceptual error. Thus, the perceptual errors that do come to be attributed to source-language users on the basis of the translation scheme will be explicable in terms of the same knowledge of perceptual error that went into the construction of the scheme.

Adapting Quine's example, suppose that the investigator pairs a source-language sentence, 'Gavagai', with the one-word English sentence 'Rabbit'. If properly done on the basis of accurately reconstructed stimulus meanings, the source-language users will assent to 'Gavagai?' in the presence of a sufficiently realistic rabbit facsimile placed in the bush, as would English speakers. Of course, the investigator probably does not test this implication of the translation scheme. But this and other deceptive stimuli are included in the stimulus meaning of 'Gavagai' as reconstructed. Equating 'Gavagai' with 'Rabbit' will provide for occasional attributions of error in less contrived situations as well, some of which are likely to obtain. And given the supposed accuracy of the reconstructed stimulus meanings, the speech behavior of speakers of the source-language will be construed as erroneous in such situations. Whatever knowledge led the investigator to the reconstruction of the stimulus meaning can be employed to give an explanation of such errors, provided that the knowledge is sufficiently developed to ground explanatory accounts.

The above discussion must be qualified in two ways.

First, it should again be recognized that the basis for the reconstruction of stimulus meanings may at times be quite ill-developed theories regarding perceptual error—even "good guesses," the ground for which may be difficult to delineate. Such are the limits of our knowledge. Ill-developed theories, or good guesses, are hardly the theoretical basis for satisfactory explanations. In such cases, the perceptual errors attributed to source-language users are not explicable within the limits of our present theories. What needs to be noted here is that translation and science are programmatic and self-correcting. Where we do not have well-confirmed theories, we tentatively use the best we have, putting it to the test. A good guess is the alternative we believe most likely to be borne out later in acceptable theory. An ill-developed theory of the sort that can appropriately be used in interpretation is some set of sentences that we believe more likely to develop into acceptable theory than any other set we can presently formulate. Thus, errors attributed on the basis of a part of a translation scheme that depends on such ill-developed theory or good guesses are beliefs that we suspect are generally more likely to be accountable for later in explanatory theory than any alternative attributable beliefs.

I will return to these themes when I discuss how interpretation and explanation can fail, and what it is to provide an empirically adequate "interpretation-*cum*-explanation" of a people. It will be important to allay fears that, given the theory-informed nature of interpretation, and given the principle of explicability, any interpretation (and any theory for that matter) is likely to prove self-vindicating.

Second, room must be made in the basic account of the treatment of observation sentences for the knowledge of differences in susceptibility to perceptual errors based in differences in acquired acuteness. Hunters may be less susceptible to the trickery of fake rabbits than city folk, and jewelers less readily taken in by simulated diamonds than others. This shows that even the general rule of pairing observation sentences according to stimulus meaning is not itself fundamental, as Quine also recognizes (1960, p. 37). The proper treatment of observation sentences in the construction of a translation scheme is *not* completely charitable—maximizing attributed truth—*nor* is it completely a matter of matching sentences according to stimulus meanings. It is a matter of pairing sentences according to stimulus meanings that roughly match and have differences that are largely limited to explicable ones. Accordingly, we can attribute errors, or the tendency to error, differently to speakers of the source-language and speakers of the target-language, if there are situations where, according to our theories, this is to be expected given different backgrounds. Here we see that the most fundamental considerations in providing for the translation of observation sentences is the explicability of what is attributed to the speakers of the source-language.

To summarize, in dealing with observation sentences, the translator seeks to match stimulus meanings, allowing for explicable differences between communities. Doing so involves the use of a more or less explicit theory of perception in reconstructing the stimulus meanings of sentences from samples of behavior and in allowing for differences in susceptibility to perceptual errors across communities. Most importantly, those errors that come to be attributed will generally also be explicable in terms of our theory of perceptions. If our theory is too underdeveloped to support explanations, then we will seek some better, successor theory (supposedly supporting many of the same attributions) to explain the errors and successes attributed to speakers of the source-language. Accordingly, the weighted charitable procedure used in providing for the translation of observation sentences leads the interpreter to attribute (presently or prospectively) explicable beliefs and utterances to the speakers of the source-language observation sentences.

The treatment of observation sentences in the construction of translation schemes is a particularly striking instance of the weighted principle of charity leading to the attribution of explicable beliefs to the speakers of the source-language. Here theories of perception obviously play an important role in the recognizably charitable procedure for dealing with observation sentences, a role that quite directly insures the (present or prospective) explicability of the errors and successes that come to be attributed under translation. In providing for the translation of many other sorts of utterances, our knowledge of explicable error does not play so direct a role in the procedure for treating the broad sort of utterance. In such cases, knowledge of error and success applies more crudely; fewer discriminations are made within the set of utterances of the broad sort at issue. In these cases, our knowledge of the likelihood of error and success leads us to weight disagreements according to the general sort of utterance involved. As I have explained, this weighted charitable treatment of broad sorts of utterances is central to the preparatory role of constructing first-approximation translation schemes. It is also central to the subsumption of weighted charity under the principle of explicability. The treatment of truth-functions exemplifies this central sort of case.

3.2.2: The Treatment of Truth-Functions

The treatment of truth-functions in constructing a translation scheme is more simply charitable, more a matter of finding agreement, than is the treatment of observation sentences. In providing for the translation of truth-functions, prevailing patterns of assent and dissent are matched with the truth-conditions for truth-functions (allowing, of course, for the sort of ambiguity familiar to English speakers).[2] This charitable search for a good fit is tempered in one major way: such fit is at a premium with a range of less complex source-language utterances (or sets of utterances); it is less important in dealing with complex utterances. Thus, the procedure is a matter of assigning a high negative weight to attributions of error involving the general sort of utterance, truth-functions, subject to one major qualification concerning complexity and simplicity. I believe that we can discern the principle of explicability in this weighted charitable treatment of truth-functions.

To begin with, truth-functions are behaviorally quite simple and generally dispositions to the prevailing patterns of assent and dissent are effectively instilled. In this situation, we can either fit such patterns with the truth-conditions for truth-functions so as to construe the source-language users as almost always correct, or fit patterns and truth-conditions so as to construe them as very widely mistaken. The fact that the source-language speakers have evidently learned their lessons well does not alone decide for us which option to take. However, the charitable option is the obvious choice for the following reasons.

To translate so as to construe the source-language speakers as widely mistaken, although they have learned their society's truth-functional patterns well, would be to construe them as mistaken either as to the meaning of their own truth-functional constructions or as suffering from a systematic logical incompetence (or both). To construe them as collectively mistaken regarding the meaning of their own truth-functions would be nonsensical (see Quine 1970, pp. 16–17). It would be to suppose that there is a correct usage, the "real" meaning, of a certain particles, independent of the use to which a particle is put by the linguistic community.

The initial response only shows that we cannot uncharitably construe source-language users as all having universally mislearned their language. There is also a reason not to translate uncharitably in association with the supposition that the source-language community members are exceedingly poor reasoners. When we understand translation and interpretation as integral parts of an explanatory endeavor—when, that is, we understand the principle of explicability as the fundamental constraint on interpretation— then we can appreciate that perversely uncharitable translation would be a great deal of trouble (with no offsetting payoff).

We are seeking what might be called "interpretation-*cum*-explanations": for each bit of meaningful behavior (verbal and otherwise) we want our interpretive scheme to provide us with an interpretation under which what is allegedly said or done is explicable. Of course, what is explicable (or even prospectively so) is dependent on our best present theories. Providing us an understanding of what is said and done is *not* the task of an interpretive scheme alone. Rather, understanding is the job of an interpretive scheme *and* sociological and psychological theories. It is this combination of theoretical and descriptive resources that allows us to account for the behavior of our subjects, and that can be empirically adequate. Choosing the relatively charitable option in dealing with observation sentences, truth-functions, and so forth, the theories we have developed in studying ourselves become available to account for minor deviations. Choosing the uncharitable option, we find what then seem to be extraordinary mistakes—extraordinary mistakes that are inexplicable and unexpected. We have no theories that will begin to take up the burden such an interpretive scheme would place on the sociological and psychological components of interpretation-*cum*-explanation. Our present theories would not combine with such an uncharitable interpretation scheme to account for the behavior and dispositions we want to understand.

While our present theories dealing with cognitive error do not allow us to account for massive logical lapses, such as would result from a basically uncharitable interpretive treatment of truth-functions, we could attempt to develop theories that combine with uncharitable translation schemes (say for truth-functions) to provide accounts of the behaviors and behavioral dispositions found in the full range of language communities. This would be an extraordinary undertaking. Rather than embarking on such an unpromising and unmotivated attempt to construct wholly new psychological theories to explain putatively pervasive truth-functional logical errors, we reasonably choose to make use of present theories (and their descendants). Thus, we choose the generally charitable option in dealing with truth-functions.

Notice that the above argument for constructing a translation scheme so as to charitably translate truth-functions has two parts. First, to interpret the speakers of the source-language as having universally mislearned at least some of their words for the truth-functions reduces to nonsense. Second, interpreting them as subject to pervasive logical failures would greatly multiply the difficulty of constructing sets of interpretive schemes and theories that are empirically adequate. Thus it is that the argument for the principle of charity in treating truth-functions is grounded in the exigencies of constructing explanatory accounts (interpretation-cum-explanations) given our present and foreseeable stock of theories. This argument is obviously of a piece with the general subsumption of the principle of charity to the principle of explicability provided above.

Attention to the limits of our ability to account for truth-functional errors also uncovers the reasons for one distinction in truth-functional utterances that is made in providing for their translation. We have relatively few ways of explaining truth-functional errors. One is to appeal to the complexity or length of the sentences or arguments in question, where they are complex and long. The length and complexity of truth-functional utterances can be gauged even in the early going. Thus, the relative explicability of error in such cases can be built into our charitable procedure. By seeking to maximize agreement in simple cases, truth-functional errors attributed under translation come generally to be localized in cases involving complex utterances or sets of utterances. Again, this is as it should be according to the principle of explicability.

Other ways of explaining truth-functional errors include noting stressful circumstances in which the sentences or arguments are encountered or contrived, and noting loyalties or biases. Significantly, such accounts of truth-functional error must often be supported by information about the reasoner that is not readily accessible in the early stages of constructing an interpretive scheme. Accordingly, while such explanations of error can be built into a weighted principle of charity for treating truth-functions, the resulting refinements in the principle have few applications in the early going. However, such accounts typically support explanations only of limited, or isolated, deviations from the general pattern being treated as indicative of the correct usage. Such effects can be ignored in charitably settling on the basic translations for source-language truth-functions by attention to the prevailing patterns of assent and dissent.

Once an approximate fit between truth-conditions for truth-functions and patterns of assent to and dissent from sentences involving source-language particles is established, and the source-language truth-functions are identified accordingly, errors will come to be attributed to certain individuals and, perhaps, in certain contexts, to many or most individuals. Most, but not all, such apparent truth-functional errors will occur in cases where the utterances (or sets of utterances) are long or complex. As the translation scheme is developed further, we will be able to bring to bear information having to do with stresses and biases in attempts to explain such errors (especially those where complexity or length is not a prominent factor. Here we will entertain the prospect of modifying the interpretive scheme, should this result in more explicable attributions, and will thus be involved in fine-tuning or refining the scheme.

I have now shown, both by general argument and by examining the treatment of two important broad sorts of utterances, that the weighted principle of charity, as applied in the construction of first-approximation of translation schemes, leads to just the results indicated by my principle of explicability. However, the subsumption of the weighted principle of charity under the principle of explicability does not depend simply on the fact that these principles counsel the same things in the construction of first-approximation translation schemes. It is supported by the realization that the weighted principle of charity follows where the principle of explicability and our empirical theories lead. This is illustrated by the treatment of truth-functions. The generally charitable treatment of truth-functions can be understood as dictated by the search for combinations of translation schemes with our scientific theories that adequately account for the observed behavior and dispositions within the community studied.

3.3: Elaboration

While the above pivotal argument seems to me telling, it can be reinforced or clarified by elaborating several points. Here I will discuss three points that bear further development.

3.3.1: Empirical Adequacy

It is not unusual to find philosophers writing about translation schemes, or "manuals," being "behaviorally adequate." Thus, Quine (1960, pp. 68–72) writes of a set of translation manuals fitting all the possible behavioral evidence, even all the behavioral dispositions within a given language community. He argues that multiple translation manuals can represent the same sets of behavioral dispositions. In view of the above discussions, we should find such presentations initially puzzling. We should wonder how interpretive schemes, taken alone, can have empirical content or represent a set of behavioral dispositions at all.

In interpretation we are faced with the holistic task of making sense out of, or giving an account of, a constellation of interrelated behaviors. Focusing on verbal behavior, we note that within a language community there is a behavioral association of sentences with both the environment and with behaviors, verbal and otherwise. This is in part a matter of the complex ways in which, with a good deal of uniformity within the language community, dispositions to utter or assent to sentences are intertwined. For example, the disposition to assent to one sentence may be associated with the disposition to assent to a second sentence or set of sentences. For concreteness, consider the following simple pairs of associated English sentences: (1) 'The barometer is falling', 'Rain is likely soon'; (2) 'This is square', 'This has four sides'; (3) 'This is a black crow', 'All crows are black'; (4) 'God loves you', 'Things will work out.' (Of course, the intertwining of dispositions illustrated by considering these linguistic cases extends beyond dispositions to verbal behavior.)

The association of sentences (with each other and with the environment and nonverbal behaviors) is, in important respects, a social matter, as there is a significant uniformity of behavioral dispositions within a language community. The connections between certain sentences may have been learned in different ways by individual members of the language community, but the overall results have come to be similar. Within the community of English speakers, one member may first have learned 'Square' as a response to certain figures and only later have been induced to count their sides, while another member may first have been taught to assent to 'Square' after counting four sides of similar length on a presented figure. In both cases, the sentences comprising pair (2) will have come to be associated. Quine (1960, p. 8) has provided an apt analogy:

> Different persons growing up in the same language are like different bushes trimmed and trained to take the shape of identical elephants. The anatomical details of twigs and branches will fulfill the elephantine form differently from bush to bush, but the overall outward results are alike.

In interpretation we wish to account for the associations of behaviors and behavioral dispositions we find among the people studied.

We may think of interpretive understanding as a matter of representing associations (at the individual and social levels) in terms of *relevance relations*. That is, when we translate or interpret others, we represent their practice (verbal and otherwise), and their behavioral dispositions, by modeling it in terms of relevance relations. For concreteness, we may imagine that an interpretive scheme gives the above four pairs of English sentences as the equivalents for certain pairs of sentences within the source-language. This interpretive scheme would represent the putatively equivalent source-language pairs in a range of ways: the equivalents to the members of pair (1) are represented as (typically) associated in virtue of dispositions to yet further sentences (a more or less large set) and inclinations to certain reasonable inferences; the equivalents to members of pair (2) are represented as associated in a rather more direct, almost definitional, manner; the equivalents to members of pair (3) are represented as associated by virtue of the recognized relation between a generalization and a piece of (confirming) evidence; and the equivalents to members of pair (4) are represented as associated in virtue of a range of further sentences comprising the relevant parts of certain religious systems. Thus, when we translate a set of source-language sentences, we represent those sentences as being behaviorally associated (with each other, with other behaviors, and with the environment) in much the same way as their putative English equivalents. (Steven Turner [1980] provides a particularly interesting elaboration on this basic view.)

The idea of modeling is important here (and it should not be given an instrumentalistic gloss). It serves nicely to capture the following aspect of interpretive schemes. We can properly treat certain sentences or actions as interpretive equivalents even when members of the respective communities are not similarly disposed to assent to or dissent from the sentences, or are not similarly disposed to doing the relevant actions. But, it must be the case that *if we were* disposed to assent to certain of the sentences that are the putative translational equivalents of certain sentences to which the source-language speakers are disposed, we *would then* also be disposed to assent to other sentences that are the translation for other relevant sentences to which they are disposed to assent. For example, we are disposed to assent to few sentences affirming the existence and working of a witchcraft substance. The Zande apparently are. However, a proper translation scheme must allow us to model in English the pattern of Zande dispositions to assent to sentences about magic and witchcraft. And a proper interpretive scheme must allow us to model their magical practices in a similar way.

When I write of representing or modeling behavior and dispositions in term of relevance relations, this should *not* be understood as saying that once we have attributed semantic content to sentences of the source-language, and have settled on descriptions of their behaviors in action-terms, we can read off the associations thereby represented simply by following out inductive, deductive, and decision-theoretic connections. (Although my examples above may have encouraged this misunderstanding.) The relevance relations that I have in mind are *not* all and only matters of normatively appropriate processing. Rather, I have in mind something that might be called "descriptive" or "psychological relevance." In representing associations in terms of relevance relations, we are accounting for them in terms of intensional states expressed in many of our subjects' utterances and actions. How behavioral associations arise out of such states is a matter of psychology—a matter of cognitive capacities or processes. Once we appreciate this fact, it becomes clear that representing the association of sentences and actions is the task of interpretive schemes *and* psychological (and sociological) theory (together comprising a global theory), *not* the task of translation or interpretive schemes alone.

When someone writes of translation schemes being "behaviorally adequate" or "empirically adequate," without mention of the psychological and sociological theory with which such a theory must be yoked, they must be thinking along one of three lines.

First, they may be thinking of interpretive schemes leading us to expect, or account for, the observed behavior using only rationalizing explanation. This is to suppose that we might account for all behavior by providing a set of translational or interpretive equivalences and then letting explanation ride normatively along on "rails of meaning"; it is to suppose that, once equipped with the interpretive scheme, we can determine some of our subjects' beliefs and desires, and then find that, given those beliefs and desires, they reason to the appropriate further beliefs and desires, and do the appropriate actions. (Putnam's compressed account of interpretation [1978] seems to suggest such a model, as does Jarvie's classic [1964] development of Popper's [1950] notion of explanation in terms of "the logic of the situation"; and Turner's [1980] account may be understood in this way.) One problem with such approaches should be immediately obvious: people just do not always reason in ways that are normatively appropriate, and just do not act in only ways that are normatively appropriate. This seems to be conceded by all. But, as a result, any attempt to account for all of what is said and done, to fully model a person's or group's behaviors, to thus provide an empirically or behaviorally adequate account, by using a set of interpretive equivalences and riding only the rails of meaning and rationality is bound to fail.

More fundamentally, it seems misleading to suppose that such an approach, in relying on rationalizing explanation, must not make use of more than an interpretive scheme. Such an approach does make use of an implicit account of human psychology. No interpretive scheme for a community will, by itself, allow us to model or account for how sentences within their language are associated, and for how all this is related to what is done. For, when nothing about rationality or irrationality is assumed, when nothing about cognitive processing is assumed, the interpretive scheme, by itself, is strictly vacuous.[3]

Second, when philosophers writing of the behavioral or empirical adequacy of translation schemes suppress mention of psychological theories, this may indicate that they believe that such theories do not play an important role. Typically, this opinion stems from an unargued for conservatism regarding the relevant psychological theories. The theory used is sometimes supposed simply too rudimentary to deserve notice. This typically leads to an unrestrained, basically opportunistic, use of rationalizing explanation combined with ad hoc excuses to accommodate cases as the need arises. There is, I think, little to recommend resting content with such an approach. Further, it seems little short of silly to talk of interpretive or translation schemes combined with such devices as empirically adequate.

Third, philosophers writing of the behavioral or empirical adequacy of translation schemes may be suppressing mention of psychological theories to achieve a simple manner of speaking with no suggestion that theories play an insignificant role. (This seems to reflect Quine's approach, for he does explicitly recognize that psychological theory of a sophisticated sort can and should be used in constructing and judging translation schemes.) A little reflection should convince us that, if we are to adequately model a people's behaviors and behavioral disposition, if we are to have an empirically adequate interpretive scheme, it must be because our scheme is yoked with substantial psychological theory. The following considerations should make this clear.

Cognitive psychologists have recently begun to study a range of apparently common heuristic procedures that can lead to systematic errors in inductive inference. (For summary discussions, see Nisbett and Ross 1980 and Slovic 1972.) Insofar as their results are correct, and human beings are generally subject to such systematic failures in inductive reasoning, we will need to use psychological information regarding such tendencies to adequately represent the behavioral dispositions among speakers of a given language, whether it is our language or another. Simply having a translation scheme for the sentences of a language and relying on rationalizing explanation will not allow us to model or account for how its sentences are associated as a result of such heuristic-induced errors. We will need to combine a translation scheme with the emerging psychological theory.

Anthropological accounts of magic provide an example of the combined use of translation and psychological (and sociological) theory to represent behavioral associations. Using first-approximation translation schemes, anthropologists have often been led to translate certain source-language sentences as accounts of the workings of magic on the social and physical environment. These translations construe source-language speakers as expressing generalizations about the effects of various rituals. However, other sentences are translated as recognizing the occurrence of certain events in the world, where these entail that the apparent intended results of magic often do not obtain. Together, these translations (taken with common assumptions regarding human rationality) suggest that magic-behavior will soon suffer extinction, which, of course, it does not. This seems to be a behavioral or empirical inadequacy in the translation manual, yoked to common assumptions regarding human rationality which typically go unacknowledged. While some modifications are sometimes made in the first-approximation scheme, psychological theories (often not recognized as such) have also come to be a common feature of anthropological accounts of magic. Malinowski (1931), for example, proposed that magic was a response to frustration borne out of the limitations of (otherwise fine) primitive technologies. Because it then serves important psychological needs, it does not become extinct. This also allowed Malinowski to account for the association of magical rituals with risky endeavors such as agriculture and deep-sea fishing where the risks could not be eliminated by existing technologies, and for the relative paucity of magical rituals in association with endeavors such as food preparation and cove fishing where existing technologies suffice.

On the view I am developing in this chapter, we are to construct interpretive schemes according to the fundamental principle of explicability. This is to say that we are to construct interpretive schemes so as to be yoked with our psychological and sociological theories to the end of modeling and accounting for the behavior and behavioral dispositions of our subjects. This combination of interpretive scheme and theory should then give rise to what I have several times referred to as "interpretation-*cum*-explanations" for particular situated actions. On this view, *the construction of interpretive schemes is an integral part of the ongoing social and psy-*

chological sciences. Their development plays an important role in the ongoing development of social-scientific and psychological theory. Interpretive schemes are needed for the cross-cultural application of more general theory. In application, a *global theory* comprised of an interpretive scheme and social-scientific and psychological theories is put to the test. If the account is not adequate, does not model what is observed, then modifications are needed either in the interpretive scheme, in the other theoretical components, or in both. If the account is successful, then the components are together supported. (The suggested understanding of testing is developed in chapter 7.)

This view of interpretation undermines the curiously conservative view that adequate interpretation must lead us to construe our subjects as rational, for psychological theory and social-scientific theory are composed of more than decision theory and serve to support more than just rationalizing explanation. Thus, as mentioned already, theories concerning the behavior of human beings under the stresses of various social and economic conditions can have an important role in interpretation-cum-explanation, as suggested by Johada's (1982) discussion of Turnbull's (1977) account of the Ik. Theories having to do with cognitive processing are, of course, essential. Thus, the work of cognitive psychologists such as that discussed in Nisbett and Ross (1980), Slovic (1972), and Wason and Johnson-Laird (1972) could usefully be employed in accounts that attribute and explain egregious inferential error on the part of some set of people. Jon Elster (1982) has made use of such cognitive psychological results in an attempt to provide the microfoundations for a theory of ideology. Such a theory could prove useful in the explanation of persistent egregious errors within the belief systems of various peoples. As already mentioned, theories of psychological needs have been employed by a diverse group of anthropologists in accounts of religious and magical practice (for example, Malinowski 1931; Spiro 1966; Beattie 1964, pp. 205–6; Geertz 1973a). This list of relevant theory can obviously be elaborated, but the point has already been made: once refined interpretation is understood as an integral part of the social-scientific and psychological explanatory endeavor, we should also recognize that the full range of our theoretical resources is relevant in constructing and judging refined interpretive schemes. Only by making use of our full range of theoretical resources can we begin to hope to adequately model what is said and done by those we study.

Because most of the theories mentioned above have to do with errors, another disclaimer seems appropriate here. I am not claiming that attributions of inconsistency, as such, are explanatory. To say that someone is inconsistent obviously does not explain why he or she believes (or does) what is believed (or done). But, we may have theories which account for cases of irrationality in certain circumstances—certain inferential errors given certain input, for example—and we can explain some behavior by showing it to be a result of an instance of the erroneous reasoning described by the theory. We have begun to develop theories capable of supporting such explanations. Further, attributions of rationality and irrationality are on a par in these respects: while I readily admit that it is not explanatory simply to show some belief or action to be irrational, neither do I think that it is explanatory just to show that some belief or action is rational. There are probably many things that it would be rational for individuals to do or believe that are not done or believed. However, there are certain descriptive theories that account for certain sorts of rationality. Insofar as such theories are drawn with sufficient care as to be empirically adequate, to show that an action or belief is rational *in a way that qualifies as an instance of the rationality described in the theory* is to explain the action or belief. Similarly, there are descriptive theories that account for certain sorts of irrationality. Insofar as such theories are drawn with sufficient care as to be empirically adequate, then to show that an action or belief is *irrational in a way that is described in the theory* is to explain it. (This view is developed further in chapters 5 and 6.)

I have argued that interpretive schemes are to be yoked with psychological and sociological theories to produce a global theory, and that this global theory is the real candidate for empirical adequacy. When this view is combined with my principle of explicability, it is bound to raise a significant worry: is the theory-informed interpretation recommended here going to render the resulting global theories, and thus the theories employed there, self-validating? While an extended and detailed response is slated for chapter 7, a general response is in order here. To begin with, I have argued that the principle of explicability provides an excellent codification of interpretive practice. However, this practice has yet to lead to any global theory (interpretive scheme plus theory) that is ultimately empirically adequate— even in dealing with individuals and groups within our own society. If following the principle of explicability made theories self-vindicating, this situation would be itself inexplicable.

The principle of explicability—interpret so as to attribute

explicable beliefs and actions to one's subjects—is not a recommendation that we force recalcitrant phenomena into conceptual molds that do not fit, awkwardly making them out to be something we can explain and ignoring anomalies. Instead, it says that where our best scientific theories are up to explaining the phenomena, we should construct interpretive schemes so as to make use of those theories. But, where our present theories are not up to the task of explaining the phenomena in conjunction with some interpretive scheme or other, we should seek to formulate new, testable, theories. As different theories are formulated and receive substantial confirmation (as applied in conjunction with interpretive schemes), we will want to revise further our refined interpretive schemes so as to take advantage of what then becomes our best theories. If the revisions are successful, and the relevant phenomena are explained, then the new theories receive further confirmation. When a refined interpretive scheme is grounded in an account that makes use of theories with little confirmation, or where the resulting account seems, on the whole, unexplanatory, even if it is the best we have, little confidence is to be placed in the interpretive scheme.

Ultimately, what we seek is a set of psychological and sociological theories that can be combined with interpretive schemes for all peoples, and when so combined, lead us to model and expect what we do observe. This, like any ideal of empirical adequacy for scientific theory, is a high goal and not easily attained. When we pause to consider the range of theory that is relevant, we see that forcing a particular interpretation on some behavior in order to make it explicable in certain respects may make it inexplicable in other respects. For example, a refined interpretive scheme might excuse a people of an inexplicable error in reasoning at the cost of making some of their beliefs inexplicable from the perspective of learning theory, or at the cost of rendering certain actions unaccounted for. And modifying our theories to allow us to account for what is found in one society may produce anomalies in our interpretive account of other societies.

Thus, far from advocating the evasion of recalcitrant phenomena, my view holds that when we cannot translate so as to construe our subjects as explicable, we should both seek to construct new theories and place commensurately less confidence in our refined interpretive schemes in the meantime. This view is forward-looking: it sees interpretation as a part of social and psychological science and science as the fallible and self-correcting search for explanation.

3.3.2: Rules of Thumb

There is a tendency to conceive of the weighted principle of charity, where it does apply in the early stages of interpretation, along the following lines. It is often conceived as applying "across the board" in Davidson's sense: for any sentence at all, there is a (more or less defeasible) assumption that speakers of the source-language are correct in their utterances of that sentence and in their assents to and dissents from that sentence. However, because some attributions of disagreement are more destructive of understanding than others, we weight sorts of cases, so that disagreement over certain sentences is assigned a negative weight in proportion to the destructiveness of the disagreement indicated. This is a matter of relative likelihood. Then the investigator simply grinds out an interpretive scheme which has the highest (or optimal) score. On this line of thought, one can only (and at best) *tolerate* attributions of disagreement, for each one counts against the interpretive scheme in some degree.

However, this view is rendered plausible only by a failure to appreciate the primacy of the principle of explicability. I have argued that the principle of charity is itself derivative on the concern for explicability. It serves a preparatory role, putting us in a position to address the pivotal issue of the explicability of those states and actions provisionally attributed to our subjects. In keeping with these points, the principle of charity should never be seen as competing with the principle of explicability. This leads us to the view of the principle of charity as a general rule of thumb about where disagreement is most readily handled within a fully adequate interpretive scheme. I say "handled" not "tolerated," because *there are attributions of serious error that properly do not at all detract from the confidence we place in the interpretive scheme* on which they are based.

As we are constructing an interpretive scheme, we will doubtless come across utterances and actions where our tentative interpretation and reconstruction of the relevant psychology indicate that error is explicable. *No* negative weight should be assigned to attributions of error in such cases. To suggest otherwise is to mistakenly put the principle of charity in competition with the principle of explicability. Of course, when dealing with other than very simple perceptual errors, this sort of treatment will typically be feasible only in later stages of constructing an interpretive scheme, for only there will we have enough information available by way of tentative interpretation to sufficiently bring to bear psychological theory.

To appreciate how the principle of charity is best viewed as a useful rule of thumb, it is needful to distinguish between two separate issues. First is the issue of whether disagreements, attributions, or error regarding *particular* utterances or actions (or particular sets of these) are necessarily destructive of confidence in an interpretive scheme on which they are based. I have argued that they are not. Of course, any "harmless" attribution of error will be so only because the error is explicable in terms of a viable theory of belief. Second, there is the issue of how to approach attributions of various *sorts of error* in initially constructing an interpretive scheme, before the explicability of the particular errors can be investigated. The weighting of attributions of errors by destructiveness has to do with sorts of errors, not with individual attributions of error.

In the course of generating an interpretive scheme, not all errors that come to be attributable to our subjects will be readily explicable; there will be anomalies. For present purposes, it is best to take attributions of error that might turn out to be explicable with sufficient time and information, given our present theories, but for which we have not yet developed an explanation, as "not readily explicable" or anomalous. The rating of errors for destructiveness is a rating of anomalies and the weighted principle of charity thus provides a rule of thumb for where anomalies may best be confined. After all, we know what sorts of error have most often proven explicable. If we need to attribute some errors that we cannot presently account for, we should do so in a way that promises to yield most readily to explanation in the course of subsequent investigation. It is in this sense that certain disagreements—or better, presently inexplicable attributions of error—do less than others to undermine our confidence in our interpretive scheme. Thus, the weighted principle of charity is a graded rule of thumb about where attributions of error should be avoided; consistent with this status as a rule of thumb, it ceases to apply when the particular error attributed can be explained.

3.3.3: Solving the Problem of Irrationality

Much of the account presented here was first developed in response to what I believe to be a problem raised by many understandings of the principle of charity, a problem that I call the "problem of irrationality." The problem is that many formulations of the principle of charity lead to the conclusion that any translation scheme which leads us to attribute irrational beliefs to the subjects of our investigations is inadequate, or, at least less likely to be adequate than otherwise. It then follows that attributions of irrationality in psychology and the social sciences are improper, or improbable, being based on evidence derived from a suspect interpretive scheme. Roth (1985, p. 156), for example, is led to conclude that "there is little to distinguish the charge that others are irrational from the claim that what one has is simply a bad translation." It would thus be requisite to withdraw, or hold in abeyance, such attributions, and that the attempt be made to revise the interpretive scheme towards the end of attributing rationality instead. In this way, the principle of charity is commonly taken to legislate, or militate, against the possibility of irrational belief or behavior, and this in spite of the seemingly substantial evidence for their fairly frequent occurrence. On this line of thought, irrationality is ruled out, or militated against, not so much on empirical grounds as on purely methodological grounds.

The problem of irrationality varies in seriousness with the strength of formulation of the principle of charity entertained. Minimally, it involves taking all attributions of obvious irrationality to be evidence against the sponsoring interpretive scheme. Thus, even if a formulation of the principle of charity is not so strong as to take attributions of obvious irrationality to fully undermine the sponsoring interpretive scheme, it can be said to give rise to the problem of irrationality if it would take such attributions as evidence against the interpretive scheme.

Taking attributions of irrationality as evidence against otherwise explanatory accounts of a society or sort of behavior does not accord well with actual reflective social scientific practice. Attributions of obvious inconsistency (inconsistency that is easily or already passingly recognized) play a role in several well thought of social scientific works, where they often do not seem to be taken as ultimately problematic. Evans-Pritchard's (1937) treatment of Zande beliefs concerning the inheritance of witchcraft provides a classic example. According to Evans-Pritchard, the Azande believe that witchcraft is a biologically inherited trait, passed from father to son and from mother to daughter. However, this belief is contradicted by an unwillingness to attribute witchcraft to entire clans. (Given the structure of Zande kinship, and given the frequency of Zande attributions of witchcraft using the poison oracle, entire clans would seem to be witches. But the Zande will not accept this conclusion.)

The apparent contradiction cannot be resolved by Zande appeals to bastardy, which are evidently not sufficiently extensive (nor persuasive). It may be that the contradiction was not originally obvious to the Azande. However, the contradiction was rendered obvious, at least to a limited number of Azande, by Evans-Pritchard's intervention. He discussed the problem with informants and reports that "Azande see the sense of this argument but they do not accept its conclusions, and it would involve the whole notion of witchcraft in contradiction were they to do so" (Evans-Pritchard 1937, p. 24). The recalcitrant fact is that the Azande see the sense of the argument, see that their beliefs lead to contradictions, yet apparently do not modify their beliefs about the inheritance of witchcraft. Short of getting someone to assent to a sentence of the form 'p and not-p', it is hard to imagine a clearer case of someone persisting in logical inconsistency once it has become obvious. (Garrett Barden [1972] has identified a rather different obvious inconsistency that he believes is found both in Zande witchcraft and in Western societies.)

Of course, Evans-Pritchard's attribution of inconsistency to the Azande does not constitute an isolated example. Edmund Leach (1954) seems to uncover inconsistent religious beliefs among the Kachin; he accounts for the nature and persistence of these inconsistencies by noting the underlying political uses of the relevant beliefs. And, in this respect, Leach's results are a model of symbolist anthropological results generally. At least at one level, most symbolist anthropologists attribute a certain amount of epistemic irrationality, even inconsistency, to those who they study (Firth 1964, pp. 227–28; 1973, p. 426; Turner 1975, pp. 146–47). Other discussions of inconsistency in religious belief are not difficult to uncover (the exchange between Horton (1973) and Skorupski (1973) concerning the former's suggestion that science as well as religion are rife with such contradiction provides a rich source of examples from the anthropological literature on religion (see also Horton 1970, 1982). Obvious inconsistency does not seem to be confined to religious contexts; the literature on political toleration in the United States is suggestive here (Prothro and Grigg 1960; McClosky 1964; Sullivan, Pierson, and Marcus 1982), as is much of the literature on political party identification.

Of course, if I am correct in my argument in this chapter, such attributions of irrationality can only be fully unproblematic and not count as a strike against the sponsoring interpretive scheme when there are explanations for the inconsistency. It is thus reassuring to find anthropologists and other social scientists offering explanations, or explanation sketches, for the inconsistencies that they impute. Thus, Evans-Pritchard feels compelled to explain why the Azande fail to perceive the "futility" of their magic. (This futility apparently includes the problems of inconsistency noted above.) Evans-Pritchard (1937, pp. 475–78) cites twenty-two reasons for this futility not becoming widely acknowledged; these have to do with limitations in the flow of putative information within Zande society, with the Zande treatment of what might be taken as countercases, with social and political supports of various kinds, and with the insulation of subsets of the larger inconsistent belief set. Such points tend to provide explanations for the prevalence of nonobvious irrationality and inconsistency in a belief system. Could an explanation of the obvious inconsistency noted above be given?

To explain an obvious inconsistency, one would need to explain how inconsistent beliefs came to be held, and how they can prove persistent. In the case of the inconsistency in political beliefs having to do with toleration, one can easily sketch an explanation here. On the one hand, one would need to notice the role of common political socialization. There are wonderfully high-sounding, unqualified principles that people have been taught since childhood in the United States—even unpopular speech is protected by the Constitution, as it ought to be in a free land. On the other hand, at times, certain people and their ideas have been thought to pose a substantial danger to the government of the United States. This perceived threat readily leads to a practical conclusion: such people must be stopped from spreading their dangerous ideas. These two processes thus generate the inconsistent political beliefs. Explaining the persistence of this inconsistency may seem to present a greater challenge.

Significantly, making such inconsistent beliefs obvious is easier than getting people to change them. We can begin to account for the recalcitrance of some inconsistent belief sets by noting that people can become wedded to, and dependent on, certain belief sets, and that, when confronted with inconsistency, they may not be able to decide where to modify these beliefs. They then go on believing as before. One might thus suppose that a general tendency to continue the relatively easy and unreflective use of ready-to-hand doctrine combines with a phenomena that is found even in more systematically reflective endeavors:

> This principle also helps us to understand the tenacity with which people hold on to "disproved" scientific theory or economic and

political dogmas. No matter how much evidence one can bring to bear that a scientific theory does not fit the known facts, scientists are reluctant to give it up until one can give them another integration in place of the old. In the absence of some other way of organizing facts, people will frequently hold onto the old, for no other reason than that (Kretch and Crutchfield 1948, p. 87).

These suggestions doubtless provide part of the story in the case of the inconsistent political beliefs mentioned here.

This crude, commonsensical, account also generalizes to cover a range of further beliefs. Certainly, religious (and magical) beliefs may serve as a basis for effective social and political actions (again a reading of Leach 1954 and Evans-Pritchard 1937 is instructive here) and the thought of finding appropriate revisions in (or replacements for) such systems, comprised of revered general "truths" backed by the "weight of tradition," will often seem daunting and baffling to individuals.

Let me mention one study that deals with deductive errors and that directly supports the suggestion that people can generate and then hold to obviously inconsistent beliefs, even when these beliefs are not particularly dear or serviceable. Johnson-Laird and Wason (1972) have studied the performance of people in what are called selection-tasks. In these experiments, subjects are presented with four cards and asked to say which of the cards must be examined further (turned over) in order to determine the truth or falsity of an English conditional. In a representative early variant of such experiments, the cards each have a number on one side and a letter on the other. They are arranged so that what is showing on the face-up sides are (1) a vowel, (2) a consonant, (3) an even number, and (4) an odd number. The sentence to be evaluated is, 'If a card has a vowel on one side, then it has an even number on the other side'. The correct response is to choose the vowel-marked card, (1), and the odd-numbered card (4). (The other cards are indifferent to the truth of the test sentence, or already favorable cases, depending on the construction placed upon the English conditional.) The two most common responses are both wrong. First, respondents often chose just the card with a vowel showing (thus ignoring the possibility that the odd-numbered card has a vowel on the unexamined side). Second, respondents often chose the vowel-marked card and the even-numbered card (compounding the first error by also choosing an indifferent card).[4] After their attempt at a solution, the subjects are shown the other sides of the cards. The vowel-marked card turns out to be an even-numbered card, a confirming instance. However, the odd-numbered card turns out to be a vowel-marked card, falsifying the test sentence. It is here that the responses of subjects making the common mistakes are telling. Very often they readily admit that the falsifying card is just that, and yet decline to alter their original attempt at a solution. Thus the subjects persist in their initial response in the face of their recognition of information obviously inconsistent with that response. Wason and Johnson-Laird speculate on several processes by which the force of the contradiction is "evaded in systematic ways."

With regard to irrational beliefs generally, it is increasingly less of a mystery how they can be generated. As I have already noted, within the last few decades, cognitive psychologists have collected a good deal of data demonstrating the existence of, and tendency to, particular sorts of systematic inferential error. Much of this work has dealt with systematic errors in inductive inference. The work on heuristics cited above is an example. Much inductive error can be accounted for as the result of the overapplication of certain heuristic cognitive strategies. The emerging theory can be used to account for particular apparently ill-grounded, and thus irrational, beliefs. For example, Nisbett and Ross (1980, pp. 124–31) use it when suggesting an explanation for how certain Zande folk-medical beliefs could arise. Further, psychological work on inferential error has not been limited to inductive errors. Some work (such as Wason and Johnson-Laird's work mentioned above) has focused on certain errors in deductive reasoning.

Of course, people are generally not reflective or critical about their belief sets, and they are generally resistant to changes that are more then complementary additions to the already held set of beliefs. For example, they seem often to have a certain cognitive "inertia," being more attuned to supporting information than to information that suggests a need to dispense with beliefs they already hold. Even when a set of beliefs are not as intimately intertwined with a range of the ways of life featured in a particular culture (as are religious and political belief systems), people often display a desire to attain or maintain a "cognitive closure," a desire to have issues settled and out of the way. Kruglanski and Freund (1983) and Kruglanski and Mayseless (1987) have studied how needs for closure can induce increasingly inappropriate strategies in settling issues. There are good reasons to believe that it should be at least as significant in inducing people to defer reopening a topic, even when there is good reason to reinvestigate.

There is, in any case, good reason to believe that people often find it harder to modify their beliefs by dropping a belief than to modify the set by adding a belief. For example, Ross, Lepper, and Hubbard (1975) show that while subjects typically are easily lead to believe something about themselves in the course of an experiment, they often can be induced to abandon the belief only by extreme measures in the postexperimental debriefing. Subjects may, for example, be led to believe they are particularly good or bad at some task by giving them predetermined feedback after they have taken a putative test for the relevant ability. Obviously, this feedback provides the information that leads the subject to form the belief in question. In the debriefing, the subject was told that the feedback received during the experiment had nothing to do with how the subject performed in the experiment, and that the feedback had been predetermined by the subject's being randomly assigned a particular treatment group. But, simply convincing the subject of this typically did little to get the subject to drop the new belief. The belief in question thus outlived the reasons the subject has for holding it, proving itself quite persistent.

When seeking explanations for how irrational sets of beliefs might prove persistent, we should not ignore the contribution that dissonance theory has made to our understanding of some cases (Festinger 1957). Particularly when the beliefs in question are beliefs that have led us to make sacrifices or beliefs to which one has devoted substantial portions of one's energies (such as political and religious beliefs) one is likely to find the thought of having been mistaken there hard to accept. As Festinger (1961) notes, "we come to love those things for which we have suffered." This effects one's cognitive stance toward one's beliefs. Thus, people will assign a higher probability to a certain possibility after betting on it than they will assign to it just prior to placing their wager (Knox and Inkster 1968). This could account for some observed adherence to ill-supported beliefs, and as described earlier, even to inconsistent but central belief sets, as suggested by Festinger, Riecken, and Schachter (1956).

Finally, it is worth noting another rather different (but in principle compatible and possibly complementary) line of social scientific thought directed to explaining even obvious epistemic irrationality. Read properly, much symbolist anthropology is an attempt to explain (and not explain away) obvious inconsistencies and epistemic irrationality in various belief systems. Symbolist anthropologists argue that, while scientific and technological thought typically developed in general conformity with well-accepted logical and epistemic standards, religion, magic, and witchcraft do not. They claim that the inferences and developments found in religions and systems of magic must be understood, not in terms of the epistemic logic of belief systems, but (primarily) in terms of the dynamics of what they call "ritual." Ritual is action; myth is its associated verbal form. Ritual is "symbolic" or "expressive" action, which is to say that it is action that stands rather abstractly for something else, typically group values (Beattie 1964, pp. 202–17, 69–71; Firth 1964; Leach 1954). Rituals thus express and inculcate various social values, including conceptions of proper or natural power relationships, the value of the group and its cohesiveness, and the significance of authoritative social recognition for some roles and relations. On the symbolist account, myths, which are the beliefs that come to be associated with rituals, are secondary. They are secondary in that, at some important symbolist level of analysis, they say much the same thing as the ritual with which they are associated. Thus, they are not to be taken simply on "face value," which would typically be to take them as a technological system of beliefs intended to direct useful interventions in the environment (Firth 1964, pp. 236–37). Still, symbolists typically admit that mythical beliefs also have an "instrumental aspect"; that is, they admit that those who hold the myths think of them as true and make some technological use of the associated rituals (Beattie 1964, pp. 72, 204–5, 215). This then makes for epistemic irrationality, even obvious inconsistency, in the belief system understood as a representation of a purported reality that could be manipulated to bring about advantageous effects. However, the posited secondary status of myth, as an elaboration on ritual, gives the symbolist a way of accounting for the persistence of such epistemically irrational belief systems. The belief system, looked at both symbolically and literally, develops according to, or is "driven by," the ritual system, and not generally by epistemic scruples.

The observations above are intended to support the claims that (1) attributions of irrationality, even obvious inconsistency, have a place in several well-received social scientific and psychological works; (2) such attributions of irrationality need not engender worries regarding the account in question; (3) in part this is so because we have commonsensical explanation sketches for how such irrational beliefs can arise and for how, once established, they might prove quite persistent; and (4) the relevant processes are coming to be subject to increasing psychological and social scientific scrutiny, with the result that the explanation sketches suggested above are undergoing improvement, particularly in cognitive psychology.

Ultimately, we can distinguish two aspects of the problem of irrationality. The first is that, on many accounts, attributions of irrationality occurring in otherwise explanatory accounts become problematic and themselves serve as evidence against these accounts. This itself seems to be an undesirable result. However, it is conceivable that this unhappy state of affairs is just one that we must reconcile ourselves to and learn to work around. Davidson, for example, apparently believes this is so. He argues that attributions of inconsistency to individuals give rise to a certain paradox of irrationality "from which no theory can entirely escape" (Davidson 1982, p. 303). Still, it seems that any interpretive scheme that we do construct will need to lead us to make some such paradoxical attributions. On this view, then, we must live with a certain amount of paradox. However, if I am correct, then there is a second aspect to the problem of irrationality: the putative problematic status often attached to attributions of irrationality constitutes a needless and misguided methodological constraint on interpretation.

My argument in this chapter has provided two bases for understanding why attributions of irrationality need not be taken as problematic or paradoxical. First, the problem of irrationality arises from a failure to fully appreciate the distinction between the earlier and later stages of constructing an interpretive scheme. In the earlier stages, the principle of charity directs us in constructing a provisional first-approximation scheme. This task prepares the way for our addressing the virtues of refined schemes. In this later task, the principle of explicability, and not the principle of charity, serves as the appropriate constraint. Thus, in these matters, the principle of charity has given way and cannot then undermine our confidence in otherwise explanatory accounts. Secondly, the principle of charity has been subsumed under the principle of explicability. As a result, the principle of charity can never really compete with our concern for explicability. Where explanation can be had, we are indifferent to whether what is explained is rational (or correct) belief and action. As we have seen, the principle of explicability is really only a rule of thumb for where anomalous beliefs and actions may best be concentrated under interpretation.

In these last few sections, I have sought to fill out several ancillary points that are particularly complementary to the central line of argument in this chapter. To insure that these discussion do not have the counterproductive effect of causing some to lose sight of the central point, let me remind my readers: the principle of explicability provides an excellent and superior codification of interpretive practice. In part, this is because it makes such fine sense of what are actually the concerns informing the various stages of interpretation; additionally it thereby allows us to understand the role for, and limitations on, the principle of charity. The principle of charity is then best understood as a derivative rule of thumb, dependent on the principle of explicability, extant descriptive theory, and the epistemic situation particularly characteristic of the early stages of interpretation. In terms of the argument of the book, this result is of the first importance, for while the principle of charity, understood as a fundamental methodological constraint requiring us to impose a normatively derived structure in interpretation, would apparently have separatist implications, the more fundamental principle of explicability, counseling the sort of theory-informed interpretation of phenomena that is characteristic of the sciences generally, can have no such separatist implications.

4

On the Supposed A Priori Status
of Minimal Rationality

A number of philosophers have recently concluded that rationality is constitutive of beliefs and desires (Loar 1981; Føllesdal 1982; McDowell 1985; Rosenberg 1985b; Root 1986; Stich 1990). There is, they insist, a certain minimal level of rationality that we know a priori will hold of any subject to whom we correctly attribute propositional attitutes, and this level is sufficient to insure that, human beings, as subjects of interpretation, are preponderantly rational. Donald Davidson's (1980c, 1980e) arguments have played a central role in forming the emerging consensus on these matters. I examine these and related arguments in this chapter.

I begin by clarifying what is at issue, pointing out that Davidson's claim that the predominant rationality of beliefs and desires is a priori is itself a more limited claim than is often supposed. Borrowing the Quinean metaphor, this claim has to do with the centrality of certain beliefs to our present web of beliefs; and thus, it has only indirect implications for the ways in which psychology and the social sciences could ultimately develop. I believe that the claim must be construed in this way to have any plausibility at all.

However, even when so construed, Davidson's arguments for this claim are not altogether successful. To make his case, he attempts to show that findings of predominant rationality are needed in order to have a viable theory of beliefs and desires as these subjects are presently conceptualized. I here consider two lines of argument to this effect, one of which is really only suggested in Davidson's writings. First, one can find in Davidson's writings the suggestion that the standard axioms of measurement enter into viable theories of beliefs and desires by virtue of the use of comparative and quantitative concepts such as "preferring x to y" and "utility." A certain, very limited, degree of rationality in the ordering of desires seems to be insured by this argument, which I will call the argument from measurement. However, the rationality underwritten in this way is too limited for Davidson's purposes. Thus he explicitly develops a distinct argument: he draws on his analytical codification of the methods of proper interpretation. Such a codification would serve to reveal the "conceptual pressures" on the attribution of intensional states. Here, he claims to find general charitable constraints on interpretation that would thus greatly expand the degree of rationality that is conceptually insured. However, this argument from charity is not compelling, for it depends on the standard view of charity as a fundamental methodological constraint (FMC) employing a normatively derived structure (NDS). Such a view was discredited in the preceding chapter.

While I repudiate Davidson's (and related) arguments insofar as they rest upon the standard understanding of the principle of charity (FMC and NDS), I acknowledge that one can properly write of an a priori minimum level of rationality. As a sidelight to the central argument of this chapter, and as aid to understanding the theory-based nature of this a priori minimum, I devote a section to a tentative investigation of whether minimum rationality is preponderant rationality. I suggest that it probably is not.

Most importantly for the purposes of my argument in this book, I show that, while recognizing that there is an a priori minimal level of rationality raises interesting questions regarding what that minimum is, this recognition does not lead us to uncover any significant difference between the human sciences and the other sciences. In the sense that there is such an a priori limit (regarding minimal rationality) in the human sciences, there are a priori limits in many of the sciences.

Finally, I take up several issues raised by Stich (1990) that are particularly relevant to my position. Stich has also argued that there is an a priori minimal level of rationality of intentional states such as beliefs. However, he believes that this minimum, and the associated charity in interpretation, are themselves connected with objectionable features of intentional idiom—features that make talk of intentional states unserviceable for scientific purposes. In particular, the minimum is taken to be a nonempirical conceptual matter of parochial similarity with ourselves. As a result, Stich argues, charity in interpretation cannot be grounded in an empirical manner. I show that interpretation, as described here, has none of the objectionable features Stich envisions.

4.1: The View that Rationality is Constitutive of Intentional States

To begin with, we must get clear on what Davidson is claiming when he insists that we know a priori that peoples' beliefs and desires are predominantly rational. After all, claims regarding a priori truths have a long and unhappy history. In order to be fair to Davidson (and to some of those who have followed him here), we must take care not to construe talk of "a priori truths" and "constitutive principles" in a way that makes Davidson's claims stronger (and less reasonable) than he would want.

4.1.1: A Priori Truths and "The Subject" as a Conceptual Matter

Davidson's remarks on a priori truth may be understood in terms of his notion of "changing the subject": a claim about something is a priori just in case denying the claim would amount to changing the subject (Davidson 1980c, pp. 216, 220–21). On this view, certain sentences represent "constitutive criteria" employed in the application of various concepts. To deny such criterial principles is to change the subject.

Davidson illustrates these matters by discussing comparative and quantitative concepts. He explains that the axioms of measurement theory are among the criteria for the application of comparative concepts such as "longer than," or "heavier than," and for the application of quantitative concepts such as "weight" and "length." These criteria insure that such relations are transitive. In application to comparative length, they imply T: for any three (rigid) bodies x, y, and z, if x is longer than y, and y is longer than z, then x is longer than z. Davidson also explains that further criterial principles that might be called "meaning postulates" combine with the axioms of measurement to distinguish particular comparative concepts, such as "longer than," form other comparative concepts (Davidson 1980c, pp. 220–21). The resulting set of criterial principles for "longer than" imply that the implementation of certain (empirical) operations (within their range) should provide transitive results.

To keep Davidson's talk of "criterial principles" and "meaning postulates" in perspective, it is important to note, as Davidson does, that were we to pairwise examine three objects for comparative length and obtain an intransitive triad of results, we could, in principle, do any one (or an appropriate combination) of four things.

We could decide that the objects were not rigid bodies, or decide that some of the pairwise comparisons had contained mistakes in the application of our methods, or conclude that the methods used to determine length were themselves unreliable (thus revising the meaning postulates), or deny the transitivity postulate. Thus, for Davidson, T is neither irrevisable nor analytic. To deny T need not be self-contradictory. Of course, to avoid contradicting ourselves, we would have to abandon the axioms of measurement theory, at least in application to the present context. This, he insists, would be to change the subject by abandoning some of what characterizes the relation *longer than.* (We might then be talking about some other relation holding between the three objects.)

For Davidson, the subject is not the set of things picked out, but a matter of the "concept(s)" used. Concepts, he explains, can be "sustained in equilibrium by a number of conceptual pressures" (Davidson 1980c, p. 221). For example, in the case of the concept of "length," these pressures are represented by the axioms of measurement theory, the relevant meaning postulates, and perhaps certain physical laws. Together these are said to be "constitutive of the system of macroscopic rigid physical objects" (Davidson 1980c, p. 221). This is to say that these principles are really constitutive of our familiar system of concepts of "physical objects," "length," and so forth, and not of physical objects themselves, which existed before the concepts or principles were contrived. (Here I am supposing that Davidson is not an idealist.) The central point, then, is that Davidson's notion of a change of subject makes this a matter of conceptual change: when we change what we say in certain ways, we thereby come to use different concepts and, thus, change the subject.

To appreciate Davidson's views on how a system of concepts is constituted, it may help to recall his discussions of interpretation and, in particular, his insistence that the content of a propositional attitude "derives from its place in a pattern" (Davidson 1980c, p. 221). To share a concept, to use the same concept, thus to talk about the same subject, involves having a similarity in patterns of dispositions. The crucial similarity here can be understood by reflecting on how we decide that someone has learned or mastered a new concept (as discussed by Wittgenstein and Quine) and by reflecting on how we decide that an interpretation is correct (as discussed by Quine and Davidson). For example, if we are to find others talking about length, using our concept, we must find them placing objects into a hierarchical transitive ordering using operations similar to ours for measuring length. They will also need to place objects on a continuum that roughly mirrors our judgments about rigidity.

Davidson's claim that there are a priori truths thus becomes the claim that there are sentences or principles that sustain patterns of behavior or behavioral dispositions, and that in interpretation and teaching we give crucial attention to whether or not the relevant patterns are realized before attributing the appropriate conceptual mastery to the initiate or to the person interpreted. The sustaining principles, articulate or not, thus go hand-in-hand with a mastery of shared concepts. Their denial constitutes a conceptual shift.

Davidson's view here is attractive. It reflects aspects of language use that motivate the old analytic-synthetic distinction, without the distortion arising from that distinction's dichotomizing of the alternatives. (For example, on Davidson's view, a priori truths, such as those mentioned above, do have empirical implications.) Neither does Davidson's view rest on false props, such as the notion of determinate meaning. Davidson's view can be understood in terms of the more graded notions of success in learning and adequacy in translation or interpretation.

4.1.2: Needed Perspective: An Extensional Notion of "The Subject"

However, despite the virtues of Davidson's notion of "the subject," there also are dangers of distortion here. Without some care, Davidson's view (and associated talk of a priori truths) threatens to rule out, or at least obscure, an extensional perspective according to which we can properly say that we have learned something about a subject (such as energy or the structure of space, for example), even when what we learn on these subjects was previously thought to be a priori false. We can, in other words, say that we have found out certain facts about such-and-such things, where those things were only most indistinctly understood in the past.[1]

On this extensional (or referential) view of the subject, it is the set of processes, states, physical quantities, or entities that we presently conceptualize in the relevant terms. It is not correct to say here that the subject is the set of things of which the sentences of our present theory (of such-and-such) are true. For, obviously, that set might be empty, and probably is. Nor, for that matter, would it be correct to say that the subject, in the extensional sense, is the set of things about which most of the sentences of our present theory are true. Presumably, what is needed is an understanding of "the subject" that comports with extension or reference as discussed in (the so-called) causal theories of reference (Putnam 1975b). Very roughly, on such a view, the subject becomes those entities, states, kinds, or physical quantities with which the relevant experts and communities are interacting. Characterizations of the subject across communities may vary in many important respects, while those within the various communities nevertheless are concerned with the same subject. Even characterizations that are justly taken to be conceptually based, or a priori, may vary (even conflict) across the relevant communities, while reference and shared subject remains undisturbed. For example, in their dealings with electrons, our contemporary physics community is interacting with with the same sort of particles as J. J. Thomson, Millikan, and Bohr, yet they would deny some of what these earlier investigators took to be basic characteristics of electrons (Hacking 1983, pp. 82–84). The atom with its electrons is no longer conceived, in the manner of Thomson, as like currants in British pudding. In fact, in view of quark theory, even so basic a putative characteristic as being a carrier of the minimum unit of electric charge is no longer thought to hold of electrons, although this was once taken to be a priori true of electrons. Despite deep theoretical differences, we can agree that contemporary physicists are talking of the same subject as these predecessors when they discuss electrons. In so doing, we overlook certain deep theoretical differences in order to come to appreciate how the work of these earlier investigators initiated a course of research into our shared subject, electrons. Here we are applying Putnam's (1975c) Principle of Reasonable Doubt.

Consider the case of energy. Putnam (1975a) has described how energy was once, practically and explicitly, defined by the equation 'e = 1/2mv²'. Supposedly, this equation sustained the concept of energy, and was thus a priori in Davidson's sense. However, with empirical work, energy came to figure in more and more deeply entrenched laws. These in turn supposedly came to sustain the concept of energy as well. (Apparently a gradual form of conceptual change.) Historically, of course, Einstein's characterization of energy treats 'e = 1/2mv²' as only a rough first-approximation for characterizing not energy (now understood in terms of the power series: $e = mc^2 + 1/2mv^2 + \ldots$), but kinetic energy. Einstein thus treated the earlier equation as just another natural law, subject to revision. The question is, did he change the subject?

There is a perfectly respectable sense in which Einstein did not change the subject. Rather, with his work, we come to find out rather a lot about that subject. Energy, we say, had only been most imperfectly understood prior to Einstein's work. His work brought our understanding of this physical quantity to a new level. From this new level, we can deny that 'e= 1/2mv²' properly characterizes energy, we can say that this equation is, at best, a rough first-approximation in characterizing a particular component of energy (which earlier investigators mistakenly believed to be all there was to energy).

I am not saying that this extensional view of changing the subject is the correct view, and that Davidson's more conceptual view is distorting. I believe both are helpful. So, we should not become so enamored with either that we lose sight of the other. We thus remain sensitive to the ways in which our conceptualizations of our subject (such as energy or electrons) can progress while we come to say different things about it. As Davidson (1980c, p. 216) says, "there is no clear line between changing the subject and changing what one says about it." If what I have said is correct, it is often not even a matter of there being a vague line to be roughly indicated. Rather, the same cases may be correctly described both ways (by employing different senses of "the subject" in each description). The same scientific discovery may both change the subject, in Davidson's sense, and also teach us a good deal about a subject we previously knew little about.

In a way parallel to the case of energy, through a progression of psychological work, we could discover that rationality is really not so characteristic of human beliefs and desires. We could find that human beings are not predominantly rational in these states that, by all accounts, we only very imperfectly understand at present. In this claim, I use an extensional notion of the subject about which discoveries are made. However, I admit that when Davidson's conceptual notion of the subject is employed, it is correct to say that beliefs and desires are a priori rational *at some minimal level.* I admit that a belief in a certain minimal rationality of such states is so deeply embedded in our web of beliefs that it is respected in translation and learning.

In light of the above, I believe there are several important points that can be established in this chapter. First, and the point of the present section, there is an important distinction to be drawn between conceptual and extensional notions of "the subject." Associated with the conceptual notion of the subject are conceptual a priori truths. I believe that there are *no good arguments to establish that there is an a priori minimal level of rationality in any but the conceptual sense.* (I do not believe that anything is a priori in any other sense.) Recognizing such conceptual a priori truths does not conflict with the claim that whatever is so guaranteed about a subject, might, as our theory changes, be found false of the subject understood in the extensional sense. For being a conceptual a priori truth is a matter of the centrality of certain principles to present theory. Second, if this is the sense in which a minimal level of rationality is a priori, then *such a priori results do not make the human sciences special, or subject to restrictions not found in the sciences quite generally*. Such a priori results, having to do with the centrality of certain principles of extant theory, are to be found in all the sciences. Third, I will argue that the level of rationality that is a priori, in this conceptual sense, is rather less than Davidson and others have supposed. Once we focus on this conceptual sense, we will find that it is still not an a priori truth that beliefs and desires are predominantly rational. Finally, Davidson's argument for preponderant rationality based on his principle of charity is misguided in two decisive respects. It is misguided in relying on a flawed understanding of the principle of charity, and it is misguided in that it is ultimately an attempt to establish an a priori result in something stronger than the conceptual sense that Davidson himself explicates.

Lest it be thought that the cautions incorporated in the above discussion are not needed, consider the implication of Michael Root's Kantian interpretation of Davidson's position:

> The norms or principles that guide interpretation are the norms of rationality. The thoughts that the interpreter attributes to the agent to explain her actions *must* rationalize them. They *must* make the action a reasonable one for the agent to have performed. Minds are, for the most part, rational because *we cannot but understand them as so* (Root 1986, pp. 227–28).

These statements express an incautious view that ignores the distinctions between the conceptual and extensional notions the subject, and thus seems to have a certain finality inappropriate to conceptual a priori truths. On Root's view, since we cannot but so understand minds, beliefs, and such, it seems we should abandon the psychological study of the rational and irrational aspects of human inference. After all, if inference has to do with beliefs (and that is the way cognitive psychologists talk) it must be rational. Root's version of Davidson's position is, I think, not so unique as not to require a response.

However, having recognized the nature of Davidson's claim, and having noted some of what it does and some of what it does not entail, we are left with the interesting question of whether or not it is a *conceptual* a priori truth that beliefs and desires are predominantly rational. I now turn to this issue. (The distinction between the subject understood as a conceptual matter and the subject understood as an extensional matter is not meant to resolve this issue, but to clarify it.) To make the case for his claim, properly understood, Davidson needs to show that findings of predominant rationality are needed to have a viable theory of beliefs and desires as these subjects are presently conceptualized. In the following sections, I consider and find wanting two arguments to this effect.

4.2: On an Argument from Measurement

It is commonplace that we desire many things, and pursue relatively few. In accounting for this within a theory of beliefs and desires, these notions are typically given comparative and quantitative forms. A failure to pursue some desire is often explained in terms of that desire's being relatively less strong than others, which are pursued, or in terms of the agent's belief that such desires are relatively unlikely to be met, despite his or her best efforts. Such explanations are also commonplaces, and presumably the appropriate associated generalizations, suitably qualified, are Davidsonian a priori truths. For, if someone does not know how to use talk of beliefs and desires in these familiar ways, we would not attribute to them knowledge of the relevant concepts. To be able to explain some portion of a person's behavior in such terms (at least in a range of particularly simple cases) is a prerequisite for having a viable theory of the person's beliefs and desires.

Thus, viable theories of individuals' beliefs and desires make use of a comparative concept of "x's desiring y more than z," and sometimes a quantitative concept. Accordingly, the axioms of measurement theory, minimally those for comparative concepts, characterize the desires of a person at any given time. This, in turn, mandates a structure of desires that is rational in certain very limited respects.[2] In particular, it follows that people's desires or preferences comprise a hierarchical, transitive, ordering. As a result, one could not simply take advantage of intransitivities in preferences to progressively bleed the individual of first one good, then another, then the first, and so on. To avoid being liable to such a "resources pump" is thought to characterize one aspect of rationality (Skyrms 1986).

Although qualifications and additions might refine this argument from measurement, it is generally compelling as it stands. However, although it is compatible with his position, and draws on considerations that he already employs in other ways, Davidson does not rely on or explicitly develop this argument. While the requirements of measurement in decision-theory are broached at places in his writings, this is typically to show that some structure must be imposed a priori in interpretation, due to holism (Davidson 1980e). Then, as discussed in chapter 2, the holistic interdependence of belief, desire, and action is taken to constitute a need to be filled by imposing a *normative* structure of rationality. Thus, mention of the requirements of decision-theoretic measurement, and the need to impose a structure in interpretation, typically leads up to a discussion of Davidson's principle of charity, and not to a discussion of the axioms of measurement theory. Similarly, while Davidson does discuss the constraints on the application of qualitative and quantitative concepts, this is done to illustrate the role of constitutive principles generally, and the examples used are taken from the physical sciences (Davidson 1980e, pp. 219–23). Little is explicitly made of the place for such constraints in the application of quantitative and qualitative psychological concepts. These observations hold for all but Davidson's earliest writings.[3] One plausible explanation for Davidson's not developing the argument from measurement is that it would seem to be redundant on his argument from the principle of charity.

In any case, the argument from measurement would seem to be open to Davidson and to draw only on what he is committed to anyway. I discuss it here because it seems to me an instructive and clear argument for the a priori status of certain sorts of rationality. In particular, the sorts of rationality under interpretation that are insured by this argument are relatively clear. However, here lies both the strengths and weakness of this argument for Davidson's purposes. For, although the argument from measurement provides a compelling case for the a priori status of at least some rationality, the rationality so insured is quite minimal. Consider: while the axioms of measurement theory require that preference orderings be transitive, they do not insure that actual choices are transitive. Tversky (1969), for example, has shown how a lexicographic ordering of preferences can give rise to intransitive choices when the series of options facing the individual varies on the dominant dimension in increments just below what is noticeable. While such intransitivity of choice need not be irrational, it serves to emphasize how little is implied by the conceptually insured transitivity of preference.

More to the point, while the axioms of measurement theory also require that the preference relation be asymmetrical, some choices between pairs of options may fail to follow suit. Tversky and Kahneman (1981, pp. 453–58) show how numerically equivalent ways of conceiving alternatives in particular cases can produce violations of asymmetry. They use the term 'decision frame' to refer to the decision maker's conception of the acts, outcomes, and contingencies associated with a particular choice. The options in a particular decision situation might be framed in various ways. To borrow one example, a choice between two health programs responding to an expected disease outbreak might be framed in alternative ways that are nevertheless numerically equivalent: one in terms of probable deaths in a population of affected people, the other in terms of expectations for saving people in the same population. How the problem is framed affects the typical choices. People tend to be adverse to taking risks when the problem is formulated in terms of gains, while tending to take risks when it is formulated in terms of losses. (Presumably then, with a well chosen third alternative, an intransitive set of choices could well result from the framing effects.[4]) In any case, these tendencies lead to violations of the asymmetry requirement on choices, as the order of the preferences between two options is reversed by such framing. Such "framing effects" are certainly problematic from the normative point of view. Tversky and Kahneman's analogy is apt:

> Veridical perception requires that the perceived relative height of two neighboring mountains, say, should not reverse with changes of vantage point. Similarly, rational choice requires that the preference between options should not reverse with changes of frame (Tversky and Kahneman 1981, p. 453).[5]

Thus, such cases remind us that the axioms of measurement theory, while insuring in some degree both transitivity and asymmetry of preferences, do not rule out important and irrational violations of such principles in actual choices. This failure to insure what might on the face of it seem a relatively direct consequence (transitivity and asymmetry of choice on the basis of transitivity and asymmetry of preference) can thus serve to emphasize the very limited extent to which such principles insure rationality.

My remarks certainly have not exhaustively surveyed the conceivable sources of irrationality in the face of the axioms of measurement and the well-ordering of preferences that is insured thereby. Beliefs might of course still be irrational (being based on sufficiently improper reasoning about what is the case or about what is likely) and the argument presently under scrutiny places no constraints on beliefs. Choices depend on beliefs as well as desires. Thus, a certain irrationality in choices could conceivably arise through the use of sufficiently irrational beliefs. Of course choice depends on inferential processes as well as on belief and desire states. Thus, irrationality could result from improper reasoning about what to do, given our beliefs and desires. Relevant beliefs might be ignored, for example. Or, as noted above, framing effects might give rise to intransitive sequences of choices. The argument from measurement does not constrain these effects of sloppy reasoning. Neither does it place constraints on the mechanisms behind changes of desires, as long as the results are transitive and asymmetrical at any time. Sufficient plasticity or volatility of desires could also give rise to a certain irrationality in choice. And, significantly, even our standard conceptions of desire do not seem to require that desires be particularly well-reasoned. For example, desires are often thought to be as much a result of attention as a result of reasoning. (To appreciate this, one need only observe the often effective work of sales personnel in temporarily modifying preferences. Few people have not had the experience of purchasing an item knowing that other purchasing plans would need to be abandoned as a result, then, upon leaving the shop finding that the preference order that dictated the abandoned plans seemed, once again, compelling.) Of course, whether much irrationality does arise through a combination of these mechanisms has not been determined. What is significant here is that the argument from measurement has not conceptually insured against this.

In several (if not all) of these matters, Davidson tries to constrain us by his argument from charity. This more ambitious argument thus becomes the crucial argument for showing that it is a priori that beliefs, desires, and actions are preponderantly rational. However, it is also less persuasive than the argument from measurement.

Before considering Davidson's crucial argument, it is worthwhile to emphasize that whatever rationality the argument from measurement insures, it does so only in the sense appropriate to his notion of conceptual a priori truths. Thus, it tells us something about the form of our present web of beliefs. However, this cannot, in any simple way, limit the form that future theories of desires and beliefs will take. It is at least conceivable that we would some-day conclude that the phenomena presently spoken of as desires cannot usefully be placed on an ordinal scale in the way now commonly entertained.[6] Still, talk of such phenomena might find a place in successful theories, which perhaps retain the terminology of "desires." I admit such developments would constitute a substantial conceptual shift in Davidson's sense (and I know of no better sense), but it would be possible to have thus learned something about that psychological phenomena that we presently conceptualize in terms of desires. Work in the social and psychological sciences could, conceivably lead to such far-reaching results. Again, this is not a prediction. But it serves to emphasize the limitations to what can be insured a priori.

4.3: On the Argument from Charity in Interpretation

As noted above, Davidson explicitly argues for the a priori status of rationality by attempting to codify the methods of translation and interpretation. He claims to uncover a fundamental principle of charity that constrains us to attribute rational beliefs and actions to those interpreted. This methodological constraint would insure that beliefs and actions are characterized as preponderantly rational. For, while isolated attributions of irrationality need not wholly erode our confidence in an interpretive scheme, the cumulative effect of such attributions in a case where we did not attribute preponderant rationality would render our scheme unacceptable.

In chapter 2, I discussed Davidson's arguments for his principle of charity. It will be rememberd that Davidson attempts a codificational argument for a principle of charity as the way of satisfying methodological needs generated by the holistic nature of intentional states. He deftly shows that we must holistically impose a structure on the beliefs, desires, and actions imputed to those we seek to understand. This need to impose a pattern in interpretation is shown to arise from the need to determine several unknowns (belief, desire, and meaning) on the basis of a rather sparser evidential base (the resulting behaviors of choice and holding true sentences).

Once we recognize the methodological needs that he uncovers, the force of Davidson's codificational argument turns on his claim that the pattern that is, and must be, projected in interpretation is a fundamentally charitable one. On Davidson's view, the beliefs attributed to our subjects must be preponderantly true and rational; we are to solve for meaning, by holding the belief variable steady, so far as practical—and this is, in part, a matter of finding beliefs steadily rational. Likewise the desires attributed to our subjects (and their interaction with beliefs to produce actions) must conform to the normative standard described in basic decision-theory. Thus he writes:

> If we are to derive meaning and belief from evidence concerning what causes someone to hold sentences true, it can only be (as in decision theory) because we stipulate a structure. . . . We individuate and identify beliefs, as we do desires, intentions and meanings, in a great number of ways. But the relations between beliefs play a decisive constitutive role; we cannot accept great or obvious deviations from rationality without threatening the intelligibility of our attributions. . . . First, then, we have no choice but to project our own logic onto the beliefs of another (Davidson 1980e, pp. 6–7).

Davidson thus identifies an important role that might be served by charitable assumptions in interpretation, and he makes a plausible case for this need actually being satisfied, *at least in part*, by a charitable procedure. Nevertheless, as we have seen, we have reason to hold Davidson's account (in terms of FMC and NDS) problematic. In none of Davidson's discussions does he provide reasons for thinking that a *fundamentally* charitable procedure is the only way of satisfying the methodological needs he identifies. Neither does he devote much attention to showing that fundamentally charitable assumptions play as great a role in the practice of constructing interpretive schemes as he seems to suggest. These lacunae in his codificational discussions are crucial. When Davidson (1984d, p. 168) remarks that "the content of a propositional attitude derives from its place in the pattern [of such states that together make sense of a person's behavior]," I can agree, while not being committed to charity in translation as a fundamental constraint. In view of the holistic character of meaning and interpretation, we must attribute propositional attitudes in accordance with some global pattern or other. The key issue is what pattern we are committed to finding in attributing propositional attitudes. Davidson insists that it is fundamentally an ideally rational pattern. However, as we have seen, one can recognize the holistic nature of interpretation without being thereby committed to finding (so far as possible) a pattern characterized by ideal rationality.

As I have argued, what have been codified as charitable constraints on translation are, more fundamentally, derivative on concerns to construe others in ways that make them explicable. The constraints that operate in actual cases are primarily a matter of concern for the explicability of beliefs and actions under interpretation. Thus, I have argued that the principle of explicability provides a better codification of the fundamental constraints on translation and interpretation than does the principle of charity. When these points are appreciated, the support Davidson's codificational argument gives to his claim that rationality is a priori is undermined. When charitable constraints on interpretation are no longer seen as fundamental, the codification of the methodology of interpretation no longer attests to the centrality of rationality to our concepts of "belief" and "desire." For, we seek to attribute propositional attitudes patterned in ways characterizable—not by "ideal" rationality—but by our expectations for both rationality and irrationality. This is the theory-laden pattern that we seek to find again as we interpret.

It is crucial to notice that the principle of explicability alone, with no supplemental information concerning our present psychological understandings, does not require that we seek to find rationality under interpretation. Thus, the fundamental constraints on interpretation and translation do not, in any direct manner, give support to the claim that rationality is a priori (as would a fundamental principle of charity).

The principle of explicability does require that we seek to attribute beliefs and desires that are explicable using our best present theoretical resources. So, while the constraints on interpretation do not directly give rise to the requirement that we find people rational, those theoretical resources we can presently draw upon may give rise to such a constraint. But *here we have come full circle.* On the view of interpretation we have come to, 'belief' and 'desire' become theoretical terms. As we noted earlier, the deepest theoretical claims in our web of beliefs involving such terms may be said to represent conceptual a priori truths. *We thus return to the question of whether such claims imply that people are preponderantly rational. What we have learned in the intervening few pages is that there is no fundamental methodological constraint on interpretation that gives direct support to the claim that there are such a priori principles.* In effect, we have found that the principle of charity, to the extent that it holds, is derivative on such theoretical principles, and not the converse.

Significantly, were Davidson's argument from charity successful, it would ultimately have given rise to an a priori minimal level of attributable rationality where this level was a priori in something stronger than the conceptual sense explicated earlier. The conceptual notion of an a priori truth turns on the centrality of certain principles to our present theories. But, the principle of charity, understood as a fundamental methodological constraint (FMC) involving the imposition of NDS is supposedly not just a matter of the structure of present theory. By way of contrast, in the above argument, I have returned our attention to the issue of whether predominant rationality is called for in the central components of our best present theories, that is, to the issue of what rationality is insured as a matter of a conceptual a priori truth.

Two objections to the basic argument given in this section warrant consideration. To begin with, while I have taken exception to the fundamental status Davidson accords to the principle of charity, I obviously recognize derivative constraints on interpretation that constitute a variant of that principle. Indeed, earlier, I discussed how, for reasons having to do with our present psychological theories and the information available at various stages in interpreting others, charitable constraints are particularly constraining in the earliest stages of interpretation. One might wonder whether the resulting "background of agreement" on which attributions of disagreement and their explanation rests is enough to make it a priori that beliefs and desires must be preponderantly rational.

Two lines of response are needed. First, what background of agreement is needed in interpretation is itself theoretically conditioned, as explained in chapter 3. Thus, the argument developed just now to show that the principle of charity does not provide a fundamental methodological constraint insuring that beliefs are preponderantly rational can be applied mutatus mutandis to show that the needed background is not a fundamental methodological matter insuring preponderant rationality. It is simply not a fundamental methodological matter (see also Lukes 1982). Second, as things stand now, the needed background of agreement is probably not so extensive as to insure preponderant rationality. For the sorts of rationality we seek to find under interpretation in the earliest stages are quite minimal. They typically involve rudimentary logical structures of a basic and simple truth-functional and quantificational form and simple forms of practical reasoning such as are represented in the rudimentary practical syllogism. Further, the rudimentary rationality insured here may be quite restricted to local belief-desire structures (as suggested by Davidson's [1982] suggestion of "quasi-independent structures of the mind"). When judged as a whole, and in terms of our best standards of rationality, the full belief-desire-action structures that are attributed in keeping with such restrictions may then yet turn out not to be preponderantly rational. (The particular psychological results discussed in the next section illustrate and give some indication of the myriad sorts of irrationality that are not foreclosed by the early results of interpretation.) Thus, the rationality we need to find in these earliest stages does not seem enough to insure preponderant rationality.

Those familiar with Davidson's thesis of the "anomalousness of the mental" will have anticipated another objection. Davidson apparently holds that there are no psycho-physical or psychological laws. If this is so, my argument in this section would be undermined. Without psychological laws, there is presumably less scope for psychological explanation of irrationality. Thus, Davidson (1982, p. 299) is led to view psychological explanation as a matter of finding conformity with non-nomic generalizations that by and large mirror our norms of rationality. Were we to know, simply on the basis of philosophical argument, that little irrationality can be explained, and that most psychological explanation must be in terms of rationality, then we could conclude, using either the principle of explicability *or* Davidson's principle of charity, that most beliefs and desires must be rational. (Without this, we would need to do as I have suggested we must: determine just how central rationality really is to our present psychological theories.) Put simply, were there no nomic psychological generalizations, the principle of charity and the fundamental principle of explicability presumably converge in their practical implications, and, as a result, it would seem to be a deeply entrenched part of our psychological concepts that belief and desire must be preponderantly rational—this would be an a priori truth.[7]

Thus, if true, the claim that there can be no lawlike psychological generalizations would be quite damaging to the position I am advancing in this chapter and damaging to the position developed in this book as a whole. However, I am convinced that there can be nomic psychological generalizations. I will not defend this conviction at this point, for the matter is given extended attention in the chapters to follow. The fifth and sixth chapters discuss the crucial role of nomic generalizations in intentional explanations, while the ensuing chapters defend the nomic status of psychological generalizations.

A final note is in order here. Some readers may wonder whether my contrast between the principle of explicability and Davidson's fundamental principle of charity accurately characterizes Davidson's views. Significantly, *if* I have misunderstood Davidson, and he holds a principle of charity more akin to Quine's, and, in turn, more akin to my principle of explicability, then his argument from charity for the a priori status of preponderant rationality fails. For reasons specified above, the principle of explicability, or a compliant principle of charity that is equally as tolerant of attributions of explicable irrationality, provides scant support for the a priori status of preponderant rationality. However, I can explain further why I believe that I have not caricatured Davidson's principle of charity, in which case his argument from charity fails because it is based on an inadequate codification of the constraints on interpretation. (Of course, the discussions in chapter 2 already have provided a good deal of support for my construction. But more can be said here.)

Admittedly, at points, Davidson has elaborated his principle of charity as a generally flexible principle. When he counsels us to construct our interpretive scheme so as to find our subjects speaking the truth, we are urged "to do this as far as possible, subject to considerations of simplicity, hunches about the effects of social conditioning, and of course our commonsense, or scientific, knowledge of explicable error" (1984e, p. 196). At the very least, this respect for explicable error should be understood as directing us to weight the principle of charity so that attributions of such errors generally do not count heavily against the interpretive scheme. When discussing the weighted principle of charity understood as a rule of thumb, I argued that such an approach to weighting the principle suggests that attributions of particular explicable errors ought not to be taken as undermining the sponsoring interpretive scheme in any way. However, there is little evidence that Davidson ever comes to adopt such a tolerant view of charity as a derivative rule of thumb. And, whatever his ultimate view of charity in interpretation generally, the difference between my principle of explicability and Davidson's principle of charity are persistent at the one significant point where he does not display respect for explicability: the treatment of rationality under interpretation.

Davidson focuses on rationality as a matter where charitable constraints are especially constraining. Attributions of irrationality, and inconsistency in particular, are viewed as especially damaging to our confidence in our interpretive scheme. Accordingly, while he finds ways of accommodating some attributions of irrationality, he insists that any attribution of inconsistency should detract from our confidence in an interpretation, *even when the inconsistency is explicable*. He suggests that one can, and probably must find, "quasi-independent structures" of the mind—belief desire structures that are characterized by "a larger degree of rationality than is attributed to the whole" (Davidson 1982, pp. 289, 299–300). These are to allow us to explain certain forms of inconsistency. However, while this "dissipates to a degree the problems," the explained inconsistency seems to remain paradoxical and problematic for Davidson, as he writes of "the underlying paradox of irrationality, from which no theory can entirely escape" (p. 303).

Davidson's perception of paradox here explains why he believes that "we weaken the intelligibility of attributions of thoughts of any kind to the extent that we fail to uncover a consistent pattern of belief, and finally of actions" (1984d, p. 159). And while this is not to ban such attributions altogether, it does treat all such attributions as evidence against our interpretation in some degree (however small). Davidson's view then is that while all interpretive schemes will be at least moderately plagued with a few such attributions, such attributions remain (at best) somewhat paradoxical and detract from our confidence in our interpretive scheme. Consequently, it seems to him that no acceptable interpretive scheme can get away with attributing a preponderance of irrationality.

Thus, on the matter of rationality, at least, Davidson fails to recognize that the attribution of explicable error does not detract from our confidence in an interpretation. Had Davidson recognized the primacy of explicability, he would have seen that the argument from what remains of the principle of charity does not support his claims regarding the a priori status of rationality, or more fully, that it cannot support such claims without a good deal more attention to the structure of present theory.

4.4: Is Minimal Rationality Preponderant Rationality: What is Central to Present Theory?

We have now determined that Davidson's argument from charity for the a priori status of rationality is a failure. However, this is not yet to say that its conclusion cannot be supported in other ways. The argument from measurement provides some support here. Still, I have argued that this supports, at best, a very limited claim about rationality, not the claim that preponderant rationality is a priori. In the absence of some relatively sweeping methodological argument, such as would have proceeded from a fundamental principle of charity, it will not be simple or easy to support the claim that we must either find people predominantly rational or change the subject. One would need to argue in a piecemeal manner, showing that various aspects of rationality are a priori. Again, the argument from measurement is an interesting beginning. The question becomes whether the results of such piecemeal work can be accumulated to the point of establishing the claim that beliefs, desires, and actions are predominantly rational.

One reason for the difficulty of this question is that in this context Davidson's remark, "there is no clear line between changing the subject and changing what one says about it," strikes home. When we get clear on the appropriate question to ask in approaching these issues piecemeal, we see that the matter turns on the centrality of different principles to our own web of psychological beliefs. This can be a somewhat vague matter, especially in view of the rather unsettled state of psychology.

Recall the standard settled on earlier for being a conceptual a priori truth. It was pointed out that some claims sustain (or are intimately associated with) a pattern of behavioral dispositions that is important in attributing conceptual mastery relative to some term contained in those claims. If, for example, someone did not behave as if length is transitive, we would balk at attributing to that person mastery of our concepts of "length" and "longer than." A claim was said to be a priori just in case it was so related to patterns of these sorts. The question becomes to what extent attributions of particular sorts of rationality are so characterizable with respect to the concepts of "beliefs," "desires," and so forth.

The piecemeal approach then is this: we need to examine a range of attributions of irrationality to determine in which cases reflective listeners suspect not just factual disagreement but unintelligibility or linguistic divergence. So far, I have only accepted the argument for the a priori status of the claim that preference-orders are rational in at least being transitive and asymmetrical. What else can be said? For reasons of space, I will consider here only the illustrative matter of beliefs. The prospects are dim for establishing by piecemeal argumentation the claim that beliefs are predominantly rational because few claims about particular sorts of rationality are sufficiently strong, precise, and central to our web of psychological beliefs.

One common claim is that people cannot believe an explicit contradiction. This is plausibly a priori. But, notice that even this claim, by itself, provides only for very minimal rationality. It would allow people to hold inconsistent sets of beliefs, as long as the inconsistency does not become, or give rise to, explicit contradiction. Just how inconsistent peoples' beliefs may be, would then depend on what capacities (or incapacities) we suppose them to possess for discovering or avoiding discovering inconsistency. If we suppose that people's cognitive processes are rather ineffective in making inconsistencies in their beliefs explicit, we could, compatibly with the above principle, attribute to people belief systems that are replete with inconsistencies while containing no explicit contradiction. These subsidiary issues do not seem to be so well settled as to be plausibly a priori. Thus, even were we to grant that the general principle above is a priori, the claim that peoples' beliefs must be rational at least in that they are (substantially) consistent does not seem to be a priori.

Additionally, as reflected in my discussion of the problem of irrationality, the claim that people cannot believe explicit contradictions must itself be treated with care. First, some inconsistency may be made so obvious to people as to be plausibly described as explicit, without thereby inducing the holder to modify his or her set of beliefs. For example, Johnson-Laird and Wason (1972) and Wason (1972) describe how respondents may be induced to provide answers to problems, recognize aspects of those problems that clearly show that their answers are incorrect, and yet refuse to modify their answers. It is not incredible to suppose that, in real-life situations, cultural wisdom that underlies valued portions of everyday life may contain inconsistencies. When these are pointed out, people might stubbornly refuse to modify the cultural wisdom. If nothing else, they may take refuge in mysticism, rather than abandon their valued beliefs. If such suggestions are not so incredible as to induce my readers to seek nonhomophonic translations for my talk of "belief" here, then even the principle that people cannot believe explicit contradictions must be carefully restricted if it is to be taken as conceptually a priori. Perhaps it may be taken to hold that people cannot believe true any sentence of the form '$p\&\text{-}p$', while allowing that they can, in some cases, believe true p and q even after being shown that these are inconsistent.

Psychologists studying human inductive reasoning have

discussed a rather impressive set of (putative) systematic failings. Significantly, there has not been an outcry that these psychologists are improperly talking about beliefs when they claim that certain "beliefs" arise by way of the fallacious inferences they describe. This suggests that (whether true or not) such descriptions of human reasoning do not violate clear principles central to our web of psychological beliefs. Yet, in the right circumstances, the psychological tendencies they have described could result in substantial irrationality within a belief system. This, in turn, suggests that whatever claims about human inductive reasoning are conceptually a priori are insufficient to insure predominantly rational inductive reasoning. From the perspective of an attempt to conceptually insure that belief systems will be predominantly rational with respect to their inductive grounding, it would seem that too few claims of any generality asserting that people are rational in their beliefs regarding probabilities can be taken a priori. We do suppose that people are disposed to enumerative inductions, for example. And, plausibly, this supposition is conceptually a priori. However, such a supposition will not insure preponderantly rational beliefs in the face of compatible dispositions to a range of inductive errors such as those already mentioned. For example, irrationality can arise from the overly free generalization from samples, and Hamill, Wilson, and Nisbett (1980) have found that people are, indeed, quite insensitive to problematic sample characteristics such as small size and clear bias, especially when the sample is itself rather vivid or salient.

As mentioned earlier, recent psychological studies of post-experimental debriefing suggest that people may regularly continue to hold beliefs for which they no longer have good reason (Ross, Lepper, and Hubbard 1975). Such stubborn persistence in believing suggests that unadvisedly acquired beliefs may not be readily removed from individuals' stocks. Of course, this would compound the failures allowed above, further reducing the extent to which people are a priori rational in their beliefs.

It is important to remember that the issue here is a matter of what claims about irrationality are a priori ruled out. Here we have noted that reflective audiences have not responded to the work mentioned above in a way that suggests that this work violates constitutive principles of intentional psychology, they have not generally suspected linguistic divergence in talk of "beliefs" in these cases. But, the cumulative effect of systematic errors such as those entertained in the sort of work just now mentioned could be striking in come contexts. People *could* have inductively ill-grounded belief systems. These might be rife with contradictions, some of which have sometimes been made explicit. Yet the systems might persist, even after their lack of inductive basis is pointed out. Now, it really has never been clear what counts as having predominantly or preponderantly rational beliefs. That is, it has never been made clear how we judge (weight and sum) the rationality and irrationality of beliefs and belief systems. But, if we are employing our best epistemic standards, it would be difficult to imagine that the set of failures entertained just now would fail to render a set of beliefs not preponderantly rational.

There is, I think, a general reason that few, if any, students of human psychology have objected to the psychological results mentioned here. It is that these results are perceived as important refinements in our folk-psychological view that people are capable of being quite stubborn, obtuse, even stupid and irrational, in their beliefs. Explaining someone's ability to believe something by showing that it erroneously follows from something else the person believes, and follows in a way we might ourselves find tempting, is as central to folk-psychological procedure as is the rationalizing explanation of beliefs. Thus, such talk of irrational beliefs draws upon and sharpens deeply rooted aspects of our talk of beliefs. In fact, it seems to me that, in much psychology, what is deeply embedded in our web of beliefs just is such rather vague positions. As a result, the refining work of contemporary psychologists runs little risk of conflicting with such positions and consequently changing the subject.

4.5: Summary and Significance

By way of summary, it is useful to set out the significance of the results found in this chapter for the argument of the book as a whole. In preceding chapters, I have argued that the principle of charity is a derivative principle, subsumable under a principle of explicability in conjunction with present understandings in the social and psychological sciences. Put simply, the constraints on the interpretation of the phenomena of interest in the human sciences are not unlike the constraints on the proper theory-laden observation of phenomena in the sciences generally. This implies that what rationality we must find under interpretation is a function of present theory, and not a function of some special constraint. But responsible thinkers have felt otherwise. They have thought that there might be an a priori minimal rationality requirement that constrains investigators in the human sciences in a way that other investigators are not constrained.

One might attempt to express such convictions by claiming that the subject of the human sciences—intentional states and their antecedents and effects (actions)—are characterized by certain constitutive principles. Violation of such principles change the subject. It then seems that investigators in the human sciences must adhere to these principles, or go out of business. However, this line of thought is flawed. Its problems stem from overestimating what can be established a priori about the limits of scientific discovery by examining "the subject" of a science. When "the subject" is understood as a conceptual matter, violation of constitutive principles does indeed change the subject, but the relevant science need not go out of business as a result. The various sciences are just not so intimately tied to particular conceptual subjects. Physics, for example, did not go out of business with Einstein. On the other hand, when "the subject" is understood as a more extensional matter, we can learn that certain constitutive principles are false of the subject.

The point of the present chapter was to address the issues raised by talk of an a priori minimal rationality requirement. I have shown that while there may well be an a priori minimum to what rationality is attributable, there are no good arguments for thinking that this a priori minimum provides or is based on a type of constraint that is not found in sciences generally. Thus, there is a minimum rationality constraint that stems from the centrality of certain principles to our present web of psychological theory. But, as Quine and others have taught us, in all the sciences there are a priori minima or limits that are matters of the centrality of certain principles within the present theory. Thus, the fact that there are such in intentional psychology has no methodological separatist implications. The argument from measurement can best be understood in this way, as it points to the centrality of the axioms of transitivity and asymmetry for the use of the comparative and quantitative concepts employed in our present theories.

On the other hand, the argument from the principle of charity (understood as a fundamental constraint on interpretation) cannot be understood in this innocuous manner. That argument does have separatist implications, and, so far as I know, it is the only tempting argument for a minimal rationality requirement with such implications. But that argument must be repudiated because it rests on a defective understanding of the principle of charity in interpretation.

Finally, I have discussed something of a side issue by addressing the issue of whether it is an a priori truth (in the acceptable sense) that peoples' beliefs and desires are preponderantly rational. Without support from a fundamental principle of charity, this becomes the issue of what sorts of rationality are crucial and central to our web of present theory dealing with intentional states. To show that preponderant rationality is insured in this way, a piecemeal approach is the only recourse; we would need to examine a range of attributions of irrationality to get some sense for which make us suspect linguistic divergence when talking of beliefs and desires. I have suggested that, given present theory, it is probably not a priori that beliefs and desires be preponderantly rational. (Of course, this depends on adding up accumulations of attributable irrationality and comparing this with the rationality that must at present be attributed.)

However, if I am wrong, and a more sustained examination were to show that minimal rationality is preponderant rationality, this would not undermine the crucial point of this chapter: the proper way of conceiving whatever minimal rationality requirement there is, is to conceive of it as resting on the structure of present theory, *not* on a fundamental principle of charity.

4.6: Further Reflection on Minimal Rationality: Stich's Concerns

Stephen Stich (1984, 1985, 1990) has developed an account of the attribution of intentional, or contentful, states that is in some respects similar to the account that I have developed here. In particular, Stich (1990, p. 38) concludes that beliefs and desires must be rational at some minimal level, and this is said to be an a priori or conceptual truth. Further, Stich (1990, p. 51) draws on Cherniak (1986) to show that this level might be relatively low, so as not to undermine contemporary psychological investigation of cognitive error. However, Stich's position also differs from my own in several important respects. Of course, Stich believes that belief and desires, as he understands them, have little if any place in scientific work. Points at which my account of intentional attributions differs from Stich's lead me to reject Stich's eliminativism as premature. By focusing here on several of these points of disgrement, I will show how interpretation need not suffer from the putatively fatal flaws Stich envisions.

One central disagreement has to do with Stich's understanding of the nature of the supposed a priori limit to irrationality. Stich understands this in a manner that would make intentional idiom, so constrained, unfit for scientific work; he eagerly points this out and draws his eliminativist conclusion. In contrast, the account of the a priori limit to irrationality given above has no such consequences. A related disagreement has to do with the basis for the a priori minimal rationality requirement. Stich believes this arises from the need in intentional interpretation to find others similar to ourselves. He argues that this need results in intentional interpretation being unacceptably parochial. There is a sense in which my account of interpretation requires that we find others to be similar to ourselves, but I believe this is not an objection to my account, when properly understood. Examining these disagreements with Stich should clarify my own position while showing it has the resources to answer Stich's concerns about intentional psychology.

4.6.1: Empirical Versus Conceptual Truths Revisited

Stich is one of the few writers who recognizes the importance of empirical psychology in grounding the principle of charity as that principle is understood by Quine. Quine, it will be remembered, seeks to ground his charitable strictures on estimates regarding the likelihood or probability of the beliefs attributed to people. Some erroneous beliefs may be psychologically plausible in the believer's situation; such beliefs are thus likely and, for Quine, the attribution of such beliefs is quite defensible. On the other hand, psychologically implausible beliefs are unlikely. The attribution of such beliefs is generally indefensible, for bad translation is relatively likely. However, Stich believes that this Quinean understanding of the matter is fundamentally flawed: "Quine's stricture against silliness is best viewed not as an empirical generalization but as a conceptual point about the intentional characterization of mental states" (Stich 1990, p. 38).

To ground charity in estimates of probabilities is to project an empirically established result to the effect that, generally, people are rational to a significant extent and in certain significant respects. But, Stich invites us to consider how we might go about collecting the evidence for the indicated empirical generalization(s). We presumably would begin by observing those for whom we have interpretive schemes. Here we seem to encounter a damning problem:

To know whether a compatriot reasons absurdly, we must interpret his words; to interpret his words, we need a translation manual; and to write an acceptable manual, Quine tells us, we must eschew the ascription of silly belief. So it looks like any inductive attempt to support Quine's precept will beg the question. In order to gather inductive evidence in favor of the precept, we must presuppose that it is true (Stich 1990, p. 36).

Thus, on pain of circularity, it seems that the projected generalization must rest on charity, and not the reverse. Bereft of nonquestion-begging empirical support, the principle of charity and the associated result that beliefs and desires must be minimally rational become "conceptual truths," for Stich.

But, is this really a decisive argument? Is the minimal rationality requirement an a priori constraint on interpretation in a way that renders it self-vindicating, empirically unassailable, and thus not an empirical matter? I believe it is no more unassailable than were the erstwhile a priori claims that e = $1/2mv^2$ and that electrons are carriers of the minimal electric charge. These claims have fallen on surprisingly hard times, even though they may once have been used to identify the objects and the physical quantities at issue. And I have argued that the same thing could happen to whatever minimal rationality claims can presently be made a priori. Historically, a priori conceptual truths have repeatedly fallen prey to empirical investigations. The world is just not a safe place for a priori truths, or so it seems. Theory (and empirical investigations) can develop in a way that renders them expendable.

To appreciate how central components of theory having to do with rationality can inform interpretation, and, at the same time, not be self-vindicating, we must recall certain features of the probability-based account of derivative charity in interpretation. When we do this, we find that there is not the sort of invidious circularity that Stich envisions. In interpretation one seeks to find others explicable in their beliefs, desires, and actions. This necessitates a partnership of interpretive schemes and theory. We seek a set of sociological and psychological theories that can be combined with interpretive schemes for the range of human societies; we seek interpretive schemes that, together with such theory, allow us to account for, or model, what is observed. In each interpretive context, then, we have theory and interpretation pulling in tandem, and at risk together. Failures to adequately model the behaviors of those we seek to understand lead us to make changes in our combination(s) of scheme and theory.

Let us survey (sketchily) some of the choices faced when deciding where to make changes in the combined scheme-plus-theory. At first, we may be particularly inclined to look to the interpretive scheme in attempting to locate the weakness. After all, the interpretive scheme is locally applied, and the theories are universally applied; changes in theory to accomodate anomolies in one context then threaten to overturn interpretive successes elsewhere. However, recalcitrant problems can induce us to look beyond our provisional interpretive scheme to question its theoretical yoke-mate. Further, there are commonly known weak points in our theories, sorts of cases where our theories have not proven empirically successful. When problems crop up in connection with cases where our present theory has proven problematic, we may be much more inclined to blame theory before blaming our interpretive scheme. (At least we will be inclined to proceed in this way when our provisional interpretive scheme otherwise works well in conjunction with our more well-established theoretical resources.) Considerations such as these are, I hope, familiar; for they are characteristic of our epistemic situation when our set of provisional beliefs "confronts experience." Generally then, it is this combination of scheme and theory that is a candidate for empirical success, and it is consistent empirical success that will vindicate the theoretical component, and recalcitrant failures that will undermine it.

We then construct our interpretive schemes with an eye to combining them with our general theoretical understanding of human psychology in order to account for what is said and done. Thus, we come to use theory-based information regarding the probability and explicability of inferential structures in deciding on an interpretive scheme. But here it should be as obvious as it is crucial that the theory that informs interpretation is not, by virtue of this, rendered self-vindicating. Failures of theories-cum-interpretation to model behavior can induce changes in theory. With such changes, even once central components may become expendable. On the other hand, successes in theories-cum-interpretation provide further support for theory. These are empirical successes and failures, and appealing in further interpretation to the theoretical fruits of such empirical work need not be invidiously circular or self-vindicating. For the theoretical components remain at risk when put to work in this new context. I believe that once we come to appreciate the range of cognitive theory that can inform interpretation, the testing or refining of such theory can be understood in terms of Glymour's (1980) notion of bootstrap testing.

Now, central portions of theory, applied in the manner just described, are the source of whatever minimal rationality requirement there is. It is permissible to describe such central portions of our theory as a priori, or as expressing "conceptual truths" (as I allow in section 4.1.1), but it would be mistaken to add, as Stich (1990, p. 38) does, that they cannot be characterized as empirical results. My point here is essentially Quine's: all components of theory, the most deeply embedded ones that we might call a priori and the ones more likely to be changed (that we would not so label), are empirical, for the theory of which they are components confronts observation as an only somewhat differentiated whole.

4.6.2: Acceptable and Unacceptable Similarity Bases for Interpretation

Stich believes he can account for the fact that there is a minimal rationality requirement on interpretation: it is said to derive from the more fundamental fact that intentional interpretation is a matter of finding others similar to ourselves. The minimal rationality requirement follows on the supposition that we are "reasonably rational" ourselves. Thus, while "it is part of what it is to be a belief with a given intentional characterization, part of the concept of a belief, if you will, to interact with other beliefs in a rational way—a way which more or less mirrors the laws of logic" (Stich 1990, p. 37), the extent to which beliefs must be so interrelated is itself a function of how they are so interrelated for us.

> [T]he link between rationality and intentionality is a by-product of a more general constraint on intentional characterization: the person's cognitive states, the interactions among them, and their interactions with the environment must all be similar to our own. The rationality requirement follows on the assumption that we ourselves are passingly rational in our inferences (Stich 1984, p. 227).

As Stich develops this view, the attribution of beliefs may be understood as a two-part process. To begin with, we are attributing to the subject, S, a set of internal states that have functional roles rather like beliefs and desires:

> First, we are attributing to S a kind of cognitive state, a belief. This

category of state can be distinguished from other categories by the role such states play in the subject's overall cognitive economy. Beliefs are the sort of states which interact with desires, perceptions, and behavior in certain systematic ways (Stich 1990, p. 49).

Additionally, there is the matter of using a content to specify what belief the subject has:

> To say 'S believes that p' then is to say S has a belief state similar to the one which would underlie my own assertion of 'p' were I just now to have uttered 'p' in earnest (1990, p. 49).

Such a procedure gives rise to the requirement that those interpreted be quite similar to ourselves:

> [S]omething akin to Grandy's principle of humanity is a direct consequence of my Quinean account of the strategy of intentional description. If what we are doing in offering an intentional characterization is identifying it by way of its similarity to a hypothetical state of our own, then we would expect that as subjects get less and less similar to us in salient respects, we will increasingly lose our grip on how their cognitive states might be intentionally characterized (1990, p. 49).

The attribution of intentional states, so conceived, is subject to several objections that render it ultimately unworkable for scientific purposes. Stich is quick to point out the problems. First, the reliance on a loose similarity relation would lead to an "observer-relative, situation-sensitive constraint that marks no natural or theoretically significant boundaries." Thus, Stich argues that a certain level of difference may render intentional characterization unworkable at some times and not at others. Second, such constraints would be exceedingly parochial. They imply that we cannot find people believing things all that different from what we believe (Stich 1990, pp. 52–53). Further, they imply that we cannot find people in other cultures "reasoning very differently from the way we do," at least if reasoning involves the manipulation of intentional states (Stich 1990, p. 35). Whatever the exact level of tolerable differences, such a parochial limit is a theoretically indefensible matter of similarity to us.

Stich (1984, pp. 230–31), of course, concludes that these results show that intentional idiom has no place in good science:

[E]ven if it were clear (which it certainly is not) that the notions of belief, cognition, mentality, and the rest presuppose intentional characterizability, this would be of no great importance to psychology or anthropology or any other science concerned to understand and explain human behavior or to chronicle its diversity. For as the [anti-pluralist] himself has argued, there is a Protagorean parochialness built into the language of intentional description. . . . But this is a positively perverse feature to build into a language in which we hope to do science.

He thus advises us to study "belieflike" states and "inferencelike" processes in a way that does not beg the question against the descriptive pluralist claim that others can and may well reason in ways quite different than do we. I believe that Stich's criticisms amply scout the sort of intentional interpretation that he envisions.

Now there is a sense in which my own account of intentional interpretation, particularly as developed to this point, requires us to find that others are similar to ourselves. I have argued that we seek to interpret other human beings so as to find others instantiating psychological dispositions characteristic of human beings. This is to find others similar to ourselves in ways characterized by our best present psychological and sociological theories. So, admitting as I do the decisiveness of Stich's repudiation of intentional idiom and its similarity basis *as he understands it*, it is incumbent on me to show that my own account escapes the sorts of criticisms just rehearsed.

We may begin by considering Stich's own summary of what it is to attribute a belief with a particular content to a person:

To say 'S believes that p' then is to say S has a belief state similar to the one which would underlie my own assertion of 'p' were I just now to have uttered 'p' in earnest (Stich 1990, p. 49).

It may seem that such Stichian intentional attribution is rather a lot like the interpretive modeling (using interpretive scheme plus extant theory) that I have described in my own account of interpretation. However, there are crucial differences. We get a glimpse of them when we ask what *single* belieflike state might induce me, as I am, to utter some expression of a belief from a rather foreign belief system. On Stich's account, either there is a state that would be responsible for such an utterance in me, or there is no belief with such a content. This is to say that no one could have a belief with the content expressed in sentence p (say, for example, no one could believe witchcraft substance travels at night to harm souls) unless there is some single belieflike state that would lead me to earnestly utter p ('Witchcraft substance travels at night to harm souls'). This is the force of saying that Grandy's principle of humanity is a corollary, for that principle supposes that we can "plug" a very few beliefs into our belief desire structures and then use ourselves as a simulator. Stich talks of single states in this manner.

Now, I really cannot imagine some single belieflike state that would induce me to utter, 'Look, witchcraft substance traveling at night!' The reason is simple: there is no such state. Thus, on Stich's account, I must conclude that the Zande have no belief about witchcraft whose content is expressible in roughly these terms (Evans-Pritchard notwithstanding). Such, he would say, is the parochial, similarity-centered nature of interpretation.

In contrast, on my account, we can attribute such a relatively foreign belief to subjects of interpretation such as the Azande. For, *we can model the relevant Zande practices and utterances by attributing to them a set of beliefs* (including one expressed in the way given above) as directed by a systematic interpretive scheme *and supposing we share certain basic psychological dispositions* as described in a set of theory. I have discussed how such a global modeling is involved in interpretation (rather than a similarity of single states). And this, in part, accounts for much of the greater flexibility, and less parochial nature, of interpretation on my account.[8] By making more use of theoretical expectations regarding shared human cognitive capacities, and more use of interpretive schemes holistically constructed against such a theoretical background, we escape the parochial limitations that plague interpretation conceived (as Stich does) as a matter of using ourselves a simple simulators.

Before proceeding further, we must distinguish between two sorts of interpretive contexts. On the one hand, there is the familiar interpretive context that has been supposed consistently in this work on interpretation in the human sciences: the interpretation of human beings. On the other hand, we may conceive of an interpretive context that is not a practical problem, but is one of substantial theoretical and "in principle" interest: the interpretation of nonhuman subjects. I will focus only on the interpretation of human beings, showing that the appropriate similarity bases for interpretation ultimately do not render interpretation unworkably parochial.[9]

My account of interpretation does require that people be found similar to ourselves, but it does not require an objectionable, question-begging and parochial, similarity. My account supposes that, at some important level of analysis, others are similar to ourselves in that they share the same basic psychological dispositions. Now, there are clearly variations in human cognitive capacities, as most teachers will attest. Some find it easier to distinguish between Modus Tollens and Denying the Antecedent than others. Some are somewhat less quick to generalize from salient (but possibly biased) samples then others. However, this variation is really not all that great in comparison with what is logically possible; there does seem to be a certain range of basic strategies to which human beings are disposed. Further, much of what variation there is seems itself accounted for in terms of more basic capacities and differences in their development in different environments. So, when I appeal to a shared psychology, I have in mind an account of certain rudimentary cognitive capacities, subject themselves to some variation, which are then explicably elaborated in differing social and physical environments. The similarity basis for interpretation is the theory-laden one constituted by our best present knowledge of human psychology. This does not seem an objectionably parochial similarity basis for interpretation in the human sciences.

As I have explained, my account of interpretation situates the construction of interpretive schemes within the context of the ongoing social and psychological sciences. We are to construct translation manuals so as to construe the speakers of the source-language as explicable. Insofar as we succeed, we will show them similar to us in ways described by our theories. Such theories will yield estimates of probabilities of various sorts of error (given the relevant conditions) and these should be borne out in our subjects under interpretation. Thus, the crucial role interpretive schemes play in the cross-cultural application of more general theory: as we employ our interpretive scheme, a global theory, comprised of scheme plus theory, is put to the test. To abandon this project, to cease to insist that we interpret so as to find those in other cultures thinking as we do, on some theory-described level of analysis, is to abandon the search for cross-culturally valid psychological and sociological theories. For such theories, ill-developed as they may now be, proceed by positing regularities in psychological and sociological processes. To posit such regularity is to posit similarities between people and across societies in social and psychological processes. Thus, to repudiate the search for similarities altogether is to repudiate the search for regularities in social and psychological processes, and to repudiate social and psychological science.

So, when we are concerned to understand human psychology and human societies, their variations and their underlying constancy, then the sort of theory-informed similarity basis I have suggested does not seem misguided. Indeed, it seems necessary. However, perhaps one aspect of Stich's concern to avoid parochialness remains to be responded to: does the procedure advocated here beg the question against what Stich calls "descriptive pluralism"? Does it methodologically legislate against, or at least stack the deck against the view that people can reason in very different ways than do we, evincing "inferential patterns . . . significantly different" from ours?[10]

It does not. The appeal to empirical probabilities in determining what attributions are acceptable need not lead us to find the overall pattern of inferences characteristic of two societies to be particularly similar. Whether of not the empirical probability approach begs the question against descriptive pluralism depends on the sorts of ways in which we insist that others be construed as reasoning like us. Were our estimates of the probabilities of instances of various inference patterns simply matters of whether or not the particular inference pattern is frequently instanced in our society, then Stich's objection would have some force. Were we to insist that such frequencies are similar, then the overall inferential patterns would be found to be similar as well. But such a reconstruction of the empirical probability approach is something of a straw man. (This reconstruction—Stich's—which limits the empirical probability approach to working with simple probabilities had no basis in Quine's writings, for example. See Quine [1970, pp. 17–19].) If, instead, we suppose that the probabilities that inform interpretation are conditional probabilities, specifying the probability of (or incidences of) various erroneous and correct inferences under varying conditions, then the empirical probability approach to interpretation is compatible with descriptive pluralism. Information regarding conditional probabilities can be used to show that, in the particular conditions obtaining in a society under study, such-and-such an inference (characterized by its pattern) is likely (or unlikely), even though such inferences are uncommon (or common) in our society.

To illustrate how reliance on such estimates of probabilities need not yield the antipluralist result that there cannot be societies whose members think in ways very different from those prevailing in Western society, consider the following two cases, both of which have already been discussed in other connections.

Many writers have suggested that witchcraft and magic provide cases of ways of thought very different from the technological, scientific, ways that typify Western society. This is one aspect of Winch's discussions and Wittgenstein's ruminations; it also is an aspect of symbolist anthropological discussions. Within a system of beliefs about magic, there are proportionally fewer logical connections between beliefs and there is less inductive grounding of the belief system than obtains in technologically and scientifically informed Western belief systems. (Even religious systems in the West are influenced by the differing habits of thought, as they typically show greater elaboration or articulation of "rationalized" doctrine, and feature set accounts of "why I believe" reflecting an "epistemological preoccupation.") If common folk religious systems of thought do evince such differences from Western technological and scientific thought, then, to the degree that magical ways have a central place in a society, much the same can be said for the belief system of that society generally—it will evince proportionately fewer logical connections between beliefs and less inductive grounding than general belief systems within Western societies. Thus, to recognize magic as quite different from Western science and technology, and to find it playing a central role in society, is to provide a moderate descriptive-pluralist account.

Now, consider Malinowski's (1931) early descriptive pluralist account of magic. It is now recognized as empirically inadequate, being overly simple. However, it has influenced many contemporary accounts. Further, its very simplicity makes it a nice showcase for an aspect of many anthropological accounts: they presuppose common human psychological mechanisms and explain the differences across communities in terms of environmental (including social) factors. Thus, Malinowski's account illustrates the conceptual possibility of a descriptive-pluralist account, attributing substantially different "ways of thought," also being an account tailored to psychological theories regarding shared cognitive dispositions.

According to Malinowski, even the most "primitive" societies have well-developed bodies of empirical knowledge in terms of which their members deal with each other and their environment, belying attributions of a general "prelogicality." However, any society's technology is limited and there are contingencies that it cannot effectively control. Where technology fails, and one is dealing with events of substantial importance to the groups involved, human beings are psychologically disposed to develop rituals to improve their luck, curry favor with (or otherwise control) hidden powers, and so forth—to control what needs controlling but cannot be controlled by other means. There is, Malinowski believes, a psychological need to be doing something, and to be thereby reassured.

What is important for our purposes is that Malinowski here predicts differences across societies in prevailing ways of thinking (in the overall patterns of inference) on the basis of differences in the technological situations within the various societies and a psychological theory postulating shared psychological principles. Malinowski thus arrives at a descriptive-pluralist result on the basis of a psychological theory and associated estimates of the likelihood of erroneous (but perhaps useful) ways of thinking.

A rather different example of descriptive pluralism being supported by employing a theory about shared psychological and sociological mechanism is provided by symbolist anthropology. As described earlier, symbolist anthropologists typically hold that religion, magic, and witchcraft are radically different from scientific and technological thought. Science and technology proceed in ways constrained by our principles of logic and induction. From the onset, both are supposedly attempts to arrive at a set of true indicative statements. In contrast, symbolists claim that the developments found in religions and systems of magic must be understood, not in terms of the logic of such scientific and technological belief systems, but (primarily) in terms of the dynamics of rituals. Ritual is symbolic action, typically expressive of group values. Myths are taken to be secondary elaborations, rather than as belief systems that "ground" what is done in ritual. This is to say, myths are not beliefs that lead people to do the rituals, at least not primarily. Rather, they are stories that spring up as another way of expressing whatever it is that the rituals already express. This said, however, symbolists typically admit that mythical beliefs also have, or come to have, an "instrumental aspect." That is, they admit that those who hold the myths think of them as true, and make some technological use of the associated ritual. But, and this is crucial for our present concerns, the entire ritual-myth system is "driven" by the ritual component, not by the myth-belief component. This means that the ritual-driven patterns evinced in myth-belief systems are markedly different from those inference patterns evinced in scientific and technological contexts. (Even within our own culture, to the degree that such thought predominates in a group—and this is not characteristic of educated Western groups—the group will evince inferential patterns that are globally different from educated Western-ers.) The symbolist position is thus a decidedly descriptive-pluralist position. Their opposite numbers in the anthropological communi-ty, the "intellectualists," hold that magic, witchcraft, and religion are much closer to science and technology than the symbolists like to let on. The intellectualist position has a descriptive-monist thrust.

Now, it will be remembered that, in the Spiro-Leach contro-versy described earlier, Leach (1969) defends his symbolist account, and attacks Spiro's competing intellectualist account, by supposing a shared psychology characterizing all the different parties to be con-trasted (ourselves and the natives). Leach objects that Spiro's intel-lectualist treatment of the Tully River natives' apparent remarks on human procreation is flawed by its attribution of inexplicable ignorance to the natives. He supposes that a commonsense psy-chology characterizes both ourselves and the natives, and argues that this psychology shows Spiro's ignorance interpretation to be "highly implausible." Leach thus employs a theory that supposes that the same psychological mechanisms are at work in all human beings. But the results are not antipluralist. Instead, Leach uses the results to support his descriptive-pluralist account by eliminating Spiro's competing account.

Stich himself cites several works collected in Horton and Finnegan (1973) as hewing to the descriptive pluralist line that he feels needs to be protected against early termination (that is, against a methodological begging of the question). Interestingly, many works collected there proceed by supposing some general cognitive or developmental psychology (applicable to all human beings) and treating some of the so-called "primitive" modes of thought as explic-able manifestations of one stage or option characterized by the gen-eral theory used. Levi-Strauss (1966) is also cited by Stich as a proponent of a version of descriptive pluralism. But even the most passing familiarity with Levi-Strauss's structuralism would reveals his repeated use of a general theory thought to be applicable to all humans in the course of his attempts to identify and describe aspect of "the savage mind." For example, he remarks early on:

> The thought we call primitive is founded on this demand for order. This is equally true of all thought but it is through the properties common to all thought that we can most easily begin to under-stand forms of thought which seem very strange to us (Levi-Strauss 1966, p. 10).

Or, again:

Both science and magic however require the same sort of mental operations and they differ not so much in kind as in the different types of phenomena to which they are applied.

These relations are a consequence of the objective conditions in which magic and scientific knowledge appeared (Levi-Strauss 1966, p. 13).

Thus, even the works cited as pluralistic by Stich belies his suggestion that appealing to psychological theory characterizing shared human capacities will somehow improperly militate against descriptive pluralism. Put simply, a concern in interpretation for what is probable, rooted in general psychological theory that we hope characterizes all human subjects, need not beg the question against descriptive pluralism as Stich fears. Empirical, theory-based expectations provide an unexceptionable similarity basis for interpretation.

Connecting the remarks made in this section to the central themes of this chapter, I have been concerned to defend my empirical approach to the level of rationality needed for interpretation against objections raised by Stich's discussions of Quine's account. I have shown (in section 4.6.1) that the empirical status claimed for the restrictions on irrationality is not vitiated by a nonempirical conceptual limitation on the relevant empirical theory. Further, I have shown (in section 4.6.2) that the theory-laden similarity basis for interpretation of humans need not be objectionably parochial nor need it beg the question against descriptive pluralism.

5

On the Supposed Privileged Place
of Rationalizing Explanation

5.1: Preliminaries

5.1.1: The Basic Issue and What Is Sought to Resolve It

I have now presented my basic account of interpretation. Of course, certain points will be clarified further in the discussions to follow. But the central points are now clear. I have argued that the fundamental principle informing interpretation is the principle of explicability. This allows us to understand the place for, and limitations on, charity in interpretation. This, in turn, allows us to appreciate the nature of whatever a priori claims can be made for the minimal rationality of beliefs and desires. Generally, these points support methodological naturalism by allowing us to view interpretation as one variant of the sort of theory-laden description of phenomenon that is familiar to philosophers of science.

However, throughout my discussions, I have supposed a very roughly hewn, but nevertheless recognizable, notion of explanation. This supposition has played an important role in my discussions, as should be expected in view of my claim that interpretation and explanation in the human sciences must be understood together. I have supposed that explanation involves the exhibition of the explanandum phenomena as an outcome of causal regularities in the producing processes. The explanandum is thereby understood as an event embedded in a web of events instancing certain causal dependencies. Applied to psychological explanation, the supposition has been that explanation involves recognizing the explanandum phenomenon as the result of human cognitive capacities (cognitive dispositions); this is to find conformity with dispositions and regularities as described in intentional or semantic terms. Here it is important that the crucial bases for explanation in the human sciences are *descriptive* generalizations, not formulations of what is *normatively* appropriate. It will be the task of this and the next chapter to develop and defend this view of explanation in the human sciences. But, there should be a strong presumption in its favor to begin with; for, as reflected in preceding chapters, it accords with much well-received practice.

This general presumption seems to be in tension with various implicit and sometimes explicit precepts regarding the important place for findings of rationality in explanations within the human sciences. For a variety of reasons, numerous writers have suggested that explanation in the human sciences must be basically a matter of *rationalizing explanation* in which the explanandum is shown to be rational in terms of the agents' beliefs and desires. Accounts of the human sciences assigning a prominent role to rationalizing explanation have been developed by an impressive range of writers, including Winch (1958), Jarvie (1964), Goldman (1970), Davidson (1980a, 1982), Turner (1979, 1980), Putnam (1978), Elster (1984), Little (1991). Several of these writers suggest that rationalizing explanation must be the exclusive, or at least the basic and strongly preferred, sort of explanation in the human sciences, and in the social sciences in particular. Davidson (1982, p. 299), for example, suggests that rationalizing explanation provides "the only clear pattern of explanation that applies to the mental." Several writers have urged that the bulk of explanations in the human sciences should either be rationalizing explanations or ultimately reduce to rationalizing explanations supplemented by attention to the often complex unintended consequences of rational actions. Now, such partisanship, such championing of rationalizing explanation, *seems* to be in tension with the view of explanation that I have relied on to this point. On my account, explanations rest on descriptive generalizations, while the proponents of rationalizing explanation seem to give normative principles, as normative principles, a crucial role in supporting explanations. Why else, one wonders, would one feel impelled to explain by finding people reasoning and acting rationally, rather than just in ways we generally expect? Indeed the suggestion of a crucial role for normative principles in such explanation is sometimes quite explicit, as in McDowell (1985) and Davidson (1987).

Still, appearances can be misleading, and the apparent tension between a preference for rationalizing explanation and the view of explanation supposed here could turn out to be illusory in many cases. *Whether or not the preference for rationalizing explanation clashes with my methodological naturalist supposition depends on how rationalizing explanation and the supposed preferred status claimed for it are understood.* If the explanatory force of rationalizing explanations is understood as deriving from exhibiting the normative propriety of what is thought or done, then there is a real tension. But it should not be understood in this manner; in section 5.2, I provide a positive account of rationalizing explanation which brings out its dependency on nomic, descriptive information. To this end, I draw upon recent work in the philosophy of mind, and on Cummins's (1975, 1983) accounts of functional analysis and explanation, to show how rationalizing explanation can be understood as a species of explanation that draws on descriptive information regarding cognitive capacities.

Further, *if* the putative preferred status of rationalizing explanation is understood as rooted in certain constraints special to intentional psychology, and a priori in some theory-independent, transcendent manner, then again there is a real tension with my naturalist view. But, there is a superior understanding of whatever preference there is for rationalizing explanations in the human sciences. I will account for such preference in terms of the theory-dependence of explanation together with the outlines of extant theory in the human sciences. Just what is at issue in this contrast between theory-dependent and transcendent preferences may well be unclear, although the general distinction is presumably roughly recognizable. So, section 5.1.3 is devoted to clarifying the issue.

The centerpiece of this chapter is the presentation of a superior positive account of psychological explanation generally, and of rationalizing explanation in particular. This account allows us to appreciate (1) that rationalizing explanation is a form of explanation drawing on descriptive generalizations, and (2) that it does not have some special sort of preferred status by virtue of theory-transcendent aspects of psychological explanation. Accordingly, properly understood, rationalizing explanation can indeed be a proper and important form of psychological and social scientific explanation without giving comfort to methodological separatists. For, the human sciences are not thereby set apart from the other sciences in virtue of employing explanations that treat normative propriety, as opposed to descriptive tendencies, as explanatory. Neither are they thereby set apart as being subject to transcendent theory-independent constraints special to them.

5.1.2: *The Rudimentary Received Model of Rationalizing Explanation*

Before proceeding to the more argumentative sections of this chapter, I should explicitly review the basic received model of rationalizing explanation. The heart of this model envisions the explanation of an action, *A*, of an agent, *S*, by listing a set of *S*'s reasons—beliefs and attitudes—in terms of which *S*'s doing *A* was rational. Thus, according to Davidson's classic formulation, to provide a rationalizing explanation of an agent's actions is to cite the agent's "primary reason," where:

> *R* is a primary reason why an agent performed the action *A* under the description *d* only if *R* consists of a pro attitude of the agent towards actions with a certain property, and a belief of the agent that *A*, under that description *d*, has that property (Davidson 1980a, p. 5).[1]

Davidson adds that to be the agent's reason for doing *A*, *R* must have been causally efficacious in bringing about that action.

Of course, for *A* to be validly indicated *by some set* of *S*'s beliefs and attitudes (desires, hopes, . . .) does not suffice to render *S*'s doing *A* rational, for there may be (and often are) competing arguments with incompatible conclusions constructible from the stock of *S*'s beliefs and attitudes. To determine what is rational for *S* to do, one must consider the full range of *S*'s beliefs and attitudes, for there is a good deal more to rationality than the ability to produce isolated valid (deductive and practical) arguments. These observations regarding rationality are presumably commonplaces.

There are several roughly parallel observations regarding rationalizing explanation that are presumably almost as obvious and indicate that the above rudimentary sketch of rationalizing explanation requires elaboration. Showing that *A* is validly indicated *by some set* of *S*'s beliefs and attitudes is not sufficient to explain *S*'s doing *A*. This insufficiency is closely related to the requirement that the reasons that explain *S*'s doing *A* be reasons that caused the agent to do *A*. If we only know of a certain set of *S*'s beliefs and desires that they provide the basis for an isolated practical argument for *S*'s doing *A*, then we commonly know too little to surmise that *S* will be or was moved to action by that set. *S* might instead be rationally moved by other reasons and arguments for doing *A*. Or, the particular case might be one in which no rationalizing explanation would be correct—having some good reasons for doing an action does not insure that the action, if done, is done for a good reason. Consequently, we really only have a justification for thinking that S was or will be moved by a certain set of beliefs and attitudes to do A when we know a fair amount about S's other beliefs and attitudes (and about how such states interact).

Of course, the need to go beyond considering small sets of an agent's beliefs and attitudes in appreciating the likelihood of various possible actions is clearly in evidence in cases of conflicting desires. In such cases, people do not and *cannot* do everything that they have some pro attitude towards, even when they believe of each prospective action that they could "pull it off." For example, imagine a person who is generally averse to involvement with "them politicians and their shenanigans." This person values being politically uninvolved. However, when faced with the prospect of a highly unattractive governmental decision affecting him or her personally (say in a zoning case), he or she might forego the accustomed and desired noninvolvement to make calls on the appropriate politicians.[2] In such a case, the individual both desires to be politically uninvolved and desires to affect a governmental decision by becoming (temporarily) politically involved. Corresponding practical syllogisms with conflicting conclusions could easily be produced. If we are to understand how the person is led to act, we will need to consider together the full range of the person's relevant beliefs and desires. Davidson (1980a, p. 16) expresses the resulting consensus, "Any serious theory for predicting action on the basis of reasons must find a way of evaluating the relative force of various desires and beliefs in the matrix of decision; it cannot take as its starting point the refinement of what is to be expected from a single desire."

To deal with such cases, many proponents of rationalizing explanation have borrowed from normative decision theory in order to have a standard for what actions are ultimately rationally indicated, and, in turn, for what actions are ultimately to be expected. This is true of Davidson (1980a, 1980e), Føllesdal (1981), Goldman (1970), Hempel (1965b), and Elster (1984), to name a few. On the elaborated account, to provide a rationalizing explanation of S's doing A is to show that A is what a rational person would do, given the range of S's beliefs and the relative strengths of S's competing attitudes.

Providing rationalizing explanations, like generating the associated interpretations, is a clearly holistic affair: any such explanation must be a member of a large set of such explanations. For any such explanation will involve attributing to the agent, S, a range of attitudes and beliefs. These, in turn, will have implications for explanations of *S*'s other actions. If this structure of explanations and attributions is not to become baroque, ad hoc, and implausible, it must be possible to assign to *S* a single set of attitudes (utility functions) and beliefs regarding probabilities such that a substantial range of *S*'s doings become explicable thereby.

The ideal here would then seem to be an exhaustive survey of a person's preference structures and beliefs to the end of demonstrating that what the person then does are a series of utility-maximizing actions. However, when discussing explanation, we must be wary of focusing too narrowly on an ideal model. For example, we are never really in a position to make the exhaustive survey suggested; consequently we are never in a position to demonstrate that the actions of an agent are maxima, all things considered. Often we settle for reconstructions of relatively autonomous (or provisionally autonomous) local structures, and for associated indications that an explanandum action was a local maximum. In fact, often we settle for the indications that a certain end was highly desired, and that the explanandum action was thought to further that end. In such a case, the fact that the end was taken to be highly desirable is taken to make probable that it was not outweighed by countervailing desires, and thus to make probable the suggestion that the explanandum action was at least a local maximum. In yet other cases, the very fact that the action was undertaken is taken to indicate that at least some of the agent's supporting reasons constituted it as a local maximum, while holistic considerations are then used to pick out what plausibly were the relevant supporting reasons.

Finally, while this model most naturally takes actions as explananda, its proponents have typically sought to explain more than just actions by rationalization. Often beliefs, and sometimes even desires, have also become explananda. This can be understood in two ways, both of which are advocated in some philosophical literature and instanced in some social scientific literature.

Probably the most common way of applying the rationalizing explanation model to the explanation for intentional states such as beliefs is straightforward: simply take demonstrations of *epistemic* rationality as explanatory of intentional states in much the same way that practical, roughly "decision-theoretic" rationality is taken to be explanatory in the paradigm cases of rationalizing explanation. When we conceive of the rationalizing explanation of *S*'s belief *B* in this way, *S*'s belief, *B*, is to be explained by reference to a set of S's antecedently held beliefs in terms of which B is rational. Whatever it is that is taken to make for the explanatory force of showings of practical, decision-theoretic rationality is then assumed to confer a similar measure of explanatory force on demonstrations of epistemic rationality. Whatever the role normative principles and descriptive generalizations have in the paradigm action-explanation cases, the same role is assigned to the corresponding normative principles and descriptive generalizations in the extended applications.[3]

The second basic approach to applying the rationalizing explanation model in connection with beliefs is to take as explananda, *not* intentional states such as the agent's belief states, but the corresponding actions of accepting beliefs. Thus, on this variant of the model we get the explanation of an agent, S's, action of accepting a belief, B, by listing a set of S's reasons—beliefs and attitudes—in terms of which S's accepting B was rational. This approach is elaborated in Jarvie's classic (1964) discussion of anthropological explanations. There Jarvie even attempts to produce rationalizing explanations for the Melanesian millenarian movements known as cargo cults. He proceeds by conceiving of the cognitive matters to be explained as actions—as positings, acceptings, and "explainings-with"—not simply as belief states, and he concludes, "The very fact that the natives use their belief to try to explain facts shows the natives to be rational about their beliefs. Rational activity is goal directed" (1964, p. 137). For a more detailed analysis of the many twists and turns in Jarvie's argument, see Henderson (1989).

When one reflects on common rationalizing explanations of beliefs, as encountered either in one's daily rounds or in the scientific literature, Jarvie's approach seems rather baroque. When beliefs and attitudes are explananda, one seldom finds circumspect treatments of them in terms of practical rationality. Instead, in keeping with the first approach to applying rationalizing explanation to beliefs as explananda, one finds the straightforward procedure of assuming that people "can put two and two together" epistemically as well as practically.[4] I suspect that the rationalizing explanation of actions (as opposed to beliefs) has only recently come to be treated as the paradigm case, and then only for a limited number of analytic philosophers. Further, I suspect this resulted from their infatuation with decision theory. In contrast, in some influential, classic presentations, the assumption of epistemic rationality seems at least as paradigmatic as the assumption of practical rationality. For example, in a discussion of historical explanation in which rationalizing explanation loomed large, Collingwood insists that man is centrally concerned with "self-knowledge," understood as "a knowledge of his *knowing faculties*, his thought or understanding or reason" (1956, p. 205, emphasis not in the original). From this perspective, what I have been describing as an extension of the basic model to accommodate important cognitive explananda is really no extension at all. From the perspective of the account I provide, much the same thing can be said: rationalizing explanation rests on an account of reasoning facilities, practical and epistemic.

In any case, it is important for proponents of a preferred status for rationalizing explanation that their model of such explanation account for explanations of beliefs, and perhaps for desires or values. For a little reflection on the human sciences reveals that many important explanandum actions are intimately associated with beliefs and attitudes which themselves ultimately stand in need of explanation. Any account of explanation that cannot provide for the explanation of beliefs and attitudes is then obviously an account of only a quite limited range of explanatory work within the human sciences. For example, in political science, attempts to explain American voting behavior have attended to such matters as party identification, the transmission of ideas and attitudes through political elites, and basic avenues of political socialization; these are taken to be either attitudes that are antecedent to voting behavior or mechanisms for the formation of such attitudes. Such matters readily become the focus of investigation themselves. Thus, at the very least, attempts to explain aggregate patterns of behavior have taken beliefs and attitudes as antecedents whose dynamic ultimately must be understood in understanding or explaining the behaviors. A similar lesson is to be had by looking at the anthropology of religion. Both intellectualists (such as Horton) and symbolists (such as Firth, Leach, and Beattie) recognize that ritual and magical activities are "commonly thought to be causally effective" by the agents (Beattie 1964, p. 204). Subjects of study are then seen as doing some ritual act to further an instrumental end, and the action would then seem amenable to a rationalizing explanation. However, despite this agreement, there remains an important point at issue in the debate between intellectualists and symbolists; the issue may be understood as turning on the question of how the development of, and persistence of, the religious and magical beliefs can be explained. If an account of explanation does not allow us to address such questions, then it misses a great deal that is important in the anthropology of religion. Illustrations could be proliferated further, but this would not be helpful here. The point should be compelling once articulated: any account of explanation which does not provide for the explanation of beliefs and attitudes could not plausibly be claimed to provide a model of the predominant or basic form of explanation in the human sciences.

In section 5.2 I provide an account of rationalizing explanation in its full range of applications. However, the following disclaimer is in order. In this discussion of the received view, rationalizing explanation of S's doing A (or believing that p) is presented as a matter of showing that A (or p) is what a rational person would do (or believe), given the range of S's beliefs and the relative strengths of S's desires. Still, such explanations could be understood in two importantly different ways, and I have attempted to take a neutral stance regarding the alternatives while characterizing the received view. However, in providing my positive account of rationalizing explanation, I cannot be neutral. One of the alternative understandings will need to be rejected in no uncertain terms. Now, it is quite possible that the alternative to be rejected is itself the most common understanding of rationalizing explanation; perhaps it is sufficiently popular to warrant including it as yet another aspect of the received view. If so, then my account is more than simply an account of why rationalizing explanations, as conceived on the received view, work. Instead, my account is revisionary. However, if it is revisionary, it is revisionary with respect to a philosophical account of rationalizing explanation only, and not with respect to explanatory practice, which I believe accords quite well with what I have to say here.

What then are the two understandings of what transpires when we explain S's doing A by citing S's precipitating reasons, thereby showing that A is what a rational person would do, given the range of S's beliefs and the relative strengths of S's desires? One might understand such explanations as explaining *by virtue of showing the rationality* of what is done. This would be to conceive of the explanatory force of such explanations as resting on the description of what is done in a way that reveals it as normatively appropriate. This is a tempting understanding of rationalizing explanations, and many proponents seem to understand such explananation in this manner. However, I deny that there is any place for rationalizing explanation, so conceived. Successful rationalizing explanations do not, and cannot, work in this way.

Alternatively, one might understand rationalizing explanations as explanations that *explain by citing the agent's precipitat-*

ing reasons—beliefs and desires—and that also *happen to* describe
what is explained in a way that reveals it as rational in view of the
agent's reasons. This is a more modest view of rationalizing explanation. On this understanding, it is quite possible that such explanations *do not explain by virtue of showing the rationality of what
is done, but do happen to describe what is done in a manner that
reveals it to be rational.* The explanatory force of such rationalizing explanations would derive from their citing causal antecedents
in terms featuring in psychological generalizations. Citing *S*'s precipitating reasons provides an *explanation* (simpliciter), given our
general psychological knowledge, while citing them provides a *rationalizing* explanation in those cases in which the reasons happen to
be good reasons. Insofar as we commonly and correctly do expect
certain limited sorts of rationality, there will be instances of rationalizing explanation conceived in this modest manner. My purpose is to develop an account of rationalizing explanation so
conceived. This will vindicate many of the particular explanations
that are characterized by the received view of rationalizing explanation, and it vindicates the class of such rationalizing explanation as a proper sort of theory-dependent explanation.

5.1.3: On Theory-Dependent Versus Transcendent Preferred Statuses

Exactly what would follow from the preferred status proposed
for rationalizing explanation depends on how that preference is conceived. Much depends on the issue (broached earlier) of whether
the preference is conceived as theory-dependent or, instead, as independent of the exigencies of theoretical context and somehow transcendent. There are several general ways in which all sciences
might be said to have theory-dependent preferences for certain sorts
of explanations. These are general ways in which, in any science, at
any time, preferences for certain sorts of explanations arise by virtue
of the general theoretical context of work in the science. Now, since
theoretically grounded preferences are a fact of life in all sciences,
the fact, if it is a fact, that rationalizing explanation has such a preferred status in the human sciences would not make for a deep difference between the human sciences and the others. To appreciate
this general point in more concrete detail, let us survey three general ways in which a theory-dependent preference can arise.

First, if our best present theories indicate that most of the
phenomena of interest in a particular science are the result of a

certain sort of mechanism or process, then we will be obliged to account for most of what is observed in terms of the indicated processes, if we are to account for it at all (given present theoretical resources). Thus, if our best present theories posit a preponderance of rationality, then this could give rise to something of a theory-based "preference" for rationalizing explanation. But, if the preferred status accorded rationalizing explanation is a matter of what general processes are posited in present theory, then this "preference" does not give rise to a separatist result, for all sciences have such theory-based "preferences." Such preferences are simply not at all unique or special to the human sciences.

By using scare quotes around 'preference' in the above paragraph, I am recognizing that it is somewhat awkward to speak of the theory-based differential production of various sorts of explanation as a matter of "preference." In the sort of case envisioned, one is simply employing one's best theory to explain what is observed, and one is not really preferring explanations in certain terms to explanations in others. This might be better described as a preference for theoretically well-grounded explanation. Still, I think a fair amount of the preferred status accorded to rationalizing explanation can be understood in this way.

However, the sort of preferred status often accorded rationalizing explanation is thought to constrain not just explanations, but, in some measure, theory development itself. It is commonly conceived as a preference both for rationalizing explanation and for the development of the appropriate supporting theory. This aspect of the projected preference is not well accounted for solely in terms of the theory-based differential production of explanations. There remain two theory-dependent ways in which such theory-development-constraining preferences arise in all sciences.

We might get such a preference for rationalizing explanation were it a priori (in the conceptual sense of section 4.1) that beliefs and desires are preponderantly rational. What is a priori does constrain theory-development (at least in the short run, if not in the long run) and, when being a priori is a matter of the centrality of claims to present theory, then a priori components of theory can give rise to theory-dependent "preferences" in much the same way theory generally can. If central components of present theory indicate that certain processes are responsible for most of the phenomena of interest in a science, then we are obliged to account for most explananda accordingly, if we are to account for them at all (given present and prospective theory).

If the preferred status accorded to rationalizing explanation is understood as a matter of it being a priori true that beliefs and desires are preponderantly rational, then again no separatist conclusions follow. While I argued that it probably is not a priori true that our beliefs and desires are predominantly rational, I also noted that this really was not crucial to my view, as long as whatever is a priori here is itself a function of what is central to our present theory. So, suppose for the sake of argument that it is a priori (in this acceptable sense) that beliefs and desires are preponderantly rational. It is not clear why anyone would find in the resulting theory-based preference for rationalizing explanation a suggestion that the human sciences are subject to unique constraints, constraints of a epistemic or logical status unlike what is found in the sciences generally. After all, there supposedly are such theory-based preferences in many, and perhaps all, scientific fields: within high energy physics, for example, there is a theory-based preference for field-theoretic explanations of interaction events in terms of exchange particles. Such theory-based preferences influence both explanation and description.

Of course, one might object that while there are direct theory-based preferences and a priori–based preferences in all, or almost all, scientific contexts, still the *content* of the preference for rationalizing explanation is unique to the human sciences and sets them apart as subject to special constraints. But this is obviously too quick. At any one time, the content of the preferences within different scientific areas will be as different as the central components of their theories. The preference in evolutionary biology for selection-mechanism explanations is quite different from the preferences found in geology, for example, and even from those in molecular biology. But we need not conclude from such differences that evolutionary biology is subject to constraints on explanation that are fundamentally different from those operating in molecular biology. Differences in the content of preferences are of a much less fundamental order than those differences entertained by methodological separatists; they do not extend to the basic "logic" or epistemology of the disciplines.

Finally, there is a third sense in which, within a particular theoretical context, there might be a theory-related preference for explanations in certain terms: one might conceive of much scientific work as taking place within the context of something like what Laudan (1977) called a "research tradition." A research tradition is a set of general doctrines and assumptions that spawns a spectrum of individual theories. For example, there have been numerous specific theories under each of the research traditions we label "evolutionary theory" and "atomic theory." Laudan argues that a major aspect of scientific rationality has to do with the choice of which research tradition to work within. One ought to choose to work within that tradition (or set of traditions) that is (or are) "most progressive" in the sense of recently having the most success at solving conceptual and empirical problems. Such choices of research traditions give rise to a preferred status for explanations in certain terms, for they commit the scientist to solving empirical and theoretical problems in terms characteristic of the chosen research tradition(s). Of course, this involves providing explanations in those terms. Thus, within the context of atomic theory as a research tradition, there is a preference for explanations in terms of bits of discontinuous matter, bits that are of various relatively simple sorts and that combine in more complex configurations to form complex stuff, and whose combinations are predictable, and so on. Similarly, within certain biological contexts, there are preferences for selection-mechanism explanations (Kitcher 1981; Darden and Cain 1989).

Arguably, explanation in terms of certain sorts of rationality provides a prominent research tradition within the human sciences. (A sense for the strength of the case here can be gotten from Little's [1991] overview of explanation in the social sciences, which emphasizes, in both discussion and numerous fine examples, the prominent place of rationalizing explanation.) As long as this research tradition is relatively progressive, the decision to work within it would properly give rise to a preference for rationalizing explanations of certain varieties. But, again, the resulting preference would not foster separatist results, for such constraints are common to all scientific disciplines.

We can conclude that *if* the preferred status claimed for rationalizing explanation is theory-dependent in one or more of the ways just now surveyed—*if*, that is, it rests on present research traditions, or on present theoretical understandings of cognitive mechanisms, or on central components of present theory, and not on other grounds—then it would *not* provide a grounds for separatism.

When we reflect on the above discussion, and the ubiquity of theory-dependent preferences that it reveals, we have, I think, good reason to suspect that the preference there actually is for rationalizing explanation can be accounted for as theory-dependent in one or a combination of these three ways. There seems no reason to postulate further sorts of constraints to account for this preference.

In particular, there seems no reason to look for special constraints resting on some unique, transcendent, a priori characteristic of intentional explanation, a characteristic which supposedly cannot be understood in terms of extant theory and the general logic of scientific explanation. Thus, an account of intentional explanation, and of rationalizing explanation in particular, is not required to account for some special or fundamental preferred status had by rationalizing explanation. It will be sufficient for it to provide room for a theory-dependent sort of preferred status. This clears the way for my account of intentional explanation generally, and rationalizing explanation in particular. For, on this account of such explanation, there is no theory-transcendent, or mysterious methodological, basis for preferring explanations in terms of cognitive processing that happens to be rational to explanations in terms of processing that happens to be irrational or nonrational. Methodologically, all such explanations are on a par. What makes one appropriate to a given case is the particulars of the case and the support that can be found in theoretical context. As a result, any preference there is for rationalizing explanation must be theory-dependent.

Before proceeding, it is worth noticing that individual proponents of rationalizing explanation can often be found to base their preference for it on multiple grounds, and, for any one writer, these need not be either exclusively theory-dependent grounds or exclusively theory-transcendent grounds. For example, Elster (1984) argues that the rationalizing explanation model provides a sort of "regulative ideal" for explanation in the social sciences. He explains that, while there clearly are cases which cannot be explained in terms of rational decision-making, regulative ideals admit of exceptions while "distributing a burden of proof" (pp. 2–3). He thus advises inquirers to first seek to find cases of decision-theoretic rationality. When such cases are uncovered, they are to be taken as unproblematically explanatory. Elster warns, however, that we should not pursue this search by positing otherwise unevidenced states that would salvage the presupposition of rationality. He thus recognizes that ad hoc rationalizing explanations are to be avoided (p. 156). All this is to assign rationalizing explanation a guarded preferred status. But, when we seek to pin down his grounds for this preference, we find that they are multiple. To begin with, Elster posits a general mechanism that should produce rather widespread rationality: a "general capacity for (nonstereo-typed) global maximization" (1984, pp. 86–87). He thus posits a mechanism that directly supports a preferred status for rationalizing explanation in the first theory-dependent manner mentioned above. He makes it clear that he believes that the success had by rationalizing explanation vindicates the general research strategy that he advocates. This suggests that he might also fruitfully be understood as treating decision-theoretic work as comprising a progressive research tradition. This would give rise to a preference of rationalizing explanation in the third theory-dependent manner mentioned above. Still, Elster (pp. 153–56) also appeals to Davidson's arguments that rationality assumptions inform interpretation in a way that makes them generally self-vindicating. This appeal to an irrevisable principle of charity points to a theory-transcendent basis for the preferred status bestowed on rationalizing explanation. (In view of the argument in the preceding chapters, we can set this suggestion aside as based on a mistaken conception of charity in interpretation.)

5.2: Rationalizing Explanation in Light of a General Account of Intentional Explanation

As I have indicated, there is nothing spurious about rationalizing explanation as such, although its explanatory force has commonly been misunderstood. In this section I draw on recent discussions in the philosophy of mind and the philosophy of psychology to set the record straight by uncovering the basic underpinnings of rationalizing explanation. It should become clear that rationalizing explanations for actions and for intentional states do rest on nomic generalizations, transition laws for a certain class of systems, or at least on prospective nomic generalizations. These transition laws are themselves stated in semantic terms and thus resemble inference rules after a fashion to be made clear in what follows. To understand rationalizing explanation and the supporting transition laws, one must understand functional analysis, for such analyses give rise to the transition laws. Functional analyses have been perspicuously discussed by Robert Cummins (1975, 1983), and these discussions provide the necessary backdrop for the present discussion.

5.2.1: Dispositions, Functional Analysis, and Semantic Interpretability

Cummins's initial (1975) work on functional analysis was primarily motivated by a desire to understand talk of "functions" in biology. Previous philosophical discussions had almost universally understood such talk as attempts to explain the presence of the organ or item to which the function is attributed (Nagel 1961; Hempel 1965a). Such accounts had, of course, also attempted to understand such explanations in terms of the Deductive-Nomological model of explanation. However, the difficulties encountered along these lines proved telling, leading Hempel (1965a) to conclude that talk of functions has a merely heuristic, not explanatory, role. Cummins objects that this conclusion simply does not do justice to the concern for functions in biological contexts. He cogently argues that, in order to better understand talk of functions, we need to recognize and understand a second explanatory strategy, distinct from the causal explanation of events. This second explanatory strategy is a matter of explaining *how* a system instantiates or has a certain property by analyzing either that system into interacting components, or the property into simpler properties of that system.

While this strategy was initially articulated in the context of a defense of biological attributions of functions, Cummins realized that the strategy is much more widespread than this focus might suggest. Indeed, it is probably employed in all sciences. Most importantly, for our concerns here, it is clearly of great importance within psychology, as witnessed by Cummins (1983). My claim is that an appreciation for the relation between the analytical strategy and the strategy of causal explanation allows us to understand both the basis for, and the limitations on, rationalizing explanation. Once we understand the analytical strategy, we find that its employment gives rise to transition laws for human psychology, and these will commonly be stated in semantic terms. These may then provide the crucial bases for causal explanations. Sometimes these explanations will happen to describe what is done in a way that reveals it to be rational, and we have a case of rationalizing explanation. Sometimes these explanations will happen to describe what is done in a way that reveals it to be irrational, and then we have what I have called "irrationalizing explanation." In either case, it is the transition laws enabling us to pick out causal antecedents, and not the finding of rationality or irrationality as such, that makes for the explanatory force of these findings.

The explanatory strategies of analysis and causal explanation are addressed to different questions.[5] Causal explanations are devoted to accounting for change, "Why did the system S change from state s^1 to state s^2?" When change is understood broadly, as is standard, we have subsumptive explanations of events generally,

"Why did such-and-such an event occur?"[6] On the other hand, analysis is devoted to explaining *how a property is realized or instantiated in a certain system or class of systems*. For example, the kinetic theory of heat allows us to address the question of how temperature is instantiated in a gas, and abstract computational theory allows us to account for how any of a range of devices can realize the property of being able to do multiplication.

Explanatory analysis can be pursued in several distinct ways. One prominent analytical approach is to *analyze the system itself into its components*. A successful analytical explanation would then show how, given the properties of these components and their mode of interaction, the system has the property of interest. Cummins calls such analyses *compositional explanations*. Molecular biology is replete with examples in which the (typically dispositional) properties of certain systems are accounted for by compositional analysis. Rosenberg (1985a) discusses several fine examples, such as an analysis of the ability of the complex hemoglobin macromolecule to transmit oxygen as needed, given the order of its atomic components. Obviously, chemistry since Dalton's atomism has produced many compositional analyses. A little reflection will reveal that compositional analysis is widespread.

The second analytical approach is to *analyze the property, as instantiated* in certain systems. Cummins calls applications of this approach *functional explanations* when the property analyzed is dispositional, and *property analyses* when it is not. This analysis of properties and dispositions may be pursued in conjunction with a componential analysis of the relevant systems. Physiological analysis in biology often involves both a functional analysis of a disposition or capacity of the system into a set of more modest capacities and a componential analysis of the system into a set of systems or subsystems possessing the simple capacities. But, in other contexts, property or functional analysis is pursued without isolating components of the system. Typically, computational analyses are indifferent to physical realization, and indifferent even to whether or not distinct physical components manage the tasks that are distinguished in the analysis. Much psychological work seems to follow along closely related lines, as psychologists attempt to discover and analyze human cognitive capacities or dispositions in terms of simpler dispositions, and often attempt to do this without pinning down the neurophysical mechanisms underlying the relevant processes, and without worrying over whether such mechanisms are themselves analyzable into components mirroring the capacities mentioned in the psychological analysis.[7]

Finally, at this very general level of discussion, we can understand how the analytical and causal strategies are interrelated and reinforce each other. Any transition law underlying a causal explanation describes a dispositional property of a certain class of systems. Such dispositions can often themselves become the explananda of analytical explanations. On the other hand, any functional explanation of a system underwrites certain transition laws and supposes a range of transition laws. Of course, the analysis underwrites the transition law describing the relatively complex disposition that it explains. Additionally, each of the simpler dispositions posited in the analysis are themselves describable by transition laws. Thus, naturally enough, the result of a successful functional analysis is a set of transition laws that can themselves underwrite causal explanations of events involving a system of the sort analyzed.

The suggestion broached several times in the proceeding remarks is that much work in psychology is directed to providing functional explanations for psychological dispositions. This is certainly true of much of cognitive psychology where investigators begin with a concern to understand how human beings solve, or at least deal with, certain classes of problems. By analysis, they seek to specify the relevant disposition (or capacity) more clearly, and to understand how it is realized by the implementation of simpler dispositions (or capacities). For example, a central theme in Nisbett and Ross (1980) is that a significant range of human inferential practices and dispositions can be understood in terms of a set of simple inferential strategies, judgmental heuristics, which, while far from foolproof, are at least effective in making many cases tractable. By appreciating how these simpler strategies are applied in context, one understands how human beings "manage" when confronted with prediction problems, for example, or how they arrive at causal claims, for another example.

I have generally shied away from referring to analyzed dispositions as "capacities" and "problem solving abilities," for such terminology suggests that the dispositions uncovered in analysis are roads to success. They may be. But the general suggestion that they are should be avoided. The more neutral term, "disposition," is generally to be preferred. For a virtue of the analytical approach is that it allows us to explain both successful and unsuccessful "problem solving." Again, Nisbett and Ross (1980) is illustrative:

The position in this book is integrative; it maintains that people's inferential failures are cut from the same cloth as their inferential successes are. Specifically, we contend that people's inferential strategies are well adapted to deal with a wide range of problems, but that these same strategies become a liability when they are applied beyond that range, particularly when they are applied to problems requiring some appreciation of the normative principles that help to guide the professional scientist's more formal inferences (p. xii).

A disposition as analyzed in functional analysis may be generally beneficial for the possessing system, and thus a "capacity," but it can also be a general liability, or a mixed blessing.

To better understand the sort of functional explanation found in psychology, we can employ yet another of Cummins's distinctions: that between descriptive and interpretive analyses. Cummins (1983, p. 32) introduces the distinction as follows:

Some analyses specify analyzing functions in a vocabulary that yields symbolic interpretation rather than description of the relevant inputs and outputs. Suppose we are analyzing the capacities of a system of relays, and suppose our analysis is specified in program form. We might write a program consisting of such instructions as 'CLOSE RELAYS A THROUGH A,' or we might write a program consisting of such instructions as 'BRING DOWN THE NEXT SIGNIFICANT DIGIT.' suppose further that in this case closing relays A through D is (instantiates) bringing down the next significant digit. Then there is an obvious sense in which 'CLOSE RELAYS A THROUGH D' describes what is to happen, while 'BRING DOWN THE NEXT SIGNIFICANT DIGIT' interprets that happening. The first sort of instruction is appropriate to an analysis of, e.g., the capacity to control an array of LED's, whereas the second sort of instruction is appropriate to an analysis of the capacity to do long division.

Here we get a fair sense of the intended distinction. In some analyses, the dispositions analyzed and appealed to in the analysis are specified in nonsemantic terms. That is to say, inputs and outputs are described either as physical states, or in a closely related way, as uninterpreted tokens. In other analyses, dispositions, inputs, and outputs are specified as interpreted symbols or states. (In Cummins's example they are referred to as "digits," which are tokens of syntactic types whose semantic role is partially specified.) When the inputs and outputs mentioned in an analysis are given in these semantically interpreted (or partially interpreted) form, we have *interpretive analysis*. Following Cummins, we can call systems that are interpretively analyzable *information processing systems*.[8]

It is important to notice that when a disposition is specified in an interpretive analysis, semantically, it is specified in terms of a generalization that *resembles* an inference rule, or a rule of reasoning. The generalization characterizes, ceteris paribus, *what semantically interpreted states will be added to, or deleted from, the system's stock* of states, given that the system begins with certain other such states. This *differs* from an inference rule in one particularly important respect: rules and principles are expressed in a *normative modality*. They either urge certain sorts of inferences on us, or give permission to undertake certain sorts of inferences. Thus, to each characterization of a disposition in an interpretive analysis, there corresponds several formulatable rules or principles. One would urge the described transformations, another would simply allow such transformations. A disposition specified in an interpretive analysis is thus a disposition to proceed in accordance with such inference rules or principles of reasoning. Of course *these might be bad principles or rules*, but as I am using the terms "inference rule" and "principle of reasoning," that does not matter. Inferences rules, like inferences, may be good, that is, epistemically desirable, or bad, epistemically undesirable. Thus, when a disposition is specified in semantically interpreted terms, it is specified in a manner that could be recast by the introduction of normative terms as a rule of inference, but not necessarily a good rule of inference.

In this last paragraph I have departed from Cummins's account in two respects. First, Cummins (1983, pp. 53–55) understands the characterizability of dispositions in terms of inference rules (or the corresponding descriptive generalization) to require more than being an information processing system. He marks this by distinguishing a system's being "inferentially characterizable," from its being interpretively analyzable. At one level, he is led to this distinction because he conceives of "inference rules" as I think of good inference rules. Roughly, he thinks that inference rules must be "cogent—epistemologically appropriate." Thus, for Cummins, to be inferentially characterizable is to be an information processing system (a system that is interpretively analyzable) that is *also* analyzable into dispositions characterized by generalizations corresponding to valid or epistemically appropriate inference rules. This is to make inferential characterizability subject to a fundamental principle of charity, whereas interpretive characterizability is not so encumbered. So conceived, inferential characterizability obviously goes beyond interpretive analyzability. But, the important point is that Cummins believes that this distinction in analyses marks an important distinction in what can be attributed to systems on the basis of analyses: a system can be correctly said to make inferences if, and apparently only if, it can be inferentially characterized. For Cummins, only preponderantly rational systems make inferences.

I believe that this charitable requirement on inferential characterizability is misguided. This can be shown as follows. Being inferentially characterizable is at least part of what it is to be intentionally characterizable. That is to say, inferential characterizability is a necessary condition for having intentionality. Anything having beliefs must be inferentially characterizable with regard to its dealing with those belief states. Now, given that inferential characterizability is a necessary condition for intentional characterizability, there *would* need to be a fundamental charitable constraint on intentional characterization, *were* there such a constraint on inferential characterization. But, we have repeatedly seen that there is no fundamental principle of charity constraining intentional characterization. Thus, there can be no fundamental charitable constraint on inferential characterizability. A system can be both inferentially characterizable and intentionally characterizable without being analyzable as instancing mostly valid or epistemically appropriate ways of reasoning.

Cummins appears to soften his charitable requirement on inferential characterizability in an endnote where he remarks that the relevant inference rule "needn't be a valid rule in the usual sense, but at least a more or less reliable rule in the context the instantiating machinery operates in" (1983, p. 199). This still seems too strong. An individual's dispositions might be analyzed in a manner partially represented by the generalization that they employ the *representativeness heuristic* as described by Nisbett and Ross (1980, p. 7). The individual would then "reduce many inferential tasks to what are essentially simple judgments of similarity." This might be a "more or less reliable rule" in the individual's initial context. For a somewhat strained example, suppose that the person is initially a farmer toiling in a benign climate where similarity judgments lead one to anticipate the sort of cyclic regularities to which farmers are supposedly attuned. Cummins would then allow that the person was, in that respect, inferentially characterizable. But, now suppose that the person goes to Las Vegas. The representative heuristic can, in such contexts where one is dealing with probabilities, lead to the familiar gambler's fallacy (Nisbett and

Ross 1980, pp. 24–25). As a result, in the context of the casino, the representativeness heuristic is probably not "more or less reliable." Yet it is surely wrong to say that the old farmer ceases to make inferences, and ceases to have beliefs, when in Las Vegas.

The second way in which my characterization of inferential characterization departs from Cummins's has to do with the sorts of inferential rules to which input-output characterizations in such analyses are to correspond. Cummins (1991) characterizes these rules as describing "functions," in the mathematical sense. This is to suppose that the inputs at each stage are mapped onto determinate outputs. The analysis is then said to characterize an algorithm for computing the function to which the analyzed system is said to be disposed. This supposes a sort of determinacy that I believe to be quite foreign of psychology. My concerns here have nothing to do with quaint scruples regarding free will or any such thing.[9] Rather, they have to do in part with the general realization that generalizations in the special sciences generally are bound to be "soft," or subject to ineliminable ceteris paribus clauses (Fodor 1981; Rosenberg 1985a, chapter 4). There is every indication that psychology should fall in step here (Horgan and Tienson 1990).

A further caution is in order along these lines. In keeping with the just repudiated assumption that the inference rules associated with an inferential analysis characterize functions, it would have been all too easy to assume that these rules are rather like rules of argument in our familiar logic. (This is also suggested by Cummins's writing of "valid inference rules.") One might then conceive of analysis as an attempt to completely model the transformational dispositions of a cognitive system in terms of generalizations corresponding to rules of argument, like Modus Ponens, for example—programmable rules.[10] This is to proceed as though one could say of a person that, if they were to believe both that *P* and that if *P* then *Q*, then they will come to believe that *Q*. But, while some of the transformation rules employed in an analysis may resemble rules of logic, such will be alone inadequate. Gilbert Harman (1986) argues that rules of *argument* are far from adequate for understanding or characterizing *reasoning*, the process by which we make changes in our views. First, consider this matter from the normative point of view. Rules of argument characterize allowable transformations in a very limited sense. They allow one to determine what is *implied* by what one believes, and this *may* be something that one can justifiably add to one's set of beliefs. But then again, it may also be something that one cannot justifiably add. One may already have good independent reasons for believing that a certain newly discovered implication of one's beliefs is false. In other words, by employing argument rules, one may discover that a certain belief, Q, is implied by one's presently held beliefs, while, at the same time, one may already believe $\sim Q$, and have what seem good supporting reasons for doing so. Then one must settle upon which of one's present beliefs are to be deleted, and whether or not Q is to be added. Rules of argument, being attuned only to implication, cannot settle such conflicts. Normatively, what one is to do must then be characterized in terms of principles that do not simply lead one to expand one's stock of belief by following out implications. One must have what Harman calls *principles of reasoning* or *rules of revision*. In this work, I will use the phrase 'rule of inference' to denote both (valid and invalid) rules of argument and rules of reasoning.

Descriptively, similar points hold. Transformations in our stock of beliefs do not simply follow out implications. While some processing may be a matter of determining some of what follows from certain beliefs, and may be partially characterized by something like rules of argument, to fully characterize our cognitive processing, we need more. We need descriptions of our dispositions when engaged in a sort of cognitive juggling act. Such characterizations, or some of them, will resemble Harman's principles of reasoning, without the normative modality of course.

Now, so far as I can see, the ceteris paribus characterization of dispositions, employing characterizations that fall short of being mathematical functions, does not rob functional analysis of its explanatory power. One can in this manner still explain how a system generally manages to do whatever it is that it tends to do. One can still clarify what general dispositions the systems analyzed have, adding to our understanding of human reasoning capacities and infirmities, for example. And one can discover simpler dispositions, and their interactions, that underlie the more sophisticated or complex dispositions. All this is possible even when the characterization of dispositions proceeds in terms of ceteris paribus generalizations such as are characteristic of the special sciences.

A summary is in order before proceeding further. Much psychological investigation is a matter of seeking functional analyses of human cognitive capacities or dispositions. This is a matter of analyzing dispositions of human reasoners into an organized set of simpler dispositions. In such analyses, the inputs and outputs characterizing the dispositions are commonly specified as semantically interpreted (or partially interpreted) states. Thus, these analyses are what Cummins would call interpretive analyses of information processing systems. In such analyses, by stipulating dispositions in terms of transitions between interpreted states, the characterizing generalizations correspond to inference rules, although not necessarily epistemically good or appropriate inference rules. Accordingly, I consider interpretively analyzable systems to be inferentially characterizable systems.

Now, being interpretively or inferentially characterizable is *not* sufficient to make a system intentionally characterizable. Real intentionality requires more. What more, I am not at all able to say with much certainty or precision. I am convinced that the answer does not lie with the principle of charity, even in part. I do suspect that intentionality requires, (1) that the system has a substantial set of states that covary with its immediate environment, states that could then be thought of as carrying information about its environment, (2) that the system's states be interactive in a way that renders inferential analyses nontrivial, and (3) that the system be capable of a range of interventions in its environment. Without (1), attributions of referents to the system's states seem all too arbitrary.[11] Without (3), notions of "wanting" or "having a pro-attitude towards" seem unmotivated. (Still, both (1) and (3) would need to be softened to accommodate special cases, such as the proverbial envatted brain. See Tienson [forthcoming] for a suggestive discussion.) Further, in connection with (2), I do suspect that intentionality has something to do with having states that are interestingly interpretable as second-order representations of the semantics of *some* of the system's first-order states.

But, happily, I do not need to be able to develop these suggestions in order to proceed with the argument of this chapter. What is needed is the recognition that, while interpretive and inferential characterizability is not sufficient for intentional characterizability as having beliefs and desires, it is clearly necessary. This allows us to get a fairly good purchase on the role and limitations of rationalizing explanation.

5.2.2: Rationalizing Explanation and Nomic Generalizations

In keeping with the above account of interpretive or inferential analysis, we can envision a great diversity of such analyses, only a relatively small number of which find application to actual systems. When such an analysis is applicable to a system, we will be able to analyze the system and interpretively characterize its states. The one task presumes the other. This is fully in accord with my earlier discussions of interpretation in the human sciences. As I have portrayed the intentional characterization of human beings, this proceeds against a background of psychological expectations that amount to a (perhaps rough and prospective) analysis. That is to say, we interpret people so as to find them reasoning in ways that we expect, instancing shared cognitive dispositions (capacities and liabilities). Of course, we recognize that there are significant variations in dispositions to be uncovered within the human population. Still, when viewed against the great diversity of possible inferential analyses, we expect that human beings are characterizable in terms of a quite limited family of analyses, a set that, taken together, posits a substantial sharing of cognitive dispositions. Our present general psychological expectations constitute a rudimentary (and generally ill-specified) beginning to characterizing the common components of this family of inferential analyses.

Now, to appreciate the basis for rationalizing explanations, we need only notice an incontestible feature of our psychological expectations: human beings are rational in some significant, although limited, respects. If this is so, then the family of analyses that characterize human cognitive systems is partially constituted of generalizations corresponding to inference rules that are epistemically and practically desirable. As we have seen, in such analyses, the generalizations specifying dispositions in terms of input and output can themselves be taken as nomic transition laws for the class of systems being analyzed. Thus, if human beings are substantially, although limitedly, rational, then there are transition laws characterizing their psychology that correspond to epistemically and practically desirable rules of inference. But this is to say that there are transition laws that characterize human cognitive processing in ways that happen to allow us to see it as (significantly but limitedly) rational. It is these transition laws that support rationalizing explanation.

Against the background of such transition laws, we can explain particular actions or beliefs. We explain by citing antecedent beliefs and desires that causally contributed to the occurrence of the explanandum action or state. We are able to determine which these are (and what their causally relevant features are) because we possess general information regarding human cognitive capacities. *Given the transition laws, we can reconstruct the causal history of the explanandum event, and thereby come to appreciate that, had the agent not have had the relevant beliefs and desires, the explanandum would not have obtained, or at least would have been less likely to have obtained.* Of course, insofar as the transition laws on which we rely correspond to epistemically or practically appropriate rules of inference, the action or belief that is explained is also shown to be rational in virtue of the explanan-beliefs and desires. Thus we have a case of rationalizing explanation. However, *it is not the exhibited rationality of the explanandum that gives the explanation its force, it is the background information regarding the responsible cognitive dispositions.* This last point will receive a great deal of expansion and support in the next chapter. For now, we can content ourselves with an illustration and a discussion of parallel irrationalizing explanations that have the same explanatory force because they rest on the same sort of explanatory background information.

Consider the following illustration, which I hope is not too implausibly naive. Suppose that we have a rough analysis of human cognitive processing that indicates that we have a limited general ability to find that *P* is implied by antecedently held beliefs, *where* the truth or falsity of *P* is recognized as important for certain further purposes, *and P* is a reasonably direct implication of antecedently held beliefs,[12] *and* these other beliefs are accessible in the memory. Of course, the characterization of such a capacity should be itself a component of a broader analysis, which should include a characterization of the structure and limitations on human memory and a characterization of the ability to recognize the prospective importance of the truth and falsity of certain claims, and the disposition to believe recognized implications of one's antecedently held beliefs (subject to ceteris paribus conditions such as those mentioned earlier). The characterization of our capacity to determine whether a particular claim is entailed by our beliefs will itself require much further analysis. For example, such an analysis might include the characterization of us as being able to readily follow out certain rules of argument when called upon, including disjunctive syllogism, for example (Cherniak 1986). We can now put such a prospective analysis to work in a hypothetical explanation.

Suppose that Billy Jean wishes to go to the game tomorrow afternoon. She would like to save money by getting general admission seats. However, she knows that if the reserved seats are sold out by this afternoon, the general admission seats will go on sale as reserved seats. In that eventuality, if she waits until tomorrow to purchase tickets, she may get undesirable seats. But, for delicate reasons I cannot go into here, she must now decide when to acquire her tickets. Thus, she believes that either she should buy reserved seats (at general admission prices) this afternoon, or she can safely wait and buy general admission seats one and one-half hours prior to the game tomorrow afternoon. She remembers that afternoon games never sell out the reserved seating,[13] and thus notes that there is no need for her to buy her tickets this afternoon (i.e., that it is not the case that she should buy her tickets that afternoon). Thus, she recognizes that her beliefs imply that she can wait until tomorrow to acquire tickets. Accordingly, we may suppose that she comes to believe that she can wait. Now we can, given our expectations as set out in our prospective analysis, explain her recognizing that her antecedently held beliefs imply that she can wait. (And, on the wider analysis, we can explain her subsequent belief that she can wait.) The explanation is that it became important to her whether she could wait and that the conclusion that she could followed by way of disjunctive syllogism from the accessible antecedent beliefs just mentioned. Of course, as with many common explanations, we probably would abbreviate all this by mentioning the antecedent beliefs and letting our general and common expectations be simply understood. In this explanation we come to see Billy Jean as an acceptably competent reasoner, and eventually, as one who, ceteris paribus, accepts the logical consequences of her antecedently held beliefs. We thus come to see her as, in these respects, rational; we see her belief that she can wait as a rational belief for her to hold, given her beliefs (and desires). We have here a rationalizing explanation.

In the simple case of rationalizing explanation just envisioned, we are explaining a belief by citing antecedently held beliefs. The explanatory effect turns on getting the causal story right, and this depends on our knowledge of the dispositions of Billy Jean as a cognitive system. The sense of explanation used here is no more mysterious than that involved in other singular causal explanations involving dispositions of a system. A rock, placed in water, dissolves. At its simplest, the explanation is that the rock was common table salt. Of course, in advancing this explanation we rely on our common background knowledge: table salt is water soluble. That is to say, the following transition law governs the physical system that is a piece of salt: If it is placed in water, then (ceteris paribus) it will dissolve. Of course, the system is subject to much more interesting analysis. This analysis would allow us to understand rock salt in terms of its components (sodium and chlorine) and their interaction (ionic bonding), which is itself explained by the dispositions of the components (chlorine has a greater tendency to capture electrons than sodium, which has a "low electronegativity"), and this in turn is explained in terms of the structure of chlorine and sodium atoms (in particular their outer electrons). This analysis, in turn, would allow us to understand how such a system can have the dispositional property of being water soluble. Water is formed by a polar covalent bond—while the hydrogen and oxygen atoms in a water molecule share two electrons, rather than exchanging electrons, they do not share them equally. This produces a partial negative charge at the oxygen, and a partial positive charge at the hydrogen atoms. When a sample of salt is placed in such a medium, the aggregate effect of these partial charges is to break down the ionic bonds of the salt, freeing the positive sodium ions and negative chlorine ions to bond with water molecules. In view of this analysis, we have a more sophisticated explanation for the behavior of our rock in water: the salt was placed in a polar covalent solution, water, and its lattice of bonded ions is broken down, and the component ions are combined with water molecules in the lawlike ways described just now. Again, our knowledge of the transition laws describing the dispositions of the system and its components supports such an explanation.

The cases of rationalizing explanation and of the chemical explanation just sketched are parallel. In both cases, we expect certain outcomes (or at least they are rendered more likely) in view of posited dispositions and their antecedent conditions obtaining. In both cases, these dispositions are characterized in an analysis of the relevant sorts of systems. These analyses differ in the sorts of terms employed, and in their degree of tentativeness. But, in both cases, it is the spawned general expectations that gives explanatory force to our citing of the antecedent conditions.

5.2.3: Rationalizing Explanation and Irrationalizing Explanation Are Epistemologically on a Par

If what I have said so far is correct, then there should be a form of explanation that is in all respects parallel to rationalizing explanation with the exception that explanations of this type do not happen to lead us to see what is done as rational. This is to say, *if* common rationalizing explanations ultimately rest on knowledge of human cognitive dispositions, and *if* only some of these dispositions are specifiable in terms of transition laws corresponding to epistemically or practically appropriate rules of inference, and consequently, some of these dispositions are specifiable in terms corresponding to inappropriate rules, then *there must be explanations that have every virtue, every explanatory strength, of rationalizing explanations, but which do not lead us to see what is done as rational.* They may even lead us to see it as irrational. Such is the case.

As I have already argued at several points in this work (sections 3.3 and 4.4), people clearly do not conform to the standards for *ideal human rationality.* By this I mean to point out more than the fact that human beings are limited in how quickly they reason and how much information they can remember and process. Of course, humans are limited in such ways. But this is no news, even to the most passionate partisans of rationalizing explanation. It is commonly recognized that reasoning takes time and can be taxing, and that some inferences are more difficult or taxing than others of equal abstract appropriateness (Cherniak 1986, Chaps. 1 and 2). It is also commonplace that not all the beliefs in the agent's "long-term" memory that are relevant to a particular decision will be recalled and brought to bear (Chaps. 1 and 3). As a result, even were the agents' dispositions otherwise in complete accordance with our ideals of rationality, implementation would be pulled up short. This results in them failing to recognize every consequence, even every useful consequence, of their beliefs. But such failings do not count as human irrationality.

Still, while the above-mentioned limitations on human reasoning capacities do not introduce anything properly called human irrationality, it is worthwhile to pause and reflect on how these limitations do reinforce the conclusion of the previous sections concerning the descriptive basis for proper rationalizing explanation. So, assume for a time that a representation of our cognitive capacities could be given using nothing corresponding to inappropriate rules of inference. Still, not all the inferences that might appropriately be made will be. While this is not a matter of human irrationality, it does put us in mind of complications in rationalizing explanations. For example, a particular action may be rational on the full set of the agent's beliefs and wants, and on several proper subsets of these as well. However, the rationality of the action may be a matter of more or less complex inferences as one deals with the different sets. Now the question is, which set of beliefs really explains the agent's doing the indicated action? To cite a particular one of the relevant subsets of the agent's beliefs, or to cite even the entire set, could be misleading. Ideally, to explain the action, one would need to cite those capacities and beliefs that were really operative in producing the action. To get at such matters one must use information regarding the relative difficulty of various reasoning tasks, the structure of human memory, and so forth. This is the sort of descriptive information represented in a proper analysis of the agent's cognitive dispositions. Thus again, we see that such information provides an indispensable grounding for rationalizing explanation.

A similar case introduces a complexity for rationalizing explanation that is only slightly more troubling to partisans of rationalizing explanation. Consider a case in which an action is rational given some subset of an agent's beliefs, but not rational given the full set of those beliefs. Now suppose that the demonstration of the action's ultimate irrationality involves a rather time-consuming bit of reasoning—perhaps one that is so difficult as not to be feasible for the agent at all. Here we might expect the agent to do the action, despite its being "irrational" on the pure ideal of rationality (specified using only epistemically and practically appropriate rules). Again, few proponents of rationalizing explanation would be surprised or troubled by such cases. After all, the action is rational on the inferences that the agent can do (and these are ex hypothesi characterized by only appropriate rules). The problem is rather that the agent apparently cannot consider together all the relevant beliefs and desires and implement completely all the ideally appropriate rules. Again, one might say that the action, while not rational as some abstract ideal, is at least humanly rational. Such supposedly is what has been wanted in rationalizing explanation. What must now be stressed is that, in order to settle on such an explanation, we must commonly rely on descriptive information acquired in an analysis of human reasoning capacities.

Cases such as these require elaborations on the simple notion of rationalizing explanation that proponents have generally already recognized. It is not enough to cite some set of an agent's beliefs and wants that make the agent's action rational. As Davidson (1980d, p. 232) insists, these must have caused the actions, and have "caused it in the right way." (See also Goldman 1970, pp. 57–63.) Sorting out such matters will require attention to various limitations in the agent's capacities, attention to the descriptive information that I have argued underlies rationalizing explanation from the beginning.

The cases just discussed involve what I call ideal human rationality, for I have supposed that none of the shortcomings of the reasoning involved there are realizations of dispositions describable with inappropriate inference rules. However, human beings do make mistaken inferences from the point of view of deductive, inductive, and practical standards. They do tend to reason according to certain epistemically and practically inappropriate inference rules. Ultimately, to provide an empirically adequate analysis of human reasoners, the set of generalizations employed will have to include generalizations that correspond to inappropriate rules of inference. Some of the relevant dispositions have already been discussed in sections 3.3.1, 3.3.3, and 4.4. Rather than recount the range of dispositions considered in those sections, I will take it that the claim that human beings have substantial dispositions to irrational ways of reasoning is already supported. Thus I will content myself with providing an illustration of an irrationalizing explanation. (A second illustration can be found in section 6.3.)

Consider the judgmental heuristics posited by cognitive psychologists. These are not explicit strategies codified into rules that are espoused and consciously implemented by agents. Their general formulations might not even receive wide support by the agents that apparently follow them. However, there are implicit strategies that agents do follow in many cases. In many of these cases the strategies might lead to correct results. The problem is that there are common situations in which these strategies systematically produce the incorrect result. They are clearly invalid rules of inference. More importantly, because they are given to systematically producing errors when used in certain contexts, they are, in those contexts, inappropriate rules. Appropriate rules would be limited in ways that are foreign to judgmental heuristics.

Now consider one hypothesized judgmental heuristic: the representativeness heuristic. As I have explained, this heuristic involves the reduction of many inferential tasks to similarity judgments. For example, the task of estimating the likelihood of a sequence is often approached by judging as to the similarity or "degree of fit" between the possible sequence and the generating process for such sequences. As a result, flipping a coin, being something of a random process, is thought more likely to generate the "random seeming" sequence HTTHTH rather than either TTTTTT or HHHTTT. However, the probability of all three sequences are the same. The first is typically judged more "similar" to the random process that "spews out" Hs and Ts. (Again, this is clearly related to the gambler's fallacy.) Imagine setting up a situation in which people are to choose sequences of six coin toss results. You explain that if their chosen sequence is realized by a set of public coin tosses, they win some attractive prize. You find that your respondents are avoiding choices like TTTTTT and HHHTTT. This is readily explained. They wish to maximize their chance of winning. To do this, they attempt to choose a sequence that is relatively likely. They avoid those nonrandom-seeming sequences because they judge them relatively unlikely because they are employing the representativeness heuristic.

The representativeness heuristic also seems to play a role in intuitive causal attributions. As Mill notes, there is a "prejudice that the conditions of a phenomena [sic] must resemble the phenomena" (Mill 1974, p. 756). If so, the representativeness heuristic has consequences that should interest the social scientist. Nisbett and Ross (1980, p. 116) note the parallel between this strategy and Zande folk medicine as described in the following report by Evans-Pritchard (1937, p. 487):

> Generally the logic of therapeutic treatment consists in the selection of the most prominent external symptoms, the naming of the disease after some object in nature that it resembles, and the utilization of the object as the principle ingredient in the drug administered to cure the disease. The circle may also be completed by belief that the external symptoms not only yield to treatment by the object which resembles them but also are caused by it as well.

On the basis of such observations, Nisbett and Ross suggest that the representativeness heuristic gives rise to the Zande belief that epilepsy can be cured using the burnt skull of the red bush monkey (whose movements are seen as similar to those of an epileptic).

Now, when accurate description of human cognitive capacities requires some use of generalizations corresponding to such inappropriate inference rules, the role of rationalizing explanation is significantly limited. Some activities will not be explicable by citing the beliefs and desires that make them rational and that brought them about "in the right way." They will not be so explicable because they were brought about by different capacities specified by generalizations corresponding to inappropriate rules. To explain them we must resort to what I have called *irrationalizing explanation*.

That there is a role for irrationalizing explanation does not show that there is no role for rationalizing explanations. Rather, it shows that there is a place for both, and that place is *determined by theoretical information regarding human dispositions* (capacities and incapacities). It is such background that accounts for whatever explanatory force rationalizing and irrationalizing explanation have. Strictly speaking, showing that such-and-such a belief or action of a person is rational, given the person's beliefs and aims, does not explain that belief or action. Nor, of course, does the demonstration of the irrationality of such-and-such a belief or action explain the belief or action. Rather, showing that the belief or action is *rational in one of the ways fostered by human cognitive capacities* explains the belief. Likewise, showing that the belief or action is *irrational in one of the ways fostered by human cognitive capacities* explains the belief. This is to say that rationalizing explanation and irrationalizing explanation are epistemically on a par; both draw on the sort of descriptive information acquired in interpretive analyses of cognitive systems.[14]

6

Rationalizing Explanation and the Scientific Explanation of Events

6.1: Restating Our Issue

As much by what they do not say as by what they say in their discussions of rationalizing explanation, philosophers championing rationalizing explanation often seem to suppose that social scientists can, with impunity, simply borrow wholesale our best normative standards of rationality and apply them in explanations. In the previous chapter, I sought to show that no such free hand is proper. By providing a superior positive account of such explanation, I argued that rationalizing explanation rests on descriptive information regarding cogntive capacities. I here seek to reinforce these conclusions by reexamining the foundations of rationalizing explanation in a way that explicitly confronts a venerable issue in philosophical work on explanation: what sort of background or explicit general information (laws or generalizations) must be had by producers and consumers of explanations? I argue that it must be as psychological theory, and not as normative principles, that inferential rules, or rather, the corresponding characterizations of cognitive strategies, provide the necessary basis for rationalizing explanation. Hence, I reject the fundamentally charitable view according to which the explanatory force of common rationalizing explanations of actions or intensional states comes by virtue of our exhibiting the rationality of the explanandum. I argue that the normative propriety of actions or events, their conformity with ideal rules of inference, can have no bearing on the why-questions that seek singular causal explanations.

When a writer claims that we must, often or primarily, explain by showing that certain actions or positions taken were reasonable or rational, we must first determine in which of various ways the proposed requirement is to be understood. Let us distinguish four quite general understandings of such claims.

Alternative 1: We may believe that certain rather rudimentary norms reflect human cognitive processing capacities. We could then expect such rudimentary rationality or reasonableness on the part of people studied. In this case, we could explain some action or belief of our subject(s) by showing that it was an instance of the rudimentary cognitive processes which we expect. As it happens, this would then lead us to see the actions or beliefs as rational or reasonable, given the agent's antecedent beliefs and desires. Of course, we could explain other actions in alternative ways. However, it seems likely that such minimal rationalizing explanation would turn out to be an important explanatory tool.

Alternative 2: In some cases at least, we may know that our subject is a member of a community that is characterized by the use of normative standards substantially stronger than the rudimentary set posited in the first alternative. We should, of course, take this into account and make more use of rationalizing explanation than would be suggested by the first alternative, unsupplemented. Suppose, for example, we were studying the work of a certain scientist or community of scientists. We doubtless believe that to become a scientist involves being socialized into the norms of a particular scientific community. The norms of such communities vary somewhat (Laudan 1984). But, supposedly the relevant community counts as scientific insofar as it holds to some fairly substantial subset of our contemporary standards for scientific rationality. At least it holds to some closely related set of standards. In such cases, we would expect to find members of the particular scientific community rational to the extent that this is suggested by their society's particular subset of our best scientific standards (and to the extent that these standards are effectively instilled). This is still a matter of expecting limited amounts of rationality. The limits here come from the limits we imagine to be endemic to human cognitive processing and from the limits of the standards learned in the historical community. (And of course we must make room for countervailing factors.) In such cases, we could explain some beliefs and actions of members of the relevant community by showing that, given the agents' other beliefs, they were rational or reasonable, in one of the limited ways we have found to be characteristic of our subjects. It is crucial to note that, in explaining a belief or action in the manner envisioned here, we would be showing it *rational in one of the ways we take to be characteristic of our subjects' cognitive processes*, and not just showing it to be rational according to our best standards.

Of course, these first two alternatives are those that are suggested by the account of rationalizing explanation advanced in the previous chapter. They make the importance or primacy of rationalizing explanation an empirical, theory-dependent matter. For our purposes here, it is worth emphasizing that both the above alternatives involve a more or less *selective borrowing of normative standards by descriptive theory*. In the first case, we would use some rather limited set of normative standards, or rather the corresponding generalizations, to represent aspects of general human cognitive capacities. It is as a descriptive theory of such capacities, and not as normative standards, that the relevant standards support explanations. In the second case, we suppose that the range of normative standards with which an agent complies is extended beyond the minimal set involved in representing basic cognitive capacities. The range of standards with which the agent tends to comply is extended by training into a particular community. To the extent that the relevant standards within the agent's community coincide with our standards, further portions of our normative theory can be borrowed and used to represent some of the standards in which the agent is trained. Stripped of their normative modalities, they then represent acquired dispositions of the agents. Again, it is in this capacity as a descriptive account of certain community standards (combined with the more rudimentary cognitive capacities) that the standards we use support explanations. (Of course, strictly, normative standards do not enter into explanation as representations of dispositions at all, rather what I have called the corresponding generalizations do. One might say that the normative standards must first be "transubstantiated," in a nonmysterious respect of course.)

Alternative 3: In contrast to the above envisioned reliance on only descriptive analogues to normative standards in explanation, where such standards must be selectively transformed into descriptive theory, writers often seem to suppose a third approach: the fundamentally charitable approach in which we simply take our best contemporary standards of rationality (scientific and otherwise) and, without selective transformation into descriptive theory, use them in explanations. On this view, there is apparently no need to take care that such standards reflect either basic human processing capacities or learned standards of reasoning. We need only show that an action or belief was rational, given the agent's precipitating beliefs and desires, in order to explain it.

Alternative 4: It is possible to adopt various imperialist versions of the third approach to rationalizing explanation in the human sciences. On such views, one would claim that *only* the third approach will serve as the basis for social scientific and historical explanation. This is to capture the claim that such explanation provides a necessary basis for such explanations. Supposedly, since rationalizing explanation is here conceived as resting on normative principles and not on descriptive general information, the role here claimed for such explanation is also not dependent on theory. Thus, in the terminology of the previous chapter, imperialist versions of the third alternative assert a transcendent, as opposed to a theory-dependent, preferred status for rationalizing explanation.

On some particularly strong variants of this view, one holds that our best contemporary standards of rationality must be employed in rationalizing explanations, and thus in the preponderance of explanations in the human sciences. Such a view would be characterized by the insistence that it is not just the case that our best contemporary standards *can* inform explanations in the social sciences, but that we must use only, or predominantly, our best contemporary standards in rationalizing explanations. It then supposedly would not do to attempt to explain most beliefs by showing that they were rationally held, when rationality is judged in terms of some set of standards other than our best contemporary standards. Both the first two approaches to rationalizing explanation, involving as they do the selective transformation of normative standards into descriptive representations, would then be ruled out as providing an inadequate way of explaining the preponderance of beliefs. (Such a view is suggested, for example, in Agassi's [1963] account of historical investigations of scientific practice, and even by Laudan [1977], pp. 164–67. It is also urged in McDowell [1985].)

One clarification of the third and fourth approaches to rationalizing explanation is in order. It is not quite correct to say that, on these approaches, we need only show that an action or belief was rational in this full-bodied sense, given the agent's other beliefs and desires, in order to explain it. This seems to adequately characterize only some (typically older) variants of these approaches. For example, it seems to characterize certain neo-Wittgensteinian views according to which common rationalizing explanations are not causal explanations at all. Such views hold that claims to the effect that "so-and-so did such-and-such because they wanted certain things" are not singular causal claims. Rather, it is said that they have a place in a sort of explanation that works by showing the "intelligibility" of what is done, where intelligibility is intimately associated with rationality and justification (for example, Winch 1958). However, since Davidson's classic "Actions, Reasons, and Causes" (1980a), advocates of the third and fourth approaches seem generally to recognize that the claims made in rationalizing explanation are singular causal claims. Still, some writers persist in writing as though it were the normative propriety, as such, of the explanandum belief or action (in light of the agent's beliefs and desires) that gives the relevant causal claims their explanatory force. This is to suppose that the relevant background for rationalizing explanation is our normative standards, qua normative standards. It is these that we are apparently allowed (or required) to draw upon without regard to whether they model actual cognitive dispositions.

It is an unfortunate fact that much writing on the importance of rationalizing explanation supposes either the third or the fourth alternative understandings of the basis for such explanation. Consider, for example, I. C. Jarvie's (1964) account of sociological and anthropological explanation as a matter of uncovering "the logic of the situation." This approach is said to rest on one very broad "hypothesis—why people acted in such and such a way can be rationally reconstructed" (Jarvie 1964, p. 35). Accordingly, investigators are urged to "attribute reasonable aims to the actors in the situation and try to show that, within their frame of reference, their actions, if interpreted as trying to realize those aims, are perfectly rational" (p. 131). It turns out that, for Jarvie, the broad hypothesis mentioned above, and the corresponding attempt to show that what is done was "the most reasonable thing to do," are dictated by a "methodological principle" (pp. 70, 73). There is here no mention of, and little place for, psychological information entering to sharpen or moderate the dictates of such a methodological principle. As a result, we are apparently free, if not obligated, to borrow our best normative standards and put them to work wholesale in social scientific explanation.

Hilary Putnam has argued that translation and social scientific explanation are intimately associated. Perhaps as a natural result of this association, the model of explanation he espouses is that of rationalizing explanation generally unrestrained by psychological information:

[W]hat we do in 'translation' is to construct a global theory which gives reasonable explanation of the speaker's behavior in light of his beliefs (as determined by the translation-manual which is *one* component of the global theory) *and* his desires and intentions (as determined by the psychological theory which is the *other* component).

To avoid one possible misunderstanding, let me say this: I am not just contending that it is *good methodology* in *finding out* what a speaker 'means' to try to *rationalize* his behavior in this way! I am suggesting that what it is to be a correct translation or truth-definition is to be the translation or truth-definition that best explains the behavior of the speaker (Putnam 1978, p. 41).

Psychological theory is ultimately given no role in specifying what "rationizing" of behavior is explanatory. Its role is apparently to be quite minimal—the only role explicitly assigned to it is the specification of "what the speaker wants or intends, at least in many situations" (Putnam 1978, p. 40). As an example, Putnam mentions attributing desires for food, drink, or sleep in the face of deprivations of such biological needs. Once it has served to constrain somewhat the desires attributed to those explained, psychological theory is notably not given a role in tailoring our rationalizing explanation itself.

Similarly, Stephen Turner's otherwise fine discussion of sociological explanation portrays this as a matter of rationalizing explanation with little or no mention of psychological theory. Thus, he describes how attributions of apparently irrational beliefs or actions can confront investigators with puzzles, or particularly problematic cases needing explanation. In his discussion of ways of dealing with such cases, one finds almost exclusively varieties of rationalizing explanation (Turner 1980, pp. 54–55, 75).

It is worth noting that Putnam's and Turner's accounts, and many others that I would find committed to the third or fourth alternative understandings of the importance of rationalizing explanation, recognize that interpretation and explanation in the human sciences are intimately connected. In fact, these accounts view interpretation and explanation as two sides of the same coin. Such a view rather naturally can lead to the third and fourth alternatives. As explained and criticized in section 3.3.1, it becomes seductively easy to think of interpretation as doing all the work of explanation simply by uncovering beliefs and desires, which are assumed to interact in normatively appropriate ways. This way of thinking should be avoided, in part for reasons to be made clear in this chapter.

However, a related reason for avoiding it is that it ignores the importance of theory-informed explanation in interpretation. Successful interpretation must lead to successful explanation, as Turner and Putnam would insist, but not necessarily to rationalizing explanation, for this is contingent on psychological theories or expectations. Thus, one can recognize the intimate connection between interpretation and explanation in the human sciences without being committed to the third and fourth understandings of rationalizing explanation.

Donald Davidson's well-known discussions of rationalizing explanation and interpretation make rationality (as such) constitutive of mental states, for example (Davidson 1980c, 1987). As a result, normative standards, as normative standards, seem to be taken a priori as explanatory. This suggestion is developed by John McDowell, who, in a sympathetic discussion of Davidson's views argues that we should recognize that it is as the *full set* of our best normative ideals that standards of rationality come to figure in explanation. He criticizes functionalists such as Brian Loar for adopting an approach to mental states and intentional explanation in which only a subset of our standards of rationality is employed (McDowell 1985). McDowell thus advances a particularly explicit and strong variant of the fourth approach:

> To recognize the ideal status of the constitutive concept [of rationality] is to appreciate that the concepts of the propositional attitudes have their proper home in explanations of a special sort: explanations in which things are made intelligible by being revealed to be, or to approximate to being, as they rationally ought to be. This is to be contrasted with a style of explanation in which one makes things intelligible by representing their coming into being as a particular instance of how things generally tend to happen (McDowell 1985, p. 389).

Thus, McDowell (1985, p. 392) urges us to see reason-citing explanations as instances of a special form of explanation: "ideal-involving explanation." At least McDowell here squarely confronts the implications often left implicit by other writers. However, when he attributes failures to recognize the force of ideal-involving explanations to prejudice, I am reminded of Meinong's dismissive view of the "prejudice in favor of the actual." I confess to both "prejudices." Some of my reasons for favoring generalization-based explanations will be explained in what follows.

6.2: Why Explanations are Nonextensional and Why Normative Principles are Explanatorily Impotent

The third (and thus the fourth) approach entails that rationalizing explanation need not rely on our descriptive (psy⸱ ⸱logical and sociological) understanding of what to expect of individuals and communities of reasoners. In this section, I develop certain observations regarding explanation generally that allow us to appreciate just how misguided the third approach is. The fourth approach is thus undermined as well. In particular, I draw on the view that explanations are fundamentally answers to why-questions. Answers to these why-questions must provide information regarding the causally relevant factors in the antecedent course of events. Such information regarding particular cases rests on general descriptive information characterizing sorts of mechanisms. The central claim of this section is that, once we appreciate what it takes to answer a why-question, and thus to provide an explanation for an action or intentional state, we find that normative principles, qua normative principles, have nothing to contribute here. When we appreciate how explanations must serve as answers to why-questions, we find that, while some causal *statements* may be extensional in the familiar sense (of permitting extensional substitutivity *salva veritate*), *explanation* is not an extensional matter. For my purposes here, *explanation* will be said to be *extensional* if and only if within any explanatory statement one can substitute coreferential and coextensive terms and phrases and thereby produce an equally explanatory statement (provided, of course, that the term or phrase substituted for did not occur within an embedded and independently nonextensional context such as an intentional state ascription).[1] By examining the referential opacity of explanation, and, in particular, *why* it matters how the explanans and explanandum are described, I seek to show that the explanation of actions rests on descriptive generalizations, not on normative standards as such.

Explanations, other than functional explanations, are answers to why-questions (see, for example, Woodward 1979, 1984, 1986; van Fraassen 1980).[2] This general approach to explanation naturally suggests that explanation is not extensional. For such questions are posed as requests for information that fills in a gap in our knowledge. Generally, in asking a why-question (regarding a particular event or state) we seek responses that allow us to appreciate what it was in or about the antecedent course of events that brought about (or helped to bring about) some particular aspect of certain subsequent events. Such an appreciation or understanding cannot just be a matter of naming or describing some causally antecedent event whose relevance to the named or described explanandum-event might yet remain wholly mysterious. Rather, the antecedent event must be presented in terms of its causally relevant features. As Salmon (1989, p. 128) puts it, "explanatory knowledge is knowledge of the causal mechanisms, and mechanisms of other types perhaps, that produce the phenomena with which we are concerned." And such knowledge is inevitably general.

One particularly venerable view in the philosophy of science provides some general support for the view that explanation is not extensional. On the covering-law account, it is not sufficient to mention a causal antecedent, C, of the explanandum-event, E. Nor is it sufficient to combine mention of the antecedent and the explanandum within a singular causal statement (of the form 'C caused E'). Rather, it is said, one must also provide (or at least allude to) a covering-law connecting things of the sort C is with things of the sort E is. On this covering-law model, if citing antecedent occurrent beliefs and desires is to explain a particular action, there must be known laws connecting beliefs and desires with actions in such a way that they allow us to (deductively or inductively) infer the action in question. On this view, those who are successfully giving and receiving explanations must either both already know the relevant laws, or the one providing the explanation must know and communicate the relevant laws to the one receiving it. On the covering-law model of explanation, it clearly matters how events are described. For expectation of the explanandum must be derivable through the essential use of scientific laws and certain initial conditions.

However, even in its most sophisticated versions, such as Hempel (1965b), the covering-law model has been found to be subject to a range of insuperable objections demonstrating that the conditions that it advances are neither necessary nor sufficient for satisfactory explanation. The objections have come to be canonized in a set of standard counterexamples illustrating the problems of relevance, asymmetry, and the explanation of improbable events. These difficulties render the covering-law model untenable (van Fraassen 1980; Salmon 1989). The covering-law model cannot serve as a basis for the present investigation.

There is an additional misgiving regarding the covering-law model of explanation. It is a concern that has led some to conclude that explanation is extensional. The covering-law model, taken strictly with common constraints on what can count as laws, has the problem that, if it is correct, there are remarkably few explanations. The reason, it seems, is that the vast majority of "explanations" we encounter are not accompanied by the requisite covering-laws of the strict sort commonly envisioned.[3] But, as Woodward says (1986, p. 233), an adequate general account of explanation must make explanations *epistemically accessible* to actual consumers of explanations. (See also Miller 1987, pp. 21–23). This concern has led to something of an overreaction. In effect, the conclusion that the covering-law account of the information needed for explanation asks too much has led some to overly liberalize the requirements on the sort of background information needed for explanation. This reaction is particularly in evidence in the claim that explanation is an extensional matter (for this claim serves as the limiting case of the reaction). Woodward (1984, 1986), for example, provides a sophisticated version of this mistaken claim. He argues that once we understand the full structure of why-questions and the associated explanatory causal claims we see that the substitution of "co-referential terms" within causal claims preserves truth.[4] Ultimately, I will grant that this is so, but it does not show that explanation is extensional.

By examining various singular causal attributions, noting what substitutions preserve truth, and drawing on Dretske's (1972) notion of contrastive focus, Woodward shows that singular causal statements are relational on the effect-side, having the form:

(1) *a* caused *b* rather than *c*.

Woodward argues that the substitution of coreferential (or coextensional) terms within the indicated places will preserve truth. Consider one of Woodward's own examples:

(2) The presence of potassium salts caused the fire to be purple.

Here it is presupposed that there is some unique fire picked out, in context, by 'the fire'. The occurrence of this fire is presupposed, not explained. The explanandum is the relational matter of the fire having a particular color, purple, rather than some other color:

(3) [a] The presence of potassium salts caused [b] the fire to be purple rather than [c] some other color.

Now, supposing that it is true that Mrs. Jones's favorite color is purple, substituting 'Mrs. Jones's favorite color' for 'purple' within (2) should preserve truth. Thus:

(4) The presence of potassium salts caused the fire to be Mrs. Jones's favorite color rather than some other color.

Further, supposing that to be purple is to emit light primarily of certain wavelengths (within the range r), the following also preserves truth:

(5) The presence of potassium salts caused the fire to emit light with wavelengths primarily within the range r, rather than some other combination of wavelengths.

All this seems correct to me, for I have no difficulty understanding many causal claims such as (2)–(5) as extensional in the standard sense (of allowing substitutivity of coreferring expressions *salva veritate*). Indeed, this seems to be the standard understanding of many such claims.[5] However, it does not show that *explanation* is extensional (in the sense described earlier).

The crux of the matter is this. Woodward uses the distinctions discussed above to show that singular causal claims can commonly be extensional in the standard sense: their truth is preserved under substitution of coextensional terms. He then proceeds as if, because singular causal explanations are commonly expressed using such statements, explanation must be preserved under such substitutions as well. That is, he believes that the substitutivity *salva veritate* characteristic of many singular causal claims shows that explanation is itself an extensional matter. This means that, if one starts with a satisfactory explanation (that is, with a satisfactory answer to a particular why-question) and one substitutes coextensional terms within this explanation, the resulting sentence is not just true, it is also explanatory. This is mistaken, for it fails to distinguish between causal statements and causal explanations. How the events are described is crucial in causal explanation, for there, the explanan-event and the explanandum-event(s) must be described in terms that reflect the manner in which systems of the relevant sorts develop and interact in lawlike ways. To appreciate this demand, we must look more closely at why-questions, explanations, and causal dependence.

Just as causal statements are relational on the effect-side, so why-questions are contrastive, or relational, on the explanandum-side (van Fraassen 1980). We seek an explanation for why a particular event has a certain characteristic *rather than* having certain other incompatible characteristics. We seek an explanation for why an event of a particular sort occurred *rather than* there being no such event. Thus, with regard to the attention-catching purple fire we could ask:

(6) Why is the fire *purple* (rather than some other color)? and:

(7) Why did the purple fire occur (rather than not occur)?

Those initial characterizations following the 'Why' are said to state the *topic* of the question, P^k. Thus, the topic of (6) is the particular fire's being purple, while the topic of (7) is the obtaining (in some contextually defined setting) of an event of the type fire. The phrases in the parentheses are said to indicate the *contrast class*, $X = \{P^1, \ldots, P^k, \ldots\}$. Formally, the contrast class is here taken to include the topic as one member. Of course, it is a presupposition of the why-question that P^k alone among the members of the contrast class obtained. Finally, such a question asks for the delineation of certain features of events that bear a certain *relevance relation*, R, to the couple, $<P^k,X>$. The why-question can then be understood as the triple $<P^k,X,R>$. Intuitively, the idea is that a proper answer to a why-question must indicate features of events that somehow favor the topic obtaining in comparison to the other members of the contrast class. So, the relevance relation is at least one of favoring the occurrence of an event with such-and-such an aspect vis-à-vis events with certain other aspects.

More must be said concerning the relevance relation. For, if the relevance relation is characterized in the above wimpy way, our account will likely end by allowing too much in the way of answers to why-questions. As Kitcher (1989) argues, a laissez-faire approach at this juncture threatens to leave an account of explanation as answers to why-questions with no advancement on the covering-law model of explanation. In fact, the covering-law model, with its problems, could be fit within the account as set out to this point. As this is obviously unacceptable, we must more fully specify the relevance relation in order to provide a more discriminating account of explanation. We have yet to bring to bear notions of "causal factors" along the lines suggested by Salmon (1984) and Humphreys (1989a, 1989b). This seems to be the missing piece: explanatory answers to why-questions must point to causally relevant factors, or to events in terms of their causally relevant aspects.

Accordingly, we will say that if an event is properly mentioned in a causal statement responding to a why-question, it will need to be specified in terms of its *causally relevant aspects* conducing to the occurrence of an event of the sort mentioned in the topic, and, in particular, *favoring* the occurrence of such an event rather than occurrences of events of the sorts mentioned in the other members of the contrast class. Thus, an explanatory causal statement will pick out an event, or aspect of prior events, that, as a causal factor, *made a difference* in the occurrence of the topic-event, rather than these others.

Recent work by Salmon and Humphreys provide good bases on which to build in understanding causation and causal relevance. As I understand the matter, causation involves relations between events, taken very broadly as interactions between, or standing aspects of, processes that develop in lawlike ways. The relevant laws may be either deterministic or indeterministic. In either case, they treat of features of the processes and events that may be called *causally relevant* or *causal factors*. Notice: *features* of events, properties, are *causally relevant* (events are, at best, only derivatively so). Drawing on Humphreys, we can distinguish two sorts of causal factors: *contributing causal factors* and *countervailing causal factors*. Strictly speaking, a causal factor *invariantly* makes a difference: A property, X, is a (probabilistic) contributing causal factor with respect to the realization of property Y if and only if X's obtaining contributes to the probability of Y's obtaining in all conditions that are physically compatible with X and Y. (For more development, see Humphreys 1989a, p. 289; 1989b, pp. 72–75). (This characterization in terms of Humphreys's *invariance condition* places a very strong condition on being a causal factor in the strictest sense.) A countervailing factor similarly detracts from the probability of an event of the relevant sort. Often, the properties meeting such invariance conditions are themselves complex, conjunctive. When they are, we can distinguish a weaker sense of causal relevance that is typically sufficient for a property featuring in explanatory causal statements: a property is a contributing causal factor in this weaker sense when it is a component of a strict contributing causal factor which itself obtains. In this case we are likely to speak of its being *causally relevant in the circumstances*. (Mutatis mutandis for a weaker notion of countervailing causal factor.)

Taking stock, the following two requirements on explanatory singular causal statements stem from the nature and structure of the why-questions to which they must provide answers. First, explanations must feature one or more (at least weak) contributing causal feature, for only then can they lead us to appreciate what is was about the antecedent course of events that, had things been different in that respect, the topic would have been less likely. Second, a satisfactory explanation must not only mention contributing causal factors with respect to the explanandum-event, but, additionally, at least some of the mentioned factors must favor the occurrence of such an event over the occurrence of the sorts mentioned in the other members of the contrast class. Notice here that not all (weak or strong) contributing causal factors relevant to the realization of a sort of event in a particular case will serve to help explain why such an event occurred rather than certain other events. For example, having latent, untreated, syphilis is causally relevant to the contracting of paresis. It can serve to explain why the mayor of philosophical lore got parasis, rather than the other citizens of his small town—given that the mayor, alone in the town, is such a syphilitic, this will make a causally relevant difference. But, assuming that the relevant individuals are all such syphilitics, it cannot explain why the mayor, rather than other members of the Committee to Re-elect the Governor, got paresis. (Still, explanatory singular causal statements may also mention some nonfavoring contributing causes, and even countervailing causes, for perspective on the operation of the contributing causes.)

Scientific work provides us with a set of nomic generalizations. Such generalizations give us an appreciation for how various sorts of systems evolve in lawlike ways. In the context of singular explanations, we draw on these generalizations in accounting for events or aspects of particular systems. These generalizations allow us to discern within those processes (that constitute the particular evolving system) a web of events that are interrelated in terms of the sort of causal dependencies to which I have appealed. This much is familiar from van Fraassen (1980, p. 124) who draws on Salmon (1978), and writes of science describing a "net of causal relations." At this point, it is helpful to distinguish two degrees of causal understanding one may have of this net, and to see how they relate to causal explanation. First, following Davidson (1980b), we can think of this web as comprised of events that are variously describable, and one can understand many causal claims as extensional descriptions of parts of the web. (This is to recognize the extensionality of some singular causal claims, as illustrated earlier.) In this weak form of causal understanding, one at least understands that certain events are related by causal dependencies by virtue of their possessing causally relevant properties, but one need not know what those properties are. Still, as we have seen, explanation is wedded to the causal relevance of features, and is thus not an extensional matter. Thus, in explanations, we must draw on a stronger form of causal understanding of a net of events. Expressions of this understanding are not extensional, for this understanding involves appreciating the dependencies between events in terms of their causally relevant properties. In this case, we not only understand that particular events are related by causal dependencies, but we also appreciate (at least some) of the causally relevant factors involved. We *selectively* draw on such stronger causal understanding in causal explanations. For, as we have seen, to answer why-questions, a causal claim must not only mention causally relevant properties, it must mention ones that favor the topic of the why-question over the other members of the contrast class.

Van Fraassen (1980, pp. 124–26) recognizes that explanation is more than a matter of citing some antecedent event in the relevant portion of the web of events. However, some of his reasons must be repudiated. Van Fraassen would say that the explanandum-event(s) cited must be *salient* in light of particular interests, and he argues that salience is a contextual matter. Thus, he understands explanation as a contextual and subjective matter. However, I believe that such pragmatic salience only serves to pick out certain explanations that are pragmatically *useful* in view of contextual interests, and this is not to distinguish explanations from what is unexplanatory. Explanations allow us to appreciate the *relevance* (in the sense described above) of the explanan-event(s), in virtue of their features, to the explanandum-event; unlike van Fraassen's salience, relevance is not a contextual matter. It is an objective matter of *how such systems tend to develop*. To *exhibit* or appreciate such relevance, the events at issue must be described using the vocabulary of the supporting law, for these allow us to pick out the causal factors. (Horgan 1989 articulates similar requirements, and see also, Føllesdal 1985; Salmon 1984, 1989; and Kincaid 1988.)

In summary, while there is a usage in which singular causal claims are extensional, causal explanations are not. While a particular true causal claim may be explanatory, another true causal claim derived from the first by the substitution of coreferential terms may fail to be explanatory. To be explanatory, a true causal claim must answer a why-question. To do this, it must allow us to appreciate features of the cause-event in virtue of which (at least ceteris paribus) it could help bring about the explanandum, favoring it over other members of the contrast class. As a result, we see that the absence of such factors or events would have made the explanandum at least less likely vis-à-vis the other members of the contrast class.

Returning now to a central point of this section, *what ultimately makes the position developed in this section important for appreciating the descriptive basis of rationalizing explanation is not the simple result that explanation is not extensional, but rather the general view of why explanation is not extensional that has been insisted on.* For those who take the third or fourth approach to rationalizing explanation could (and probably often would) agree that explanation is not extensional and claim that in intentional explanation the explanans and explanandum must be described in a way that reveals the logical relevance of the explanans to the explanandum. They could hold that explanation is not extensional because the explanans and explanandum must be described in a way that allows us to appreciate the rationality of what is done or believed. On such a view, explanation is nonextensional as a result of the need to make the rational relations between explanans and explanandum manifest in light of our normative principles of rationality. However, the untenability of this approach to intentional explanation is obvious as long as we do not lose sight of the demand that explanations allow us to appreciate what it is in the antecedent course of events that was causally relevant to (and favored) the explanandum.

A reliance on descriptive generalizations rather than on our normative principles is clearly indicated once we consider what bearing normative principles might have on the question of what events can help to bring about what other events, and on the question of what it is about the course of antecedent events that, had it been different, the explanandum would have been less likely.[6]

Of course, when a normative standard reflects certain rudimentary cognitive processing capacities, then we would expect cognitive and intentional events to proceed accordingly. That is, when the normative standards are taken to reflect the way people do, as a matter of general fact, reason, then we can appreciate how certain cognitive events or states can bring about certain other states. But this view of the significance of normative standards is just the first alternative approach to rationalizing explanation described in section 6.1.

Additionally, when a normative standard reflects certain learned cognitive strategies, then we would expect cognitive and intentional events to proceed accordingly. That is, when the normative standards are taken to reflect the way a certain group of people do, as a matter of fact, reason, then we can appreciate how certain cognitive events or states can bring about certain other states in the relevant people. And this is just the second alternative approach to rationalizing explanation.

But, what does the normative status, the propriety, of a cognitive process have to do with its occurrence, when we ignore the effects of rudimentary and learned cognitive processes that happen to be normatively appropriate? *When a normatively appropriate cognitive strategy is neither a rudimentary ability within a set of reasoners, nor a learned disposition, there is no reason for thinking that those reasoners' cognitive processes will conform to the relevant norm of rationality in any given instance.* The fact that a given belief, *b*, is normatively appropriate in light of a set of antecedent beliefs, *A*, is *no reason* to believe that *A* helped to bring about *b* and that *b* was less likely to have occurred had *A* not obtained, *if we do not also suppose* that there was a disposition of the reasoner to make inferences of the relevant normative type.

6.3: Applications to Intentional Explanations

We can illustrate the application of the above results by considering a relatively concrete set of normative principles and our general expectations with regard to actual practices. Consider our normative principles regarding forming generalizations on the basis of samples. Some of our standards for such inductive inference have to do with sample size and sample bias. They dictate that we should seek to make inferences from samples that are representative of the relevant population or random. When provided no information bearing on a sample's representativeness or possible biases, a reasoner is placed in a normatively difficult and somewhat cloudy situation. But, when one is provided information indicating that the sample is decidedly nonrepresentative, biased, one clearly should forebear from generalizing on the basis of it. I trust that these principles are sufficiently uncontroversial as to comprise one small part of our standards for inductive reasoning.

However, there is a fair amount of psychological evidence suggesting that untutored reasoners commonly ignore such principles. In particular, Hamill, Wilson, and Nisbett (1980) report that when reasoners are presented with a vivid case, in effect a sample of one, they are quite insensitive to information regarding sample bias. For example, a vivid magazine article about a "career welfare mother" in New York City produced marked effects on attitudes and beliefs regarding welfare recipients, regardless of whether the subjects also received along with the article simple statistical information indicating that the case recounted there was representative or clearly not representative. Similarly, watching a videotaped interview of a "humane" or "inhumane" prison guard significantly affected attitudes and beliefs regarding prison guards, regardless of whether the subjects were told nothing about how the interview shown was selected, or were told that the interview was selected for its representativeness of the population as a whole, or were told that it was selected because it portrayed an unusually good or bad guard. Such results indicate that common reasoners are disinclined to follow our basic norms for generalizing from samples, at least when they are confronted with a vivid case suggesting a generalization.

In the terminology used earlier, we would say that our normative standards for generalizing from samples cannot simply be borrowed and employed in a descriptive generalization regarding human processing capacities. On the basis of empirical studies, we should conclude that the rudimentary norms that enjoin us to determine whether or not a sample is biased (when this is feasible), and that prohibit us from generalizing on the basis of samples known to be biased, probably do not reflect common processing capacities. As a result, we should not expect common cognitive dispositions to produce such behavior on the part of just anyone studied. Employing such standards is then *not* sanctioned by the first alternative approach to rationalizing explanation. In contrast, a principle that is emphatically *not* a part of our best standards of inductive reasoning does seem to reflect common human processing capacities: namely the principle that we generalize from salient and vivid cases. (Of course, to some degree it is possible to train reasoners to be concerned with sample bias, and to withhold assent from generalizations that might otherwise be induced by vivid cases. But more on this complication anon.) To illustrate the force of our results in this and the previous chapter, and their ultimate agreement with our explanatory practice, we can consider a series of hypothetical cases inspired by Hamill, Wilson, and Nisbett's results.

Suppose that we present someone vivid footage of a person being dined on by a certain type of shark, and that the person we show this footage to comes to believe that sharks of that sort are dangerous "man-eaters." We might readily account for this new belief by drawing on the generalizations advanced above, pending new information regarding the individual involved. We would note that the cognitive processes involved were sensitive to such vivid scenes; thus, exposure to such footage favors the drawing of the conclusion here, rather than the drawing of more cautious conclusions. Had the subject not viewed the vivid film, their forming the belief in question would have been markedly less likely. We would then say that viewing the vivid footage caused the subject to generalize, the explanandum belief being the obvious result.

Assume that we did not give the subject information on the representativeness of the behavior portrayed. We would probably not want to say that this lack of information was causally relevant (or if causally relevant, it is probably an exceedingly weak factor). After all, the general information we possess regarding such cases suggests that common reasoners are not sensitive to such information, and would readily form the relevant general beliefs regardless of whether information is provided along these lines. In this regard, it is worth noting that we would proceed in much the same way in the case where we showed someone the vivid footage, gave them information indicating that it was not representative, and the person still formed the belief in the sharks' man-eating proclivities.

Next, suppose that we present someone with the vivid footage and claim that it portrays fairly typical behavior for such sharks in the presence of human edibles. Suppose, as is likely, that this person also comes to believe that such sharks are man-eaters. How should we explain this belief? Some are probably inclined to attempt to explain it by noting that the person had a good reason to believe this way after being provided a putatively representative sample of such shark's behavior around people. But, such rationalizing explanation, depending as it does on the indiscriminate importation of normative standards into intentional explanation, is mistaken. We should use descriptive generalizations, not normative principles as such, to inform our causal understanding of the relevant processes and events, and, in turn, in intentional explanation; and we should transubstantiate normative principles into descriptive representations of cognitive dispositions only where we have empirical reason to do so. Based on what we know so far, we have no reason to believe that the person is much influenced by information regarding sample representativeness. Little of the variation in beliefs observed by Hamill, Wilson, and Nisbett was due to such information (1980, pp. 581–82, 585). So, explaining the new belief in terms of rudimentary and common human cognitive dispositions, we should explain it as the result of the person's viewing the vivid footage (as in the earlier cases). For, given what we know, it is probably false that the explanandum belief would not have occurred had the information on sample representativeness not been given; it is probably false that the information really contributed significantly to bringing about the belief. However, it seems very likely that the explanandum belief would not have occurred had the subjects not been shown the vivid footage, which clearly helped to bring it about in this case.

Now, it is supposedly possible to train people to be concerned with sample biases, and to behave more appropriately. At least this is possible to some, as yet empirically undetermined, degree.[7] One might then naturally use the norms for generalizing from representative samples in characterizing these acquired dispositions. Now, suppose that a person who has been subjected to the appropriate training is shown the vivid footage and provided information indicating the representativeness of the behavior there portrayed. Such a person would probably form a belief that sharks of the sort shown are liable to feast on humans, given the opportunity. *Ex hypothesi*, this person would not have come to believe this had they not been induced to believe that the sample was representative of the behavior of the relevant sharks. Coming to have this belief about the sample then was an important aspect of the antecedent course of events helping to bring about the belief regarding the sharks. Thus, the descriptive generalization regarding the individual's acquired dispositions can here be used to appreciate the fact that the belief about this sample was causally relevant to the belief to be explained. Put simply, the belief about the sample explains why this person comes to believe that sharks of the relevant sort are man-eaters upon being shown the footage. (If the person really has been trained so that, when it is feasible, they check for bias before making inferences, then this is not a case of causal overdetermination.)

It seems to me that the above relatively concrete examples *reflect how we do actually proceed in intentional explanation*, and this a way that fits very well the general approach to such explanation for which I have argued. This significantly strengthens my position, for it *shows that the claim that intentional explanation* (and rationalizing explanation as a special case) *rests on descriptive generalizations, is not the product of forcing certain general considerations from the philosophy of science onto a practice in the human sciences that really does not conform.* Rather, our judgments about concrete cases do conform to the general position developed in this and the preceding chapter.

Here I have argued that explanation generally, and thus psychological explanation in particular, rests on descriptive generalizations that allow us to appreciate what it was about the antecedent course of events that helped to bring about the explanandum and that, had it not obtained, the explanandum (probably) would not have obtained. Consequently, intentional explanation cannot rest on normative principles as such (that is, cannot properly be understood in terms of the third and fourth approaches to rationalizing explanation as distinguished in the first section), but must rest on descriptive generalizations, some of which may selectively employ normative principles to represent particular cognitive dispositions (as is suggested in the first and second approaches to rationalizing explanation).

This chapter, and the surrounding chapters, focus quite heavily on psychological explanations and their bases. Some readers may wonder what has become of the concern for sociological explanations, and for other explanations at the level of social groups. My intent certainly has not been to ignore such explanations, but to argue for a needed perspective regarding the sorts of psychological explanations that inform, at least in general ways, such social-level explanations as well as psychological explanations. My point has been that expectations regarding ways of reasoning and interacting inform all explanations in the human sciences, and that an appreciation for the place of such expectations reveals that what I have called "irrationalizing explanations" are importantly on a par with what are commonly called "rationalizing explanations." The preference for one sort over the other must be a theory-based preference. In social-level explanations, we seek to show how the explanandum is itself an intended or unintended aggregate result of such reasoning and interactions as we would expect, or we seek to show that it is accounted for in terms of certain social-level patterns (that are, in context) themselves ultimately grounded in explicable reasoning and interaction. Earlier chapters have featured several examples of such social-level explanations. Little (1991) provides useful discussions of the relations between psychological expectations and social-level aggregations.

7

The Nomic Status of
Psychological Generalizations:
Handling Rosenberg's Refinability Problem

7.1: Rosenberg's Challenge:
Nomicity and Refinability

On the account of psychological explanation developed in the preceding chapters, it is crucial that there be nomic information regarding the cognitive capacities of human beings. This is needed to support both rationalizing and irrationalizing explanations. Further, were there no such nomic transition laws to be had, this would undermine more than the account of psychological explanation I have provided, it would ramify to call into question the account of interpretation I provided, by calling into question my principle of explicability. The purpose of this and the following chapter is to address misgivings one might have regarding the nomic status of psychological generalizations. In this chapter I take up a recent, and particularly challenging, variant of one venerable misgiving. There is a long tradition in which challenges to the scientific status of social and psychological inquiry proceed by harping on the requirements of the interpretive understanding that would need to inform any such inquiry. The idea is that the constraints on interpretive understanding interfere with uncovering really nomic psychological generalizations. While much that is relevant to such misgivings has already been said in this book, I address the issue head on here in order to demonstrate that my account of interpretive understanding provides the resources to deal with such misgivings, even in the particularly sophisticated form it takes in Alexander Rosenberg's (1985b,1988) writings.

By drawing on Davidson's thesis of the anomalousness of the mental, and, it seems, by reflecting on the venerable tradition just mentioned, Rosenberg produces an argument to the effect that

183

psychological and social scientific generalizations cannot be law-like, at least to the extent that the human sciences use intentional idiom and seek to explain actions, beliefs, and attitudes. The argument begins with the supposition that such inquiries would proceed on the basis of an intentional generalization linking belief and desire states as causes with actions as effects. Rosenberg envisions the following as representing the rudimentary form of such a generalization:

[L] Given any person x, if x wants d and x believes that a is a means to attain d, under the circumstances, then x does a (Rosenberg 1988, p. 25; cf. 1985b, p. 402).

Of course [L] can be commonsensically refined. But the crucial question becomes whether or not [L] (or its commonsense refinements) can, in principle, be empirically tested and refined in a significant way. If such empirical refinement is impossible, then [L] (and its commonsense refinements) would be disanalogous to laws in the sciences generally, they would seem to be non-nomic (Rosenberg 1985b, p. 36; 1988, pp. 36, 47–49). For, "what is characteristic of science is its capacity to provide generalizations that are improvable beyond what common sense provides" (Rosenberg 1985b, p. 404).

Now, if refinability is to be taken as a necessary condition for a principle's being nomic, or potentially nomic, and for its having a place in scientific theorizing, as Rosenberg here suggests, then what it is to be refinable must be examined carefully. First, we must acknowledge the holist's lesson: a sentence is neither refinable, nor irrefinable, in any interesting sense, when considered in isolation. Rather, the refinability of a sentence, S, is a matter of S's being embedded in a system of sentences that can be compared to the results of observation, where one possible result is that we could be led to make changes in S. (See Rosenberg 1988, pp. 46–47.) This essentially Quinean formulation can, of course, be elaborated. Philosophical accounts of empirical evidence and confirmation, such as Glymour's account on which I draw in this chapter, provide the basis for more detailed characterizations of the refinability of S in a context. Second, there is a sense in which the laws of an ideal theory would not be refinable, for no physically possible evidence would lead us to make revisions in such a theory. But, clearly, this is not the sense of refinability that concerns us here. Again, refinability is a matter of how a sentence is situated in a theory, and of how users of that theory would respond to recalcitrant observations. Roughly, given recalcitrant observations, would or could they be led to entertain abandoning the sentence or adopting revisions of it? If so, then the sentence is refinable in the relevant sense. Conceived along these lines, being refinable is required for a given general principle if it is to be a candidate for the status of nomic generalization, and it is to have a place as a law in a given scientific theory. Conceived in this manner, Rosenberg's claim that [L] is not refinable is the claim that, as the central principle of intentional psychology, it is not situated in a theory in a way that would allow recalcitrant observations to lead us to entertain other than commonsense refinements in it.

Rosenberg's argument can be stated as follows:

1. There are only three broad ways that access to the intentional phenomena of interest in the human sciences and relevant to generalizations such as [L] might be obtained:

    (a) Typically, intentional states are attributed in an [L]-*dependent way*: interpretation. Interpretation is a matter of imposing a pattern on the beliefs and attitudes attributed to those interpreted. Significantly, the pattern is that indicated in [L]. Thus, in standard interpretation, attributed conformity with [L] becomes a measure of success.

    (b) One might imagine [L]-independent access to intentional states coming through neuro-physical measuring instruments. This would require supporting psycho-physical laws.

    (c) One might (perhaps) imagine behaviorist identifications of intentional states.

2. Behaviorist approaches have proven to be obviously inadequate.

3. There cannot be [L]-independent, interpretation-independent, measures of intentional states. The basis for this is Davidson's arguments for the anomalousness of the mental: there can be no psycho-physical laws that serve to give us access to mental states of the sort at issue.

4. *Lemma* (following from [1]–[3]): There really is only one way of getting at the intentional phenomena of interest: the [L]-dependent method of interpretive understanding. There are no [L]-independent ways.

5. If [L] is to be refined, there must be ways of comparing pre-

dictions or retrodictions derived using [L] with the relevant phenomena.

6. In order to compare [L] with the phenomena of interest, we obviously must have ways of identifying the phenomena to see what obtains. But, comparability in the relevant sense requires [L]-independent access. For, on the (charitable) [L]-dependent procedure envisioned in (1a), failure to find conformity with [L] indicates problems with the interpretation, and thus, with the data that would supposedly serve as the basis for checking and refining [L]. Accordingly, there could be no phenomena (under interpretation) that indicated the need for refining [L].

7. *Therefore*, (on the basis of [4]–[6]) [L] is not refinable.

As a result, Rosenberg (1988, p. 40) concludes that psychological generalizations having to do with intentional states are not nomic causal generalizations, and that, "even though desire/belief explanations of actions do link causes to their effects [as Davidson has argued], their explanatory power does not consist in this fact." Naturalists thus seem driven to espouse changing the traditional subject of the human sciences, becoming eliminativists. Antinaturalists, on the other hand, contentedly embrace a separatist understanding of hermeneutics.

While Rosenberg draws on Davidson's discussions of the principle of charity, overall, and not considering the way in which particular premises rely on the principle of charity, the argument's general structure makes no use of that principle. Rather, it turns on the claim that the principle that supposedly controls in intentional explanation, [L], also serves as the standard for successful interpretation. *Were we to suppose that some less charitable principle informed intentional explanation, this would not interfere with the general argument as long as we also suppose that the same principle also serves as the pervasive guide to the interpretation of the data on which its own appraisal rests.* Consider my view that the fundamental constraint on interpretation is the principle of explicability. Rosenberg's basic argument can be easily reconstructed employing the principle of explicability, *if we assume that some principle—*[L] *or some alternative—exercises as dominant an influence on intentional explanation as Rosenberg envisions* for [L]. Supposing that [L] (or some alternative) constitutes the pervasive guide to intentional explanation, we would be led to take it as an equally pervasive guide to successful interpretation. [L] (or the alternative) would then seem irrefinable, for no evidence could indicate a substantial need for refining it, as the only credible evidence would conform to it. At least, we can reason this way as long as we can suppose that there is no interpretation-independent way of identifying the relevant intentional states. Of course, this last claim is what premise (3) asserts.

It is in premise (3) that we find some reliance on Davidson's principle of charity in interpretation. For Davidson's arguments for the anomalousness of the mental rely on that principle. According to Davidson, there cannot be psycho-physical laws because mental and physical predicates are "not made for one another" (1980c, p. 218). When such predicates are combined in generalizations the results are said to be akin to that paradigm both of non-nomic generalizations and of combining predicates not made for one another: 'All emeralds are grue'. Davidson insists that mental and physical predicates are not made for one another because the central constraint on the use of mental predicates, namely the principle of charity, has "no echo in physical theory" (1980d, p. 231). Because I do not believe that the principle of charity is a fundamental constraint on interpretation, I am not convinced by this argument.

However, such reservations regarding the principle of charity and Rosenberg's third premise are not where I will concentrate my fire. For, as a matter of fact, our stock of nomic psycho-physical generalizations is none too impressive; at least it is not sufficient to yield anything resembling a "neuro-physical measuring instrument" for beliefs and desires. There is, as Rosenberg says, no way of identifying our subjects' beliefs and desires other than interpretation. Nevertheless, we do manage to make empirically motivated refinements in psychological generalizations. We do subject psychological generalizations to scientific tests. My goal here is to examine how we can manage this. My strategy is to concentrate on a supposition repeated several times in the preceding paragraphs: the supposition that there is a principle, [L] or some alternative, that exercises as dominant an influence on both intentional explanation and intentional interpretation as Rosenberg envisions for [L]. The resources that inform interpretation are greater than what is reflected in Rosenberg's argument, and this provides a basis for interpretations that can induce and support refinements on [L].

We can begin to appreciate our epistemic situation in the human sciences by considering what sorts of generalizations feature in psychological research in addition to Rosenberg's [L]. Obviously, [L] represents a rudimentary version of the ceteris paribus generalizations that inform our rationalizing explanation of actions. As such, [L] can doubtless be refined somewhat to accommodate further aspects of our common sense rationalizing explanations. (Of course, insofar as refinements produce precise, unified, accounts, these will typically incorporate elements that are not, strictly speaking, parts of our common sense. But I will not quibble with Rosenberg's argument on such grounds.) Some would say that one prominent natural refinement is at least roughly that obtained by taking normative decision theory as informing rationalizing explanation. This much is suggested by Rosenberg (1988, pp. 25–26, 65–74), and I will not here dispute the naturalness of formulations in decision theory, applied descriptively and selectively, as proposed refinements of [L]. I will refer to proposed refinements of [L] as [L^a]. I argue here that [L^a]-generalizations can feature in both explanation and interpretation in important ways that contribute to the refinability of psychological generalizations including [L].

It is important to notice the range of further generalizations that inform our explanations (and interpretations) in the human sciences. As I have noted, proponents of rationalizing explanation also seek to explain intentional states themselves—peoples' beliefs, desires, and other attitudes. This involves the use of further principles (as generalizations) having to do with the relations between such intentional states. Let us denote this complementary set of generalizations [L^c]. Now, as I have also argued, not all intentional explanations are rationalizing explanations. Some are informed by general expectations for cognitive processing that is not rational, and some are informed by expectations for actions that are not rational in light of the agents' beliefs and desires. The relevant generalizations may be denoted by [G^a] and [G^c] respectively. (Nothing in my reasoning will depend on categorizing the generalizations informing intentional explanations in this particular fourfold way. The purpose of the categories is simply to have some way to begin to reflect on the complexity of our resources outside of Rosenberg's [L], or even [L^a].

7.2: An Illustrative Case

I believe that it is clear that we do manage to refine generalizations within each of the four categories, including [L^a] (thus refining on [L]). We can, and do, contrive situations in which peoples' responses give us empirical reasons for revising our general expectations, including our [Lᵃ]-expectations. Consider, for example, a set of situations and results produced by Amos Tversky (1975). The situations in question here are of the common sort involved in studies of decision making: choices between gambles. (Using the common notation, [X,P,Y] will represent a gamble where one will receive X with a probability of P, or Y with a probability of 1–P.) Subjects are presented with the choice between gambles A and B:

$$A = (\$1,000, 1/2, 0) \; B = (\$400)$$

In situations of this first sort, almost all subjects prefer the "sure thing": B. They do this despite the fact that A has a greater expected actuarial value: $500.

Of course, such results are not themselves news within standard decision-theory. It is common to distinguish between the amount of goods or money to be had and its *utility*. The latter is conceived as a subjective, nonlinear, function of the former. The common postulation of decreasing marginal utility—a concave positive utility curve—is clearly enough to accommodate the results obtained in situations of this first sort: one need only claim that, for many subjects, $u(\$400) > 1/2u(\$1,000)$.

This standard response is just what Rosenberg would expect: standard decision theory is not impugned by Tversky's results in the first situation because we interpret our subjects on the basis of its basic principles. We attribute to our subjects preference structures that conform to [Lᵃ].

However, *we follow this line only to a point, after which such [Lᵃ]-informed identification of values comes to clash with other constraints.* This begins to occur with the second situation, which is produced by multiplying the probabilities of the gains in A and B by 1/5. Subjects are now asked to choose between:

$$C = (\$1,000, 1/10, 0) \; D = (\$400, 1/5, 0)$$

If the explanation of the choices found in the first situation were the concave shape of the subjects' preference curves, then we could expect these curves to produce preferences for D over C. However, most subjects now prefer C over D. As Tversky (1975, p. 166) notes, within the confines of standard decision-theory, the overall pattern of choices observed in the two situations is "incompatible with any utility function."[1] Such results indicate a "positive certainty effect" in which "the utility of a positive outcome appears greater when it is certain than when it is embedded in a gamble"

(Tversky 1975, p. 166). Tversky goes on to provide evidence of a negative certainty effect when losses are in the offing instead of gains. Such interaction of utility and probability of options violates aspects of standard decision-theory, where it is supposed that there are utility functions (unique up to a certain transformation) associated with particular goods and that such utility functions interact simply with subjective probabilities according to rule: $u(x)p(x)$. Thus, if Tversky's apparent finding of certainty effects is borne out, it will constitute a significant refinement within $[L^a]$.

Tversky's results do seem to put a certain amount of empirical pressure on standard decision-theory as $[L^a]$. To begin to appreciate how this is possible, we should consider several responses that might tempt proponents of descriptively applied decision-theory.

Defenders of decision-theory might suggest that Tversky's subjects just did not understand the situations in the way that he understood and presented the situations. In keeping with Rosenberg's argument, they might even cite Tversky's own results as evidence to this effect, arguing that investigators are obliged to interpret their subjects so as to find conformity with $[L^a]$. However, I think we are then entitled to a plausible account of just what it is about the situations that the subjects understood differently. Tversky's subjects were college students. Is it plausible to suppose that they do not understand talk of "dollars"? Or, that they did not understand the relative sizes of amounts such as 1,000 and 400? Is it then plausible to suppose that they did not realize that whatever common commodity can be purchased with $400 can typically be gotten in a matched pair with $200 left over from $1,000? On these counts I believe that it is implausible to postulate misunderstanding. The reason, it seems, is that we have, in addition to $[L^a]$, expectations regarding roughly when people learn rudimentary matters of importance within their society. Elementary arithmetic and monetary units are matters we expect are learned much before college-age. *Such relatively mundane (but nevertheless empirical) expectations effectively block positing significantly different understandings of the relevant aspects of the situations presented.*

It may seem more plausible that the subjects understood the probabilities involved differently than did Tversky. But even this seems to me to be implausible. To begin with, the gambles were not made to depend on events regarding which the subjects might have antecedently acquired subjective probability estimates. Such antecedent probability estimates could conceivably serve as an anchor, effecting the subjects' subjective probability estimates even after the situation is stipulated by the investigator.[2] However, in the absence of such antecedent expectations, it is likely that their subjective probabilities conform to the stipulated probabilities, assuming that the subjects understand talk of a "probability of 1/2," "of 1/5," and "of 1/10." Now, while many of the subjects may never have reflected on whether "probability" should be understood as a matter of relative frequency, or of propensity, or in both ways, and so on, it is not unlikely that they know well enough how to apply such descriptions to simple cases: coin tosses, urns with balls of mixed colors, the weather, their car starting on a cold morning, and so on. This would reflect enough shared understandings to make Tversky's results telling. (These relatively mundane expectations, like those above, are testable enough. So, the empirical case above could be buttressed somewhat.)

Again, we see that *in the particular situations produced here, we have expectations in addition to* [L^a]*-expectations that constrain us from gerrymandering our interpretive scheme too much.* What I have thought to appeal to here are socially applied crude generalizations regarding learning, something of a marriage of crude learning theory and information about socialization. Such presumably belongs to either [L^c], or to [G^c], or has components from both.

In a related vein, Tversky and Kahneman (1981) have produced a distinctly nonstandard decision-theory, called "prospect theory," designed to accommodate a range of experimental results, including certainty effects. In prospect theory, there are "values," which are rather like utilities of outcomes (gains and losses) judged in terms of a neutral reference outcome. There are also "decision weights," which are nonlinear functions of probabilities. These are what is used to account for certainty effects. For, commonly, a weighting function, π, for an individual is such that $\pi(0)=0$ and $\pi(1.0)=1.0$, but a fair portion of the intermediate probabilities are undervalued: $\pi(P(x)) < P(x)$. Now, continuing the thinking of the preceding paragraph, a defender of standard decision-theory might propose taking these weighting functions as a way of representing empirically determined "subjective probabilities." After all, Tversky and Kahneman's choice problems typically stipulate probabilities and one might then take decision weights as representing what such and such a probability "feels like" to an individual. In view of the above, this would be to say that, although the subject may cognitively recognize simple applications of probabilities, decisions are made using a less well-behaved, almost gut-level, response to such probabilities. However, if one wished to retain most of the standard theory by calling the values arrived at by way of these decision weights "subjective probabilities," then one would need to also hold that subjective probabilities need not be probabilities at all. (For, unlike probabilities, the decision weights attached to an event and its complement will often not sum to 1.0.) This would involve a rather substantial modification of [L^a] after all.

While Tversky's work discussed above may not lead inescapably to the conclusion that [L^a] must be modified, there is also a sense in which all empirical work is likely to be strictly inconclusive. What is more to the point is that this empirical work is generally compelling, it puts significant pressure on standard decision-theory descriptively applied as [L^a]. The most straightforward interpretation of the subjects in the experiments leads us to attribute to them violations of principles of decision-theory as [L^a]. We could abandon this interpretation of the experiment, but only at the cost of abandoning certain non[L^a]-expectations as discussed above. As Quine has emphasized, we can hold any part of our web of beliefs constant—including [L^a]-parts—if we are willing to make radical enough compensating adjustment elsewhere in our beliefs. This sense in which any experiment is not absolutely decisive is the sense in which Tversky's is not decisive. Still, often it seems unreasonable to make the adjustments elsewhere in our beliefs, and Tversky's work seems to put us in just this situation. In this situation our non[L^a]-expectations—our mundane [L^c] and [G^c] resources—constrain us to retain the more straightforward interpretation.

What we find illustrated here is that a wider range of our expectations or generalizations constrain us in interpretation then is generally appreciated. This range is an epistemological resource of importance. For it allows us to test some generalizations using others in particular situations. We are then not left employing [L^a] alone, nor, for that matter, is [L^a] itself monolithic. Part of our set of general expectations can be played off against other parts in situations where those other expectations are relatively constraining. In this manner, [L^a]-generalizations, and others, can be empirically refined. This, in rough form, is the account that I propose to develop. In effect, the central basis for the initial plausibility of Rosenberg's argument against the refinability of psychological generalizations is his failure to appreciate the complexity or richness of our resources both in addition to [L^a] and internal to [L^a] (cf. Rosenberg 1988, pp. 70–71).

7.3: Bootstrap Testing: Using our Theoretical Resources

My central concern in this chapter is to show that empirical results can be used to test the acceptability of particular intentional psychological generalizations, such as those in [L^a]. To this end, I now draw on Clark Glymour's bootstrapping account of scientific testing, a particularly promising account of how empirical results can be evidentially relevant to particular parts of our theories. The ability to distribute praise and blame has proven difficult to account for in terms of the Hypothetico-Deductive approach. Glymour takes accounting for it to be an adequacy condition on accounts of scientific evidence and testing (1980, p. 3). He shows that his own "bootstrapping" account succeeds here, and argues that it provides a basis for an accurate understanding of some (but not all) important episodes in the history of science (1980, pp. 169–72).

According to the bootstrapping account of scientific evidence and testing, data provides evidence for theoretical claims, hypotheses, by providing instances of the hypotheses (where an "instance" is understood in something like the way developed in Hempel's work on qualitative confirmation). Of course, when the hypothesis under test employs vocabulary not used in statements of the data, a very common situation, the data can provide an instance of the hypothesis only when an instance of the hypothesis can be derived from the evidence in conjunction with further theoretical claims. Thus, confirmation becomes a triadic relation: certain data confirms (or disconfirms) hypothesis H with respect to theory T (Glymour 1980, p. 110). The theoretical claims connecting data to hypothesis are not here thought to be analytic truths. Rather, they are themselves subject to testing (confirmation or disconfirmation) against data with respect to some bits of theory (Glymour 1980, pp. 145–51). (Thus the notion of bootstrapping.)

Glymour's account raises a familiar worry—how can we guard against mutually compensating errors:

> Suppose that bit A is used together with evidence E to justify bit B; and suppose that bit B is used with evidence E' to justify bit A; then might it not be the case that E and E' determine neither a real instance of A nor a real instance of B but provide instead *spurious* instances, which appear to be correct because the errors in A are compensated for in these cases by errors in B and vice versa? (1980, p. 108)

Glymour responds: "Indeed it might be the case, but it would be wrong to infer straight out from this that E and E' provide no grounds at all for A and B" (1980, p. 108). He seeks to build into his account ways of guarding against compensating error and concludes that "[t]he only means available for guarding against such errors is to have a variety of evidence, so that as many hypotheses as possible are tested in as many different ways as possible" (1980, p. 140). Such variety in testing any one hypothesis involves computing the values involved in that hypothesis in different ways, using different sets of theoretical generalizations and computing them from different sets of evidence.

To test a hypothesis, H, on the basis of evidence E with respect to theory T, then, it must be possible to compute or determine the value of the quantities occurring in the hypothesis so as to obtain a positive instance of it on the basis of E and generalizations of T.[3] However, while this is a necessary condition, it is clearly not sufficient for testability. For it is also necessary that evidence of the sort E is puts H at risk. That is, E contains values for certain quantities (understood broadly), and it must be possible to have gotten from the procedures used in obtaining E a data set E' with values of those same quantities that would, when used in the same computations that produced the positive instances, produce a negative instance of H (Glymour 1980, pp. 115–17).

Rosenberg's worry is just that all possible attempts at finding negative or positive instances of [L^a] fail this last requirement of bootstrap testing. In particular, his argument can be understood as an attempt to show that the following undesirable state of affairs, as described by Glymour, characterizes [L] and [L^a]: "it may turn out that some hypothesis or other has to be used in every computation in such a way that that hypothesis itself cannot be tested from the evidence" (1980, p. 134). This ultimately does not characterize the epistemic situation of [L^a], but the case has to be made with care. We will see that a bootstrapping model can incorporate the observations already made in connection with Tversky's illustrative work.

First, however, we need to recognize one respect in which the basic characterization of bootstrap testing provided so far is clearly too demanding. I have followed Glymour's original presentation in requiring that the values of the quantities in the hypothesis be completely determinable from the evidence together with the relevant additional theoretical generalizations. Now, it is clear that this requirement is very seldom, if ever, met in the human sciences. However, the human sciences are certainly not alone here. This has prompted van Fraassen (1983) to provide a flexible reconstruction of Glymour's account in which it is not supposed that the values of the quantities in the hypothesis must be completely or exactly determinable in order for that data to provide even a moderate test of the hypothesis with respect to the relevant theory. It is necessary to allow for approximations in which the ranges of values for the quantities in the hypothesis are significantly restricted. Here a range of somewhat weaker positive tests are achieved when the ranges obtained are fully compatible with the hypothesis, while different possible evidence would have produced ranges incompatible with the hypothesis. Such testing is clearly in evidence in the work by Tversky already discussed, where we find appeals to what is "plausible" and "implausible" to attribute to subjects, and talk of what is and what is not "likely." It is worth noting that such a narrowing of ranges of values for quantities of interest is also found in the interpretation of experiments in physics, for example. This is clearly seen in accounts of experiments devoted to the detection of solar neutrinos (Pinch 1986; Shapere 1982).

Of course, provision must also be made for developing theories in which "more and more quantities may become empirically determinable; conversely, a good deal of testing is already being done, while some of the crucial quantities still remain indeterminate" (van Fraassen 1983, p. 32). Indeed, Glymour's own discussion of atomic theory in the nineteenth century reflects ways in which progress can be made in such situations (1980, pp. 226–63).

Alison Wylie has convincingly argued that certain research in archaeology "does conform to Glymour's model in intent and, in broad outline at least, in practice" (Wylie 1986, pp. 314–15). Such a guarded positive conclusion can also be drawn for important work in cognitive psychology. However, the implementation of bootstrap testing here is complicated somewhat by the much remarked-on holistic character of intentional states.

To appreciate the complications, consider the failure of a naively straightforward application of the bootstrapping model. We may begin by asking what sort of information would count as data and what sorts of predicates would count as representing quantities whose values are to be determined. The most plausible candidates for data are characterizations of behavior, verbal and otherwise. The hypotheses to be tested are supposedly generalizations about intentional states, and intentional states and actions. Providing instances of such generalizations will then be a matter of attributing states (or ranges of states) to subjects on the basis of their utterances and other behavior. To do this, we supposedly would need further generalizations that connect the observed behaviors with the intentional states mentioned in a given hypothesis. This naive bootstrapping model of psychological testing would have us proceed as follows: We observe some behavior in the course of a particular experiment. Then, we employ a set of relevant psychological generalizations to that rather limited set of observations in order to derive intentional attributions that cumulatively constitute either negative or positive instances of some hypothesis stated in intentional terms.

The problem with this naive approach is that there are no plausible candidates for the role of interesting psychological generalizations that will get us from a set of characterizations of behavioral events to characterizations of intentional events and states. At least this is so when we look for generalizations that would connect relatively discrete sets of behavior with intentional states—for example, grabbing behavior with wanting to have the thing grasped. Does the battlefield hero really want the grenade that he grabs up from among his fellows? Such an approach to applying the bootstrapping model is entirely too behavioristic (not in the sense of a methodological program that would forego intentional idiom, but in the sense of a program in the tradition of philosophical behaviorism that would take relatively discrete behaviors as indicative of mental states).

As already indicated, the reason for the failure of the naive approach is the holistic character of the mental. But, such holism need not foreclose producing instances of intentional generalizations on the basis of psychological generalizations and data that is more or less behavioral. It is just that, in keeping with it, psychological generalizations will have to be put to work in a much more cooperative manner than that envisioned above. My model here is the account of theory-laden translation and interpretation advanced in earlier chapters. At the most general level, the relations between the holism of the mental, interpretation, and our psychological generalizations can be understood as follows. The holism of the mental is basically a matter of the type and content of intentional states depending on their place in a pattern. Thus, whether we can attribute a particular state to a person may well depend on what other states we attribute to that individual, as well as on the person's behavior. The cooperative use of psychological generalization is, in effect, the basis for the pattern we seek to find in interpretation. In this way, a range of our psychological generalizations provide a basis for interpretation, and thus for the provision of instances from more or less behavioral data. If I am correct, we test and refine psychological generalizations by producing negative or positive instances of such generalizations under interpretation, when interpretation is both holistic and theoretically informed.

The challenge in developing this general position is obvious: an adequate model of bootstrapping in psychology must reveal how the holistic nature of interpretation *does not* result in "some hypothesis or other," say those of [Lᵃ], needing "to be used in every computation in such a way that that hypothesis itself cannot be tested from the evidence." It must provide for holistic, theory-laden, interpretation that does not result in the theory informing the interpretation being self-verifying in the way Rosenberg envisions.

In developing such a model, we should consider two intimately related tasks: the construction of translation manuals or interpretive schemes generally and the application of such schemes in the course of empirical work. A proper account of the first matter will allow us to subsume the second matter as a special case in a way that provides for bootstrap testing in psychology.

I have argued that the fundamental constraint on interpretation, from start to finish, is that we should seek to attribute to our subjects intentional states, beliefs, desires, and actions that are patterned in certain general ways, specified by our best present psychological theories, and that thereby account for subjects' behavior as a whole (at least so far as we can sample it). Thus, significantly, the relevant pattern is dictated by our general psychological expectations. (The role of [Lᵃ]-informed expectations here will need to be considered with particular care.) At this general level of analysis, interpretation is quite naturally viewed as the theory-based attribution of states, and, in this respect, fits nicely into the bootstrapping account, as suggested above. But, again the question is, does the theory inform such interpretation in a way that allows for bootstrap testing?

In everyday contexts, and in the context of typical psychological investigations, our interpretations will proceed in terms of the application of a rough but workable interpretive scheme. (In Tversky's work that is discussed above, the implicit translation manual was basically homophonic.) In these cases, then, we are employing an empirical scheme which has been produced in the course interpretive work in the relevant culture. This work has found that, in the particular society, certain behaviors are generally indicative or expressive of certain intentional states under interpretation. That is, such work can be understood as finding certain utterances expressive of states that, when attributed to utterers in a society, fit their behavior (at least so far as we can sample it) into a general pattern informed by our psychological expectations. Such an interpretive scheme does not stand in place of interpretation; rather, it gives us a running start at interpretation. (In effect, it spares us the task of repeating the earlier interpretive work.) It thus seems that, in order to address the concerns regarding the applicability of the bootstrapping model, we will need to investigate how components of our psychological theories can enter at various stages in the interpretive enterprise.

If we are to overcome Rosenberg's worries, it is important to recall what was determined earlier when distinguishing between the earlier and later stages of constructing an interpretive scheme. The distinction itself is required by anthropological practice and reflects significant differences in the constraints facing actual investigators. In the earlier stages, we seek to construct a first-approximation scheme. In this task, the application of sophisticated theory informing interpretation is pretty much out of the question. Rather, we seek to attribute beliefs and desires (and actions) in a way the accords with rudimentary expectations, and expectations whose antecedent conditions require little information to determine whether they hold.

Having generally satisfied the above constraints in the early stages of interpretation, we have access to presumptively or generally correct information about a fair range of our informants' beliefs and desires. With this in hand, we can go on to apply more and more sophisticated psychological theory to address more adequately the explicability of surprising beliefs, desires, or actions that we occasionally find ourselves led to attribute to those who are being studied. This is the essence of the later stages in translation or interpretation. If we find that our subjects are explicable as interpreted according to our first-approximation scheme, this reinforces the scheme and adds another, if somewhat yet tentative, confirming instance for the relevant theory. If however, certain phenomena under first-approximation interpretation proves recalcitrant to explanation using more sophisticated theory, we face the choice: modify the interpretive scheme at some relevant point (taking care not to create other recalcitrant anomalies), or treat the case as a negative or disconfirming instance of the relevant theory, or employ a mixed response—placing less confidence in both scheme and theory.[4]

For our purposes in this chapter, the importance of the distinction between the earlier and later stages in constructing interpretive schemes is that, without employing sophisticated theoretical expectations, we can in the reasonably early stages of interpretation learn a good amount about a people's categories, beliefs, and values. Although some cases will remain puzzles awaiting further investigation, we can generally learn a good deal about what sorts of things they take to be consequences of what other sorts of things, and about what they take to be the case. Of particular importance for our concerns here, we can learn a fair amount about *how they express preferences and choices*, and about some of their preferences.

Again, it must be emphasized that this can be done without using sophisticated theory, such as variants of [L^a]. The more rudimentary patterns reflected in common everyday explanations seem to suffice in many cases. In association with identifying source-language expressions for wants and desires, we typically seek to understand indigenous explanations of behaviors, source-language users' own requests, and expressions of choices. (Of course, we need to be able to translate our informants categorizations of what is wanted.) In this interpretive endeavor, we seldom need to construct elaborate representations of our subjects' utility preferences, "unique up to a linear transformation," as they say in decision-theoretic work. (Indeed, I can think of no ethnography that is supported by a demonstration that the interpretive scheme used leads us to attribute beliefs and utilities in anything resembling full keeping with decision-theoretic expectations.) Instead, we seek to construct a rather rudimentary explanatory model of those who we interpret—one that allows us to attribute some enduring or "standing" wants (wanting to acquire horses, wanting a spot in close to the river to camp, wanting to be admired) and "occurrent" wants (wanting a drink, wanting that horse), and all this in a way that allows us to make use of rudimentary explanations. Often, but not exclusively, these simple explanations will be rudimentary rationalizing explanations. While this will sometimes involve some information on the relative strength of the wants we attribute to those we study, typically it will not involve much precision here. Much might be (and typically is) done without anything but crude ranges into which we have sorted the desires of our subjects. If we can do this much, it is *enough to give us the confidence that our interpretive scheme generally allows us to determine what is wanted* (assuming a modicum of candor of course) *and to determine when a choice is made*. The crucial point is that these accomplishments seem to be attainable without the use of anything of a sophisticated nature in the way of [L^a].

When we investigate the thoughts and thought processes of people, or of a particular group of people, by employing an interpretive scheme for their society, we are engaging in the later stages of interpretation. Tversky's study discussed above can be understood in this way. In practice, Tversky relied on an implicit first-approximation interpretive scheme. I think it is safe to say that his implicit scheme measures up to the standards for a serviceable first-approximation scheme. (And, doubtless, he designed his experiment so that the threat of linguistic divergence was minimized by a selective use of the supposed scheme.) Thus, there is a prima facie case for the general reliability of his characterizations of his subjects' choices. And, as we have seen, there are further considerations that support this presumptive case. This is typical of the later stages of interpretation as described above, for there further theory is typically brought to bear in determining the plausibility of possible modifications (or nonmodification) of the first-approximation scheme employed.

The above way of conceptualizing matters has important implications for the possibility of bootstrap testing of [L^a]-generalizations. For it turns out that [L^a] must now be understood as internally complex, having a rudimentary core that does not go much beyond [L] together with rough provision for competing desires. Such a core is then elaborated within [L^a] by clauses of various sorts, stipulating the shape and nature of utility curves perhaps, or the nature of subjective probabilities, or how these interact in cognitive processing. Because [L^a] is internally complex something substantially less than the whole of it can be used in arriving at a basic, or first-approximation, interpretive scheme. Only a rudimentary component of it needs to be used or supposed in constructing the interpretive schemes on which tests of sophisticated variants of [L^a] are based. Thus [L^a] *is not so fully involved in the computation of values—the attributions of intentional states— that it interferes with its own testing.*

At the very least, Tversky's accomplishment is obtaining a set of choices (under interpretation) that are incompatible with the principles of standard decision-theory as discussed earlier. He can "calculate" roughly the conditions of interest—choices, preference— cautiously using his homophonic manual, buttressed by further empirical considerations (generally taken from [L^c] and [G^c]). It then seems infeasible to find in the choices actually obtained an instance of the hypothesis under test: standard decision-theory applied as [L^a]. Thus, a negative test.

One possible response is to suggest that, while refinements of [L] may be testable in the way I have suggested, [L] itself is not testable. But this misses the point. The response admits that [L] *is empirically refinable*, in the sense that elaborations on it that are empirically stronger and more precise could be tested. If any elaboration were to prove empirically adequate (or even a substantial improvement) we would certainly want to employ that generalization in scientific contexts. Thus, the claim that [L] itself is an untestable core principle of intentional psychology would not preclude there being scientific refinements in psychology. (Rosenberg [1988, p. 47] would agree that refinability is the central issue.)

However, the claim that [L] is untestable is quite mistaken. It is reminiscent of Davidson's claim that it is a priori that beliefs and desires are preponderantly rational. As we saw in the fourth chapter, Davidson makes this a conceptual matter: if we do not attribute preponderant rationality to those we interpret, we would not be using talk of beliefs and desires in the now standard way, we would thereby "change the subject" (even though from a referential point of view, we may still be referring to the same psychological states). Of course, this would not insure that people are preponderantly rational. It shows at most that, given how beliefs are presently conceived, what beliefs people have are preponderantly rational. Even accepting this much, for the purposes of argument, it does not follow that people are preponderantly rational, for they may have few, if any, beliefs as these are presently conceived. Similarly, if the claim that [L] is untestable is the claim that [L] is such a contraint on interpretation as to be a conceptual a priori truth, and that thus we could never be led to abandon using [L] in psychology, then the argument is not sound, and its conclusion is probably false. However, if we were to abandon [L] (understood as a rough generalizaton endowed with a spectacular ceteris paribus clause), it is plausible that we would no longer be doing intentional psychology, *strictly* speaking. From the perspective of much of psychology and the human sciences, this would be to change the subject in Davidson's conceptual sense of the subject. But, as long as we are being so strict about what counts as the subject of intentional psychology, we should also recognize that the new subject that emerges need not be all that different from intentional psychology as presently understood. We might have as internal states "B-states" and "D-states" that are recognizable as conceptual descendants of "beliefs" and "desires." We could still be doing psychology, and need not have changed the subject at all, in the referential sense.

If my argument is correct to this point, we can conclude first that [L] is refinable, for refinements of [L] are testable, and second that [L] itself is testable in the sense that we could be led to finally give up on intentional psychology, insofar as it is understood in terms of [L].

My discussion to this point has focused on one way in which the complexity of the generalizations underlying the rationalizing explanation of actions provides a basis for tests and refinements of such generalizations: only a rudimentary core is involved in the provision of a first-approximation interpretation or translation. Relying on this, one can produce enough of an interpretation to justify the conclusion that no positive instance of the candidate refinement can be obtained in some concrete case. Thus, a proper part of $[L^a]$ can be used in testing putative refinements on it.

Other cases of parts of $[L^a]$ being used to test distinct parts are certainly conceivable. Suppose that certain refinements on [L] have proven empirically supported and have come to be accepted as reasonably well confirmed. We might then use these as a constraint on further interpretation. Thus we might encounter a case in which we face a choice: attribute a violation of this well-confirmed refinement, or produce an interpretation that is a disconfirming instance of another proposed refinement. In this case, it is reasonable to use the well-confirmed refinement as a part of the theory with respect to which the proposed additional refinement is tested. We then "calculate" a negative instance of the hypothesis, the proposed additional refinement. These reflections suggest that refinements in psychological generalizations add to the resources we have in psychological testing. This is simply an instance of what van Fraassen described as a "developing theory becoming ever *more testable*" (1983, p. 33).

Having now sketched the way in which the internal complexity of $[L^a]$ allows us to use parts of it to test other parts of it, we should explicitly note the place for psychological generalizations other than those in $[L^a]$ in providing for psychological testability— that is, the place for generalizations from $[L^c]$, $[G^a]$, and $[G^c]$. All such generalizations can contribute to the testability of other psychological generalizations in the capacity assigned above to [L] and to well-confirmed $[L^a]$-generalizations: they can provide constraints on interpretation. (This role was already in evidence in the concrete psychological studies discussed earlier.) In this way, they provide resources for the "determination" of states mentioned in yet other proposed psychological generalizations, thus becoming part of the theory against which hypotheses can be tested. For example, refinements in our general expectations concerning human inductive reasoning can serve to make psychological theory more testable by serving in turn as a constraint on interpretation.

Further, such refinements may be obtained in much the way that we have found for refining [L^a]-expectations. Thus, if, for example, one were to consider recent psychological work on the sort of heuristics posited by Kahneman and Tversky (1972; Tversky and Kahneman 1974) one would find that those investigations (and their apparent positive tests) take a now familiar form: an implicit first-approximation interpretive scheme is employed here, and a rich enough set of data is elicited to allow checking for some possible deficiencies. The questions addressed to the subjects are designed so that, if the subjects' understandings of the tasks given them differ from the investigators' understanding (based on the implicit translation manual) then some clue or hint to this effect should appear in the pattern of responses. Additionally, one could point to the relatively straightforward nature of the task given to the subjects and ask just what it was that was supposedly not understood. Again, we would find a set of relatively mundane (but empirical) expectations strengthen our confidence in the implicit first-approximation interpretive scheme employed. Thus, the account developed focusing on [L^a]-generalizations can be applied mutatis mutandis to the testability of these other classes of generalizations and to their role in the testability of yet other generalizations.

Before summarizing my results, I must acknowledge what seems to me the most serious limitation of the model of psychological testing developed here. It will be remembered that the one limited defense against mutually compensating errors in bootstrap testing was to "have a variety of evidence, so that as many hypotheses as possible are tested in as many different ways as possible." But the holism of the mental and what I called the cooperative application of psychological generalizations lead to limitations on the variety that is attainable here. One way in which tests are relevantly different is in using "different calculations"—resting on different sets of supporting theory, in producing instances of hypotheses. However, attaining a basic first-approximation interpretive scheme seems to rely on the constraints imposed by a characteristic set of rudimentary theory that is applicable in the early going.[5] Thus, all tests will apparently be similar in resting, in part, on this rudimentary core. However, even so, there remains some place for a variety of tests. For, significant differences will arise in the sort of tests described here as, in different cases, different additional generalizations become particularly relevant as further constraints on interpretation.

In general then, we find that an appreciation for the complexity of our set of psychological generalizations, combined with an adequate account of interpretation as a theory-informed endeavor, allows us to account for the testability of psychological generalizations as a matter of bootstrap testing. In particular we find that empirical refinements in [Lᵃ]-generalizations are possible when we take into account how a generally adequate first-approximation interpretation can be developed that does not rely on those refinements in attributing the relevant states to subjects. Further, we find that a range of other types of psychological generalizations can similarly be tested and can be resources in psychological testing. Theory-informed interpretation here amounts to the determination of values of the "quantities" mentioned in the psychological hypothesis being tested. A negative test occurs when a rich set of (roughly behavioral) data is produced that, (1) when straightforwardly interpreted according to a first-approximation scheme, produces a negative instance of the hypothesis, and (2) cannot be reinterpreted to provide a positive instance without violating other psychological generalizations.

In fairness to Rosenberg, I should mention an aspect of his interesting argument that has been neglected to this point. I have considered his argument (as formulated at the start of this essay) on its own internal merits, challenging the premised understanding of interpretation, and arguing that a close examination of our epistemic resources in psychological work reveals leverage for scientifically refining [L]. However, Rosenberg (1988, p. 30) seems to conceive of his argument, premises and all, as at least in part supported by what it allows us to explain: the alleged lack of progress in the social sciences when compared with progress in the natural sciences. This relative lack of progress is to be explained as the result of the social sciences relying on folk psychology through much of their history, while folk psychology is said to be wedded to empirically irrefinable commonsense variations on [L]. Rosenberg's argument, including its premises, is thus to be supported by an inference to the best explanation. Rosenberg can then justly demand of me whether I would deny that the explanandum phenomenon obtains, and, if I do not, what alternative explanation I could supply.

I believe that the appropriate response is a guarded one along three lines. First, inferences to the best explanation are appropriate only when the potential explanation that is to be supported in this way is not just the best among present competitors, but is also a meritorious potential explanation itself. But, if a potential explanation supposes that a certain state of affairs obtains when there is good reason to believe that it does not, then that potential explanation as it stands can hardly be meritorious (although some related potential explanation might yet prove meritorious). Thus, the fact that there is reason to believe that a potential explanation relies on false suppositions renders that explanation not meritorious and not supportable by argument to the best explanation, even if it is the best explanation we presently have. Now I have here presented reasons for believing that the explanation Rosenberg advances for the paucity of social scientific progress rests on a faulty view of [L] as not empirically refinable. I have described our epistemic situation in a way that allows us to appreciate how such principles can (in principle) be empirically refined. Further, I have discussed cases where empirical pressures are brought to bear on such principles. Thus it seems that Rosenberg's argument does not provide us with a meritorious explanation.

Second, to the extent that the social sciences and even psychology have seen little progress, compared to the natural sciences, this seems to me best explained by noting a range of complementary factors. To begin with, rather than claiming that the central generalizations of intentional psychology are wholly irrefinable by empirical work, one might account for the *relative* lack of progress by noting that the generalizations are *relatively difficult* to so refine. In view of my discussion above, this would seem to be a reasonable conclusion. In addition, other factors surely contribute to the frustratingly slow pace of social scientific progress. It is obvious that certain social scientific debates have been initiated and perpetuated by concerns to protect or further certain ideological sacred cows; this has doubtless hindered progress. Further, some social scientists have taken a studied conservative stance to the variants of intentional psychology that they might draw on as psychological work does progress; they thereby have treated common rationalizing explanation and [L] as privileged, if not sacrosanct. There are, of course, other factors that might be cited here. Together, these observations seem to me to comprise the best present explanation of the paucity of social scientific progress.

Third, while progress may have come relatively slowly to psychology, and to the social sciences in particular, it seems to me to have come. And empirical work has proved an inducement. Cultural anthropology *has* progressed from the days of Frazer and Taylor. And empirical work (properly understood) has played its part. With extended field work, observations showed that earlier accounts of magical and religious belief as socially elaborated childishness were inadequate. Observations also showed simple symbolist accounts inadequate (Geertz 1973, p. 101). More directly to the point, my concern here has been primarily with the pivotal case of psychology, and it seems to me that empirical work in cognitive psychology, such as that discussed earlier, is resulting in empirical pressure being exerted on traditional psychological principles. The results are proposed refinements. Some of these may well survive further empirical work, and this, so far as I can see, is what empirical refining generalizations largely amounts to.

8

In Defense of Heteronomic or Soft Laws

8.1: The Issue: Can Psychological Generalizations Be Nomic?

Typically, when we explain some event or phenomenon, we find ourselves relying on general background information that we know could well stand for some refinement. This is so if for no reason other than the characteristic epistemic fact that we find ourselves in possession only of theories that we know will eventually be either refined or replaced. Generally, then, we have no choice but to rely on such approximate and improvable information. Working within a research tradition, such improvable background is, at best, taken to provide us with rough, or approximate, formulations of the relevant laws, generalizations that we will continue to refine. Still, if an explanation drawing on such rough generalizations is to be successful, the generalizations must be nomic, or lawlike. The characteristics commonly thought to reflect the nomicity of generalizations include: (1) being confirmed by their positive instances, and (2) supporting subjunctive and counterfactual claims about individual cases. Were our generalizations in a particular domain not to possess such characteristics, we could not have empirical, scientific grounds for explaining phenomena in that domain by showing that, had certain antecedent events not occurred, then the event to be explained would at least have been less likely. Further, in view of my discussion in chapter 6, we could suggest a somewhat more fundamental characterization of nomicity, holding that a generalization is to be nomic when it mentions causally relevant features of processes, and assigns to them roughly correct contributions to the features for which they are causally relevant. After all, it is in virtue of such generalizations that we can reconstruct the network of counterfactual and causal dependencies as required by (2), it is in virtue of this that we arrive at the sort of causal understanding on which causal explanation draws. In any case, in typical explanations, we rely on rough generalizations that are known to have some exceptions, but which are nevertheless nomic.

Now, while most, if not all, explanations rely on somewhat rough generalizations, several writers have felt that there is particular reason to despair of the quality of the generalizations one finds in the human sciences. The challenge has been raised: despite the refinability of psychological generalizations (demonstrated in the last chapter), is there some deep problem with psychological generalizations (and other generalizations in the human sciences) that makes them ultimately non-nomic? Are their exceptions irremediably too sprawling and unmanageable to allow them to be really nomic? This formulation is preliminary, as we should wonder what sort of "sprawl" or "unmanageability" is at issue, and why it might render refinable generalizations still non-nomic. The point of this chapter is to take up the most plausible variant on this challenge, and to show that it is not telling.

Even among those who believe that generalizations in the human sciences (including psychology) are non-nomic, there is not a settled account of what the supposed infirmity amounts to, although there seems to be one influential and initially plausible suggestion. The infirmity envisioned is commonly thought to be associated with the rather sprawling nature of the exceptions to the generalizations we can produce. Davidson (1980c, 1980d) picks up on this line of thought when he characterizes the problematic generalizations as *heteronomic*, meaning that refinements will require attention to factors from a range of subject matters in addition to the phenomenon of primary concern in the initial generalization. Davidson's writings contain several suggestions regarding why such heteronomic generalizations might be non-nomic. On the other hand, Horgan and Tienson (1990) have responded by repudiating the suggestion that the sprawling set of exceptions to psychological generalizations renders them non-nomic; they defend what they term *soft* laws, laws with ineliminable ceteris paribus clauses.[1] LePore and Loewer (1987, 1989) and Fodor (1989) provide complementary discussions. Members of these classes can indeed be nomic generalizations that directly support explanations.

8.2: Davidson's Suggestion that
Heteronomic Generalizations Do Not Cite
Causal Factors and Thus Cannot Be Nomic

As with several other issues that I have considered in this book, so also, in connection with the suggestion that psychological generalizations might have a special infirmity rendering them non-nomic, Davidson's writings have been quite influential. So, it is appropriate to reflect at the beginning on his distinction between heteronomic and homonomic generalizations. On one natural reading, his discussion of this distinction reveals a very general, but rather vague, "intuition" or suspicion regarding the central problem with heteronomic generalizations. However, this warning is in order: I am not concerned with whether or not my discussion here characterizes exactly what Davidson ultimately holds. Rather, I seek to reveal a suggestion to be found in a package of his doctrines associated with his thinking on heteronomicity. Further, I believe that the suggestion strikes responsive chords in numerous philosophical discussions. Accordingly, in this section, I put the suggestion on the table so that it can be evaluated.

Davidson ennunciates his distinction between heteronomic and homonomic generalizations in the context of a defense of his principle of "the Anomalism of the Mental," which is the thesis that "there are no strict deterministic laws on the basis of which mental events can be predicted and explained" (p. 208). Subsequent discussion makes it clear that, for Davidson, the issue is not really one of determinism, but of "strictness." A *strict law* is a generalization that has been refined to a point that renders it closer to being deterministic than any other true generalization dealing with the relevant phenomenon: "This ideal theory may or may not be deterministic, but it is if any true theory is" (p. 219). The claim that psychological phenomena are necessarily anomalous is thus the claim that psychology cannot produce such ideal theory, with its attendant strict laws.

To better appreciate what Davidson may be driving at here, it is helpful to recall his "Principle of the Nomological Character of Causality": "where there is causality, there must be a law: events related as cause and effect fall under strict deterministic laws" (Davidson 1980c, p. 208). As already noted, the important qualifier here is 'strict', not 'deterministic'. When Davidson (p. 215) restates the principle as, "when events are related as cause and effect, they have descriptions that instantiate a law," this suggests that, *on his view, laws—real laws—are strict generalizations that are not susceptible to further refinement.*[2]

One might plausibly reconstruct the underlying approach to causality as follows, if one's generalization makes reference to the real causal factors, and not just correlated factors, then when one has done what can be done by citing such factors, there is no room for further improvement. In the terminology of Salmon's (1978) Statistical-Relevance Model of explanation, one could say that, in such a case, all further factors are "screened off" as causally and explanatorily, as well as statistically, irrelevant. Of course, these irrelevant factors would be needless clutter, having no place in nomic generalizations. *On this picture, real laws are strict by virtue of their mentioning all and only real causal factors.* It is on the basis of such generalizations that we can come to appreciate the causal history of particular events, thereby explaining them. *Nomic generalizations* are then naturally taken to be those generalizations that are at least *viable present candidates for this status* of being a strict law, or generalizations that are *viably taken as partial specifications* of such strict laws, generalizations that may well need only the added mention of a few further causal factors to be strict laws. In view of what we presently know they are lawlike in that they are plausibly taken to get at the real causes, and not just some factors that are correlated with the real causes. Such nomic or lawlike generalizations may need refining, but the envisionable refinements supposedly are not such as to reveal causal factors that may serve in the stead of the ones presently mentioned in the generalizatation.

Now, it is against the backdrop of the above picture of laws and nomic generalizations that we can understand Davidson's heteronomic/homonomic distinction. The distinction is introduced after Davidson admits that there are psychological (and even psychophysical) generalizations that do support explanations. Such generalizations are projectible in the sense that they give us reason to believe that the regularity they describe is not accidental,[3] and that events will continue to fall in line. Further, it seems that, in order to have this sort of status, such generalizations must receive some confirmation or support from their positive instances. Thus, one is led to wonder why, recognizing this much, Davidson yet denies that psychological generalizations can be nomic. After all, such generalizations seem to possess two of the characteristic marks of nomic generalizations. Davidson then introduces his distinction. For him, it serves to block the threatened conclusion that there are psychological laws by allowing him to hold that there are weakly confirmable, explanation-supporting, generalizations that are nevertheless not nomic. It does this by purporting to distinguish between those rough and relatively robust generalizations that might be developed into strict laws, "real" laws, and those which could not be so refined:

> In our daily traffic with events and actions that must be foreseen or understood, we perforce make use of the sketchy summary generalizations, for we do not know a more accurate law, or if we do, we lack a description of the particular events in which we are interested that would show the relevance of the law. But there is an important distinction to be made within the category of the rude rule of thumb. On the one hand, there are generalizations whose positive instances give us reason to believe the generalization itself could be improved by adding further provisos and conditions stated in the same general vocabulary as the original generalization. Such a generalization points to the form and vocabulary of the finished law: we may say that it is a *homonomic* generalization. On the other hand there are generalizations which when instantiated may give us reason to believe there is a precise law at work, but one that can be stated only by shifting to a different vocabulary. We can call such generalizations *heteronomic* (Davidson 1980c, p. 219).

One natural understanding of all this is that *heteronomic generalizations are not susceptible to being developed into strict laws which deal with real causal factors.* It is the foreign vocabulary imported in their refinement that supposedly indicates the sort of factors that are the *real causal factors* underlying the rough regularity formulated in the heteronomic generalization. Heteronomic generalizations thus seem to traffic in *epiphenomena*.[4] Something like this seems to be required to reconcile Davidson's admission that certain generalizations can deal with *events* that *are* causally related, and deal with them in terms that render the generalizations both supportable by positive instances and counterfactual supporting, with his insistence that they are somehow yet not nomic.

Thus, the central suggestion is that, whatever their practical virtues, heteronomic generalizations in general, and psychological generalizations in particular, do not get at the real causal factors, but rather traffic in epiphenomena. This suggestion captures a central strand in several writers' misgivings regarding the status of psychological generalizations. Admittedly, my reconstruction imports a realist notion of a "causally relevant factor" into Davidson's discussions. This notion may seem foreign to Davidson's views, for he conceives of causality as completely a matter of a relation between events, and he insists that there is no more story to tell. Indeed, his discussions contain remarks that are obviously at odds with my reconstruction, as when he claims that "every property of every event is causally efficacious" (1987, p. 46). However, I am convinced that the increasingly common concern for distinguishing between causally relevant and irrelevant *features* is important: any account of mental (or other) causation *must* come to terms with this distinction by allowing us to appreciate the causal relevance of mental features such as intentional states. Thus, insofar as Davidson fails here, his own suggestive discussions are inadequate, although they may raise a worthy issue. Further, despite conflicting claims, such as that (obviously false) claim just quoted, I believe that this distinction between causally relevant and irrelevant features helps to make ontic sense out of Davidson's suggestions that heteronomic generalizations cannot be lawlike, and that all causal relations between events fall under homonomic laws which are the "precise law[s] at work" in those cases.

I think we have managed to locate an important issue, and it is one that seems to resurface in yet other aspects of Davidson's philosophy of mind. For further light on how one might conceive of heteronomic generalizations as inherently trafficking in epiphenomena and passing over the real causal factors, one can reflect on Davidson's thesis that mental events are identical with physical events whose causal relations are strictly formulated in physical laws. According to Davidson (1980c, p. 211), to be a mental event is to be truely describable in terms of some open sentence that contains at least one mental verb essentially. To be a physical event is to be picked out by a description that contains only physical vocabulary essentially. Davidson argues that all mental events are physical events (the token-identity thesis). He reasons that mental events are causally efficacious, entering into causal relations both with other mental events and with nonpsychological events. But, his principle of the Nomologicial Character of Causality informs us that all causal relations between particular events are describable in terms of strict laws. Now, if we add that there are no nomic psychological or psychophysical generalizations, the causal relations into which mental events enter must be describable in terms of physical, not psychological or psycho-physical, laws. To be so describable, their relata, including the mental events, must be describable in only physical terms. Thus, these mental events must be physical events.

What is important for our purposes here, is the way in which Davidson's view of the relation between the mental and the physical can encourage one to view mental *factors* as epiphenomenal, while still recognizing that mental *events* can be real causes. It does not provide an argument to the effect that heteronomic generalizations do not get at the causal factors.[5] Rather, it provides a model for understanding mental properties as epiphenomenal, and, in turn, a model for understanding macro-level factors generally as epiphenomenal. All this encourages one to view heteronomic generalizations, being characteristic of generalizations at the macro-level, as trafficking in epiphenomena.

The relata of causal statements are commonly events, and such causal statements are extensional. If a mental event is identical to some physical event that causes some other event, then the mental event is a cause of that distinct event. But, of course, not all the properties of the event are relevant to the causal relations into which it enters. For a property of an event to be causally relevant, it must be the case that had an event with that property not occurred, an event with the property of interest of the effect-event would at least have been less likely to have occurred. Quite generally, with respect to a given causal relation between two events, not all the properties of the cause-event are causally relevant.

My behavior at 4:15 p.m. 6 November 1990 may cause a basketball to go through a particular hoop, but the behavioral event is variously describable. It might be described as a particular, physically situated, bodily movement. Described in this manner, it seems to be both the cause and to be described in terms of causally relevant factors. But the behavior is also describable as the salient event in the life of Jewell Henderson's eldest boy at 4:15 p.m., 6 November 1990, or as a basketball launch by Mrs. Henderson's eldest boy. So described, it is still the cause of the momentuous basket, but it is not described in terms of causally relevant factors. Once the bodily movement is taken into account, its being a basketball launch by Jewell Henderson's eldest boy is screened off as irrelevant. Being a shot taken by Mrs. Henderson's boy isn't a causally relevant factor. Supposedly the real causal factors are what has a place in laws, real laws (for Davidson, strict laws). Thus, even if basketball launches by Mrs. Henderson's boy tend to go through the hoop, there are no laws to this effect.

Now, one way of understanding what Davidson says of the relations between the mental and the physical is to say that mental (psychological) characteristics of events seem to be in much the same situation as are properties like "being a basketball launch by Jewell Henderson's eldest boy." Even as a certain bodily movement may be a basketball launch by Jewell Henderson's boy, so a certain physical event may be a certain mental event (say a remembering, or seeming to remember, that there is beer in the fridge). And even as the characteristic of being a basketball launch by Mrs. Henderson's boy is found to be causally irrelevant in view of the physical properties of the hypothetical event, so the mental characteristics are screened off and rendered irrelevant by the physical properties. They are then not the real causal factors, as that role is reserved for the physical factors mentioned in the strict physical laws. On this view, the real causal factors in any transaction involving mental events are not mental or psychological factors. Instead, the causal factors are (among) the physical aspects of the relevant events.

Thus, Davidson's identity thesis of the mental and the physical seems to give rise to the view that, while mental events are identical with physical events, the causal relations between mental events and other (mental or physical) events are ultimately grounded in whatever (perhaps sprawling) physical factors are mentioned in the cluster of physical laws relevant to the complex physical events in question. It is then inferred that the mental factors are themselves not causal factors, but are causally irrelevant. The resulting view then serves as a model for the supposed non-nomic status of heteronomic generalizations as a class, and for the causal irrelevance of the factors mentioned in such heteronomic generalizations.

These reflections on Davidson's identity thesis are reinforced by considering his account of how heteronomic generalizations feature in explanation. It will be remembered that Davidson (1980c, p. 219) introduces the notion of a heteronomic generalization by referring to "generalizations which when instantiated may give us reason to believe there is a precise law at work, but one that can be stated only by shifting to a different vocabulary." Such generalizations are taken to be important in that they can provide support for singular causal explanations in those cases where we do not know or employ a strict causal law or a nomic approximation. According to Davidson, they can do this because they often "give us good reason to expect other cases to follow suit roughly in proportion," for they "provide good reason to believe that underlying the particular case there is a regularity that could be formulated sharply and without caveat" (Davidson 1980c, p. 219). They thus have an oblique role in explanation. On this view, true singular causal statements can be explanatory, even when they do not mention the real causal factors of the relevant events. They can do this because of the somewhat oblique role non-nomic heteronomic generalizations can play here. Such generalizations can formulate regularities that we believe to be relatively robust by virtue of underlying causal factors which are not mentioned in the generalization. Supposedly, such heteronomic generalizations do not point to the relevant causal factors, but do give us reason to believe that there are such factors to be found, and that those factors make for the relatively nonaccidental character of the heteronomic generalization itself.

I am not recommending this package of doctrines suggested by Davidson's work. (In fact, for my purposes, it is not even important that it constitute the best reading of Davidson's own views.) I am setting it out because I believe that it raises a misgiving that ultimately informs many contemporary discussions of whether psychological generalizations can be nomic. While even a passing familiarity with Davidson's view is enough to appreciate that Davidson believes psychological generalizations to be non-nomic, less has been made of the intimately related suggestion that mental factors are not causally relevant. Many readers have been too easily comforted by his insistence that mental events can be causes. But, we have seen how various familiar features of Davidson's view seem to point to the conclusion that psychological generalizations, and all heteronomic generalizations, must be non-nomic and fail to get at causal factors. We have found this strongly suggested by his discussions of strict laws and causality, of heteronomic versus homonomic generalizations, of the relation of the mental to the physical, and of the role of heteronomic generalizations in causal explanations. Recently, the suggestion has come to be recognized and has spawned increasing critical scrutiny (Sosa 1984; Honderich 1982, 1984; Føllesdal 1985; Kim 1989b; Fodor 1989; Horgan forthcoming).

It must be noted that, in these reflections on Davidson's identity thesis, I have yet to articulate a strong reason to conclude that all heteronomic generalizations must be non-nomic by virtue of failing to get at the real causal factors. I have not even set out a telling reason for accepting such a conclusion, *were* we to grant that psychological generalizations do not get at real causal factors. In reflecting on Davidson's identity thesis we have focused only on one special class of heteronomic generalizations, psychological ones.

When we connect the indicated view of psychological factors and psychological generalizations with Davidson's insistence that heteronomic generalizations play an indirect role in supporting the relevant explanations, we see how Davidson seems committed to extending the model to all heteronomic generalization. But, we must wonder how plausible or defensible is the view that all heteronomic generalizations focus on causally irrelevant factors, and are thus non-nomic. Once we examine this issue, we will find that such an unqualified judgment regarding heteronomic generalizations as a class is quite untenable. Only some heteronomic generalizations seem subject to indictment; the general condemnation of heteronomic generalizations must be significantly qualified. When the needed qualifications are in hand, we will need to reconsider the Davidsonian line of thought regarding psychological generalizations set out in this section. That is, once we have a better grip on what makes some heteronomic generalizations nomic and others not, we will need to reconsider whether there are grounds for the purported causal impotence of psychological factors.

8.3: The Prima Facie Case for There Being Nomic Heteronomic Generalizations Citing Causal Factors

To make a strong prima facie case that not all heteronomic generalizations need traffic in epiphenomena, and that at least some such generalizations can be lawlike, we need only consider a select generalization from a special science and find it apparently both heteronomic and nomic. In this section I consider a particularly unproblematic heteronomic generalization from biology. The generalization to be considered is heteronomic by virtue of dealing with open systems in a manner that is characteristic of the special sciences. To appreciate the significance of the example, it is needful both to understand this manner of dealing with open systems and to appreciate how this is a source of heteronomicity that is characteristic of generalizations in the special sciences. We will then see that if being heteronomic renders a generalization non-nomic, then any generalization dealing with the properties of open systems, and, quite generally, the generalizations of the special sciences, must be non-nomic. This is implausible. (But more argument will follow, in any case.)

There is, of course, a respect in which any science, even the most general and fundamental, can deal with open systems, systems whose processes are subject to interruption by exogenous factors. All that is needed is to use the vocabulary of the science to characterize a set of initial conditions for some limited portion of the universe and to then consider what will transpire within that portion if no other portions of the universe exercise a significant effect on it. But, it is significant that, when using the resources of a general and fundamental science, such treatments can deal with progressively more inclusive systems without employing different sorts of terms.[6] Thus, it is not as though the general science itself deals with a particular sort of open system—an ecosystem, a biological organism, a geological plate system, a physiological system—in terms that are fitted to dealing with such an open system (and not to exogenous factors). Physical systems, we might say, can be open systems, but physical systems are not a particular sort of open system, as the more inclusive systems are each physical systems as well.

On the other hand, the special sciences develop vocabularies that treat of components and capacities of open systems of particular sorts (ecosystems, physiological systems, and so forth). They deal with *properties of the relevant sort of open system.* For example: the carrying capacity (with respect to a population) of an ecosystem, or low glucose levels in a circulatory system, or savings levels in economic systems. Obviously, moving to a more inclusive system need not be a move to another system of the same sort. A more inclusive system for a given physiological system may be another physiological system, but it need not be. In these respects, the manner in which the special sciences deal with open systems contrasts with the manner in which fundamental, general, science does.

Developed to treat of processes *within* open systems of a particular sort, theories in the special sciences lay no claims to completeness (not even to potential completeness as the ideal theory in that special science is developed). Instead, they are developed with the goal of accounting for orderly development within the systems on which they focus. They characterize likely developments, provided certain parameters or initial conditions (of systems of the relevant sort) and no interruption. Their special vocabulary is tailored to this end.

For our purposes here, we can suppose that "the vocabulary of the special science" is just that *developed within* the special science to characterize the factors and processes within the sort of open systems of special interest in that science, and *not borrowed* from some more inclusive science. There is no more precise and principled way in which to distinguish the vocabulary of a special science from that of other sciences to which it helps itself.[7] Of course, the special sciences do not confine themselves to such a special vocabulary. Generally, further vocabulary becomes relevant in two ways.

First, there is the matter of taking some account of interruptions in the processes of the open systems at issue. Anthropologists, economists, psychologists, physiologists, ecologists, geologists, thermodynamicists, and so on attempt to understand how impinging processes can affect the systems on which they focus. Interruptions are typically treated as resetting some of the relevant (special scientific) parameters, which are then treated as new initial conditions. Accordingly, impinging processes are typically characterized in terms borrowed from some other science whose province is processes of the relevant sort. Thus, exogenous factors are typically characterized by employing an imported vocabulary.

Second, many practitioners of the special sciences seek to understand how the processes on which they focus are themselves realized in physical systems as characterized by a more inclusive science. As Fodor recognizes, workers in the special sciences commonly seek to "explicate the physical mechanisms whereby events conform to the laws of the special sciences" (1981, p. 138). Again, we find an imported vocabulary, although one that often eventually becomes second nature within the special science—witness the intimate relations between biochemistry and molecular biology.

Thus, typically, some of the possible interrupting exogenous factors are not characterizable in the vocabulary of the special science, strictly drawn, for that vocabulary is developed to deal with events and processes within certain open systems. Further, accounting for how systems, as described in the vocabulary of the special science, are realized in keeping with physicalism leads naturally to the use of borrowed vocabulary in the special sciences. In either case, the generalizations of any such special science that result from these inquiries will be heteronomic.

The suggestion that heteronomic generalizations cannot be nomic thus entails that generalizations in the special sciences, tailored as they are to dealing with open systems and properties of open systems, cannot be nomic. One can find this consequence openly embraced in Davidson's writings. Psychological generalizations cannot be strict laws, he says, because they deal with open systems:

> Physical theory promises to provide a comprehensive closed system guaranteed to yield a standardized, unique description of

every physical event couched in a vocabulary amenable to law.

It is not plausible that mental concepts alone can provide such a framework, simply because the mental does not, by our first principle, constitute a closed system. Too much happens to affect the mental that is not itself a systematic part of the mental (Davidson 1980c, p. 224).[8]

But, the general suggestion should be puzzling and troubling. Why cannot the generalizations of a special science dealing with open systems pick out relevant factors in causal processes? The processes that are the focus of the special science seem to be causal; to use Salmon's criteria, apparently they can carry or transmit a mark. Of course, the factors mentioned in such generalizations are typically macro-level factors in macro-level processes. Such macro-level factors are supposedly realized in lower level processes, as is the macro-level process itself. But why should this render the macro-level factors causally irrelevant?

One answer, suggested by earlier discussions, is that the macro-level factors are statistically screened off by micro-level properties. But, we will need to proceed cautiously in deciding what to make of this point. It cannot, of itself, be dispository, for this would lead to the incredible conclusion that the only acceptable causal explanations are those couched exclusively in terms of our most fundamental micro-physics. This, to put it mildly, would be silly. Neither social, nor psychological, nor neurophysiological, nor biochemical, nor any other factor short of those dealing with the most elemental factors of fundamental physics could claim a place in explanations. The problem would not be limited to macro-levels of particular relevance to psychology. Neither astronomical, nor geological, nor general chemical, nor any other level short of the most fundamental of micro-levels would be respectable, were the screening off test taken to be, of itself, dispository. Further, as LePore and Loewer (1987) point out, the simple screening off test could conceivably be applied to render micro-level features irrelevant in much the way that it would render macro-level properties irrelevant. For now I will simply note that the screening-off (partial) test for causal factors must be applied so as not to rule out all macro-level explanation, and let the matter rest. I expect wide agreement. (See also LePore and Loewer 1987, and Fodor 1989.) In a later section, I will discuss what relation between micro-level factors and macro-level properties must obtain if the macro-level properties are to be causally relevant. In any case, the example to be considered here seems to me to provide a clear case of a nomic generalization that is both couched in macro-level terms and heteronomic by virtue of dealing with open systems.

Once we have repudiated the suggestion that macro-level properties must be causally irrelevant, the claim that generalizations dealing with open systems must be non-nomic can in turn be seen to be quite extraordinary and unmotivated. It entails that merely by virtue of characterizing open systems in terms of components and capacities of such open systems, merely by virtue of characterizing processes that are interruptible by exogenous factors characterizable only in terms borrowed from another science, one must be trafficking in epiphenomena. This is a difficult claim to credit. To begin with, setting off interruptible processes seems clearly not enough to render a property causally irrelevant. After all, in the strict sense, a causal factor contributing to the production of the given effect is *not* a property whose instantiations invariably have that effect, it is rather one whose instantiations invariably change the chance of events of the sort the relevant effect-event is (Humphreys 1989a, 1989b). When such a contributing causal factor is conjunctive, we also recognize the component properties as causally relevant in that they contribute in the circumstances. This, somewhat looser sense of causal relevance is the most common, and it is that use that concerns us here. Obviously, such causal factors could set off interruptible causal processes. In macro-level cases such as are our focus here, we may then say that causally relevant factors are those that leave a "mark" on a structure or process, where, as a result, certain effects tend to issue, *provided* that the process is not subsequently "marked" in offsetting ways. For example, exerting a certain force in a certain direction is obviously a causal factor, as it leaves its mark on the process that is the affected object and its propagation. As a result, the object will tend to arrive at some point or state at a later time. However, the process is interruptible. Second, it is hard to find much significance in the fact that "refinements" on the generalizations at issue here would need to rely on an imported vocabulary to characterize interrupting processes. For example, why suppose that, in order to be a causal factor, (instantiations of) a given biological property would have to set off processes that were only interruptible by (instantiations of) other biological properties? There is no good reason to be found. Third, there should be a strong presumption against accepting any claim that entails the claim that biological talk of chlorophyll in chloroplasts, or of cells, or of genes must miss the real causal factors because these ways of talking deal with components of open systems and their interruptible processes.

It may help to consider a concrete case. So, let us consider a biological factor—having chlorophyll in the chloroplast structures of leaves—and a biological generalization to the effect that light striking the leaves initiates a process resulting in the production of carbohydrates. Of course, this is subject to refinement. For example, light with wavelengths 620–720nm striking chlorophyll in chloroplasts initiates a process (involving many intermediate steps) that results in the production of carbohydrates such as glucose, starch, or dihydroxyactone phosphate (DHAP). My claim is simply that such generalizations are nomic, and that they point to real causal factors. They can properly serve as the grounds for explanations of a leaf producing a quantity of one of certain carbohydrates.

The biological process of interest is roughly as follows: light of the relevant wavelengths falls upon two (slightly different) forms of chlorophyll. One is responsible for using the light energy in the breakdown of water and the capture of electrons. (Substances to which electrons have been added are said to be "reduced." Reduced substances provide stores of energy that can be used when they donate electrons to substances that more readily capture electrons.) Through a series of electron transfers, the reduced chlorophyll donates its electrons to the second sort of chlorophyll. Here, light striking this second sort of chlorophyll provides yet further energy that makes its reduction possible. Again, a series of ensuing electron transfers leads to the production of reduced NADP+ (NADPH). In the course of the electron transports mentioned above, more energy is produced than is needed for the reduction of NADP+. This energy makes possible the phosphorylation of ADT to form ATP. The production of NADPH and ATP is the work of the "light phase" of photosynthesis (so called because it is initiated by light energy enabling the reduction of chlorophyll which in turn serves as a reducing agent). In the "dark phase," the NADPH and ATP produced in the light phase are used as energy resources in reducing CO_2 during its incorporation into carbohydrates. A prominant process here is the Calvin cycle. In this cycle, two three-carbon molecules are produced by a catalyzed reaction combining a five-carbon precursor and CO_2. (This initiates the cycle in which five of every six resulting three-carbon molecules will be reconverted into the five-carbon precursor.) The three-carbon molecules then undergo two distinct reactions: in the first, they are phosphorylated by ATP; in the second, NADPH is reconverted into NADP+ and the resulting energy is used to produce Glyceraldehyde–3–phosphate (GAP). Finally, within the chloroplast, GAP may be converted to glucose phosphate, and, in turn, into starch, or it may be converted into DHAP for export to the rest of the cell (where DHAP is converted into sucrose).

So, put simply, light falling on the chloroplast, and in particular on component photosynthetic units containing the chlorophyll, initiates a rather involved causal process in which important carbohydrates are ultimately produced. As an initiating event of a causal chain, it is appropriate to say that light striking the chlorophyll causes carbohydrate production (both generally and in particular cases). Further, there being illuminated chlorophyll in photosynthetic units seems undeniably to be a real causal factor. Were the biological property of being illuminated chlorophyll not instantiated, there would be no carbohydrate production; the causal process in the relevant systems depends on it. Considering the matter in terms of Salmon's mark criterion, we find that there being (appropriately) illuminated chlorophyll is indeed causally relevant. It leaves it mark on processes that clearly transmit marks: the chlorophyll itself and the energy economy of the cell. It tends to produce a characteristic set of electron transfers in which energy is captured and then used in the production of carbohydrates. Employing Humphrey's account we come to much the same result, although we may on that account be led to conclude that the the illumination of chlorophyll in the photosynthetic units is causally relevant as a component of a conjunctive causal factor. It, along with the presence of the appropriate further cellular context, and the absence of interruptions, increases the chance of the relevant carbohydrate production in all treatment conditions. Further, anticipating a theme soon to be developed in the following sections, it would be confused to think that it is shown to be causally irrelevant when a description of the relevant macromolecules is provided. For the explanation in terms of chlorophyll in chloroplasts being exposed to light does not compete with an explanation in terms of a lower-level biochemical description of the relevant structures and their being exposed to light. The one explanation is not excluded by the other.

But, it is obvious that the generalization mentioned above to the effect that light striking the chlorophyll causes the production of the relevant carbohydrates is heteronomic. The relevant process provides many opportunities for interruption from outside the biological system. At any point, the process might be arrested by being exposed to extreme temperatures, for example, or by the introduction of further interactant chemicals, or by exposure to extremes of pressure, and so on. As is to be expected, the characterization of these possible interrupters clearly outruns the vocabulary of plant physiology, strictly construed.

Thus, we have a clear case of a generalization that is heteronomic and yet seems to get at a real causal factor in some causal chains. Again, this should amply motivate abandoning the suggestion that all heteronomic generalizations are non-nomic and fail to get at the real causal factors. We thus duly note that at least some generalizations that are heteronomic basically by virtue of dealing with open systems are nomic. Again, we are led to wonder what makes some heteronomic generalizations nomic and others not.

8.4: Psychological Factors Can Be Causally Relevant: The Basic Solution to the Explanatory Exclusion Problem

In view of the preceding discussions, we are left with two pressing issues: First, there is the general issue of how we can tell which heteronomic generalizations must fail to be nomic, and which can be nomic. Second, we must determine whether psychological generalizations can be among the chosen, or must be excluded.

The first issue can be framed as the problem of characterizing the class of generalizations and explanations that focus on real causal processes and factors, and distinguishing it from the class of generalizations that focus on pseudoprocesses and epiphenomenal features. Recall that this issue becomes a concern when reflecting on whether or not purported macro-level factors and processes must be causally irrelevant by virtue of being statistically screened off by lower-level causal factors. Accordingly, the issue might be fruitfully addressed by considering what relations between micro-level causal factors and macro-level factors must obtain if the latter are to be causal factors, and not just correlated epiphenomenal characteristics. This is how Kim approaches the issue when developing his principle of explanatory exclusion and his related notion of supervenient causation.

It was once common to insist that macro-level theories must ultimately be reducible to micro-level theories, in which case one would also say that the macro-level properties were reducible to micro-level properties. Classically conceived, in the fashion of Nagel

(1961), reduction requires that there be very strong systematic connections between the properties employed by two theories. Reduction was to be undertaken by providing correlations between the properties (vocabularies) of the two theories that enabled one to derive the laws of the reduced theory from the reducing theory. To fully succeed here, the reduction-enabling correlations would need to provide micro-level necessary and sufficient conditions for the macro-level properties. Further, it is commonly required that such necessary and sufficient conditions be manageably simple. For example, it apparently would not do to employ a sprawling disjunction of complex micro-level conditions in one side of the biconditional.

However, the tall order of providing such biconditional "bridge laws" commonly cannot be filled. As a general rule, macro-level properties are multiply realizable. Even relatively tractable macro-level properties such as temperature, are realized differently in different cases (thus we have temperature in gasses and temperature in solids). The bridge laws then become modestly disjunctive. When we turn to sophisticated functional capacities of systems, the number of possible realizations becomes unmanageable (perhaps endless). For example, there are in principle many microphysical systems for removing and adding glucose to the blood (blood-sugar regulators), or for the transport of nutrients and wastes (circulatory systems), just as there are many possible physical systems that can keep time (clocks). Thus, reduction often seems out of the question. Instead, a weaker connection between properties in related theories is in order. Supervenience seems just such a relation. Kim (1984, p. 262) explains the general notion of supervenience as follows:

> [T]he supervenience of a family A of properties on another family B can be explained as follows: necessarily, for any property F in A, if any object x has F, then there exists a property G in B such that x has G, and necessarily anything having G has F. When properties F and G are related as specified in the definition, we may say that F is *supervenient* on G, and that G is the *supervenience base* of F.

Thus, while the supervenient macro-level property, F, may be realized in multiple supervenience bases, G, G^1, G^2, and so on, in any given case of F, it is realized in a particular instantiation of micro-level properties, G^k, and there G^k determines that the particular case is a case of F. (See also Rosenberg 1985a, pp. 111–16.)

Suppose now that we are considering a particular macro-level sequence that we suppose is causal. How must it relate to the micro-level causal processes if it is to be properly so taken? Kim's answer, which I take to be essentially correct, is that the causally relevant properties of the macro-level process must at least supervene on the causally relevant properties of the micro-level process. The basic motivation here is that, if the purported macro-level factors depend in an appropriate way on micro-level causal factors, then they too will bear the marks of being causally relevant, and may properly be taken to be higher-level causal factors realized in the particular lower-level causal factors. With regard to causal explanation, mentioning such macro-level factors does not produce a competing, or alternative, explanation, but rather provides further perspective on, and appreciation for, the causal processes. Mentioning the macro-level causal processes can provide new information and an appreciation for a further set of counterfactual dependencies. As Kim formulates the resulting suggestion, if an object's (x's) having the macro-level property C is to be a causal factor in an object's (y's) coming to have macro-level property E, then x's having C must supervene on certain micro-properties of x, (m)C, and y's having E must supervene on certain micro-properties of y, (m)E, and there must be a micro-level causal connection between x's having (m)C and y's having (m)E. When this happens, and there are the appropriate dependencies between C-events and E-events generally, then we can conclude that x's being C is not rendered causally irrelevant to y's being E, even though it is statistically screened off from y's being E by x's being (m)C. We then have a case of *supervenient causation*.

Thus, at the macro-level, a change in the temperature of an object can cause a change in its dimensions (volume). For, temperature supervenes on, and thus is realized in, physical properties of the aggregate of the object's micro-physical constituents, and so does it's dimensions; and the supervenience base of the object's dimensions is causally affected by the supervenience base for the object's temperature.

Kim's basic idea can be fleshed out somewhat by thinking in terms of macro-level functional states. A physiological explanation might mention certain events involving subsystems described in terms of their functional roles. (For example, the liver as a glycogen-glucose interconverter serves as the organ which decreases or increases blood sugar levels, while the pancreas as the source of glucagon and insulin, and the adrenal medulla as the source of epinepherine, serve as components of a feedback loop partially modulating the liver's activity.) The relevant functional capacities of the relevant subsystems, and their macro-level states, are *not in competition* with the underlying causal micro-level factors; they are *not alternative causes.* They *are macro-level properties of the system whose realizations in the micro-level properties and organization of this system serve to bring about the explanandum-event.* It is *by realizing such macro-level properties* that the *micro-level properties of the system conspire to bring about the event to be explained.* Encapsulating this line of thought, the important distinction is between those macro-level properties that are realized in the causally relevant micro-level properties, and whose realizations at the micro-level is thus the relevant micro-level causal process, and those macro-level processes that are not so based. Kim's notion of supervenient causation builds on just this point, employing the common concept of a set of properties supervening on another set of properties.

However, to allow these exceedingly plausible applications of the basic idea to go through, the formulation of the notion of supervenient causation given above must be liberalized somewhat, for the above formulation is rather too constraining. In particular, it renders problematic any causal role for functional properties of object as embedded in a more inclusive system. An object's having a certain functional property is a matter of its dispositions within a wider system. Having a functional property is a matter of being a component of a system that has a certain functional (and often componential) analysis. Accordingly, the supervenience base for an object's having a certain functional property will include not just lower-level properties *of the object* in question, but also certain lower-level properties of *the rest of the system* in question. In such a case, realization is said to be "non-local," as the property is then realized by *the object as embedded in the system.* This is nicely illustrated by certain physical devices that can be either electric generators or electric motors, depending on how they are hooked up in a wider system. Such a device will realize the property of being a generator in one system (in which the movement of magnets or coils are mechanically produced, thus yielding electrical current in a circuit), and yet realize the property of being a motor in another (in which flow of current through its coils produces a rotation in the relevant parts).

Reflection on such cases suggests the following somewhat loosened characterization of supervenient causation. An object's (x's) having macro-level property C can be said to be a supervenient causal factor in an object's (y's) coming to have macro-level property

E, when x's having C supervenes on certain micro-properties of x together with its containing system, (m)C, and y's having E supervenes on certain micro-properties of y together with its containing system, (m)E, and there is a micro-level causal connection between x-in-x's-system's having (m)C and y-in-y's-system's having (m)E. The earlier characterization can then be taken to treat of those cases in which realization is local; in those cases, x-in-x's-system can be understood as just x.

Consider an example from recent molecular biology provided by Kincaid (1990a). Once proteins are synthesized in the cytoplasm, they must be transported to destinations within and at the boundary of the cell where they can be further employed. Biologists have wondered how proteins can "know where to go." In several cases, it has been found that the protein is synthesized from a larger precursor and that the precursor contains an amino acid sequence that is instrumental in directing the resulting protein. It seems that "the information determining protein transport is contained in a signal sequence—a particular sequence of amino acids incorporated in the protein precursor itself" (Kincaid 1990a, p. 11). Now, clearly, being a "signal sequence" is a matter of cellular biology, a matter of the functional role played by an amino acid sequence in the cell as a biological system: a signal sequence "targets" the synthesized protein for a particular cellular location. Further, being a signal sequence is multiply realizable. More than 100 sequences have been found to serve in various cellular contexts as signal sequences, and there seems to be no single biochemical property characteristic even of all and only these known cases, and what serves as a signal sequence in one cellular context need not function in this way in a different context. Of course, as complex macromolecules within an environment of many other macro-molecules, we surmise that any physical *system* that is identical in all (or even select) chemical respects to *a given signal sequence in a given cell* would provide a case of a signal sequence carrying the same information within its containing cell. Being a signal sequence is thus a cellular biological property that supervenes on biochemical properties, and in particular it supervenes on biochemical properties of a component as situated in a larger biochemical system.

Suppose that we have a generalization to the effect that a particular sort of signal sequence is responsible for depositing a certain protein at the endoplasmic reticulum. This generalization seems to make a general causal claim: the presence of such-and-such a signal sequence on the relevant precursor is a causal factor in the relevant protein being deposited at the endoplasmic reticulum. We find here a set of supervenient causal episodes. The generalization would seem to support singular causal explanations. Suppose that we seek to explain a particular case of the relevant protein being deposited at the endoplasmic reticulum. The association of the relevant signal sequence with that protein is causally relevant, for it is a macro-level factor realized in the causally relevant micro-level factors of the signal sequence, the protein molecule, and their containing system. Had it not obtained, an event with the property of interest of the explanandum-event would have at least been less likely to have obtained. This is is a case of supervenient causation.

This notion of supervenient causation does not vitiate the distinction between causally relevant and irrelevant properties. Similarly, the use of supervenient causation in the defense of the causal relevance of factors that might otherwise be eliminated by the screening-off test does not interfere with the use of the screening-off test in its classical applications distinguishing between causal processes and pseudo-processes, and distinguishing between real causal events and spurious causes, such as events that are correlated by virtue of being the results of a common cause. Common macro-level causation supervenes on common micro-level causation. Just as the relevant micro-level events may be screened off from each other by a common micro-level antecedent, so the supervening macro-level factors can be rendered causally irrelevant by the macro-level event that is their common supervenient cause.

Recently, Kim has returned to the question of "whether the same bit of behavior, say an action, can be given both a 'mechanistic' explanation, in terms of physiological processes and laws, and a 'purposive' explanation, in terms of 'reasons'" (1989a, p. 77). The particular issue had been addressed in an earlier exchange between Malcolm (1968), who tentatively concluded that such multiplication of explanations must be disallowed, and Goldman (1969), who defended the thesis that the explanations were compatible. Kim recognizes here the general issue of whether or not there can be multiple explanations for a single explanandum. He seeks to address the issue by formulating his "principle of explanatory exclusion": "No event can be given more than one *complete* and *independent* explanation" (1989a, p. 79). But, this suggestive formulation is in need of much clarification. On some readings, it is obviously unacceptable, as it conflicts with his (and my) own appreciation for supervenient causation. On others, it is unexceptionable. Much depends on how "completeness" and "independence" are understood.

While Kim never provides a general characterization of either completeness or independence, he at least considers important classes of cases.[9] The most important class for our concerns is that comprised of explanations that appeal to events supervening on events that are causally related within a single causal process. Kim explicitly recognizes that such cases of supervenient causation provide the basis for explanations that do not violate the exclusion principle (1990, p. 90). Because the supervening events are dependent upon, and realized in, the events on which they supervene, the explanations pointing to the supervenient causal relation are taken to be dependent on the explanations pointing to the relevant lower-level causal relation. Given such dependence, the macro-level explanation is not rendered problematic by the explanatory exclusion principle. It does not compete with the relevant micro-level explanation. Thus, in the psychological cases, because the psychological events "work through" the physical process on some of whose events they supervene, "we cannot regard [the psychological events] as constituting *independent* explanations of [the explanandum events]" (Kim 1989a, p. 87).

Again, Kim's discussion leads us to the result that has seemed reasonably indicated throughout this section: there is a place for macro-level explanations for phenomena that might also be redescribed and explained at a micro-level. What is required is that the macro-level process be a case of supervenient causation. In this case, macro-level features supervening on causal micro-level features can be real causal factors, and generalizations mentioning them can be nomic. As a special case, psychological generalizations can mention causal factors and be nomic insofar as these generalizations describe supervenient causal relations.

Problems arise when Kim attempts to connect up the exclusion principle to an account of the proper relation between theories. Surprisingly, Kim's own ruminations on this score lead him to a more pessimistic evaluation of the status of psychological generalizations. In the next section, I consider Kim's misgivings and argue that his (tentative) pessimism is not justified. This discussion may seem quite specialized and technical to some readers. Since it is intended to defend and elaborate on the line of thought in the present section, readers who have wearied and are averse to following a more specialized argument repudiating reductionism can safely bypass the following section. For such readers, we can round out the argument of this chapter to this point.

I have developed and evaluated the suggestion that psychological generalizations must be non-nomic due to the characteristic "sprawl" of their seemingly endless exceptions. I developed this suggestion by reflecting on Davidson's influential distinction between heteronomic and homonomic generalizations. We found in Davidson's discussions the suggestion that heteronomic generalizations could not be nomic, for their heteronomicity itself reflected their failure to key on the causally relevant factors. In application to the case of psychological generalizations, the suggestion is that their heteronomicity reflects the fact that the physical features mentioned in their sprawling and open-ended exceptions are the real causal factors. References to the psychological features are supposedly second-rate proxies for references to such causally relevant features. If we wanted to get at "the precise law at work" in the relevant cases, we would then ultimately need to move to using only the physical vocabulary. These suggestions were associated with a way of conceiving of the relation between macro-level and micro-level features of processes according to which only the micro-level features could be causally relevant.

These lines of thought have been called into question. To begin with, the suggested causal irrelevance of macro-level features mentioned in heteronomic generalizations is extremely implausible, as it would render typical generalizations in the special sciences non-nomic. This implausibility was brought home by attending to a case of a prima facie unproblematic heteronomic causal generalization from biology. This led us to seek principled ways of distinguishing those heteronomic generalizations that do get at causally relevant features from those that do not. To this end I have developed Kim's suggestion that (heteronomic) generalizations at the macro-level can deal with causally relevant features when these features supervene on causally relevant micro-level features. At the very least, then, we can conclude that the fact that psychological generalizations are invariably heteronomic, subject to sprawling, open-ended, exceptions, should not, of itself, lead us to conclude that psychological features are not causally relevant.

Now, not only is such supervenience sufficient to vindicate a feature's causal relevance, it may be necessary for causal relevance as well. It is, so far as I can see, the only defense against a macro-level feature being screened off as irrelevant. Without such supervenience, a purported explanation in terms of the higher-level properties would seem to compete with an explanation in terms of lower-level properties. As Kim makes clear, the higher-level features are bound to lose this competition.

Such considerations lead me to be sympathetic with Fodor's

(1987, pp. 27–44) argument that only "individualistically individuated" features of mental states can be causally relevant. At least this seems plausible at the level of individual psychology. (To be so individuated is for the relevant state-types to supervene on physiological features of the individual.) When discussing Burgean hypothetical cases of molecularly identical individuals in differing speech communities (cases which seem commonsensically to call for differing descriptions of mental states and actions, despite the identity of behavioral effects and dispositions), Fodor argues that the states of such individuals must have the same "causal powers." For, if the causal effects of such (physiologically identical) states are to differ:

> [t]hen, there must be some mechanism that connects the causal powers of [one of the individual's] mental states with the character of the speech community he lives in *and that does so without affecting* [that individual's] *physiology* (remember that [the two hypothetical individuals] are molecularly identical). But there is no such mechanism; you *can't* affect the causal powers of a person's mental states without affecting his physiology (Fodor 1987, p. 39).

Fodor's point then, is that to be a causally relevant feature of a macro-level process, it is necessary for there to be underlying causal mechanisms and processes in which the feature is realized; these making for the causal relevance. When we are concerned with effects at the level of individual psychology, this does seem to require that causally relevant features be realized in individual physiological mechanisms. Thus, at the level of psychological regularities and processes, all the causally relevant features are supervenient on physiological features. In Salmon's terms, it is by being so realized that psychological processes can "carry a mark." Thus, if two individuals were to be alike physiologically (or molecularly), their psychological causal features are determined as well.

Thus, for there to be causal psychological laws formulatable at the level of semantics, there must be a notion of content according to which content supervenes on the physiological. (The projected notion of content is commonly referred to as a notion of "narrow content.") Functionalist accounts of mental states have traditionally attempted to satisfy such constraints. The (perhaps modestly revisionist) account I have provided in earlier chapters is, in effect, a descendent of functionalist accounts, and it is intended to be compatible with the requirement just suggested. (In particular, see

sections 4.6 and 5.2.) Accordingly, if supervenience on causally relevant features at lower levels is indeed necessary for the causal
relevance of high-level features, and if, at the level of psychology,
the causally relevant lower-level features are physiological, this
poses no problem for my account (and its dependence on there being
nomic psychological generalizations).

At the same time, my own account could serve as a flexible
basis on which to tease out, or reconstruct, closely related notions
of content and interpretive success. For, even as there are multiple levels of analysis appropriate within the human sciences, so
there may be multiple notions of content. From the point of view
of sociology, anthropology, and the other *social* sciences, aggregates
of interacting individuals may instantiate causally relevant factors. For example, the fact that other members of a speech community would generally assent to a certain sentence in a situation
where a given speaker might not, may be quite significant. For,
within the community, a deviant speaker may be disposed to readily conform his or her behavior to that of the group once the deviance
becomes obvious. Here, we may desire an interpretive scheme
tuned to such patterns of deference within the group, and keying on
social patterns of usage. Such a scheme might, for example, reflect
the linguistic division of labor by attending to the usage within certain expert communities. Here, we seem to find a set of social features and facts supervening on (narrow) psychological features and
facts. In this way, something even more akin to commonsensical
"wide content" may perhaps prove rehabilitatable.

The upshot of all this is that psychological generalizations
seem be nomic, and psychological features can apparently be causally relevant. Their heteronomicity does not indicate that psychological features are causally irrelevant, for they can be understood
as treating of supervenient causal relations within macro-level
open systems. They are thus characteristic of the sort of heteronomic
causal generalizations found in the special sciences.

8.5: Kim's Misstep into Reductionism

Kim begins by calling our attention to two notions of theory
reduction. First, there is the common account of *conservative reduction* that received its classic formulation in Nagel (1961). On this
account, biconditional "bridge laws" connect the theoretical vocabularies of the reduced and reducing theories. This allows us to

regard the reduced theory as a subtheory of the reducing theory (and the bridge laws). In this situation, explanations afforded us by the two theories do not compete. Second, Kim draws attention to a notion of reduction elaborated by Kemeny and Oppenheim (1956). On this account, reductions need not conserve or vindicate the reduced theory, but rather could pave the way for the elimination of the reduced theory in favor of the reducing theory. Basically, this obtains when the reducing theory accounts for the data accounted for by the reduced theory, and for a good deal more data in addition.[10] Kim enunciates what I will call his "reduction test" regarding the proper relations between theories: *"If a theory is confronted by another that explains more, the only way it can survive is for it to be conservatively reduced to the latter"* (Kim 1989a, p. 99, emphasis in the original). This is just where Kim seems to go wrong. This reduction test leads him to repudiate supervenient causation indirectly, for it leads him to embrace a demanding reductionism with regard to the special sciences.[11] He ultimately would have us abandon and replace any theory that is not reducible to more fundamental theories that might be said to deal with the same phenomena.[12] This is to eliminate talk of putative properties mentioned in the abandoned theory. Common theories in the special sciences, and the properties they posit, are apparently to be replaced by radically fragmented theories for which conservative reduction is possible.

Generalizations are only as good as their home theory. So, Kim correctly reasons that, if a theory or line of theories must be abandoned, then its generalizations must likewise be junked, or at least recognized as non-nomic. The generalizations of an eliminated theory are, at best, accidental generalizations, like a mechanic's generalization that all Chryslers are lemons. This could be true, but it would not nomic. Alternatively, they might be false, by virtue of mistaken existential commitments, as is the generalization that all fires give off phlogiston. In either case, it follows from Kim's reduction test that any theory in the special sciences that fails to be conservatively reducible to more fundamental theories must be abandoned, and its generalizations must be non-nomic. But, as we have noted, intentional psychology is apparently not so reducible to more fundamental sciences, for its states are, in principle, multiply realizable in a rather spectacular manner. Accordingly, on this line of thought, intentional psychology must be replaced, and its generalizations must be recognized as non-nomic:

[V]ernacular psychology and neuroscience each claim to provide explanations for the same domain of phenomena, and because of the failure of reduction in either direction, the purported explanations must be considered independent. Hence, by the exclusion principle, one of them has to go (Kim 1989a, p. 101).

Kim (1989b, forthcoming) suggests that something of intentional psychology may be preserved by a radical fragmentation of that theory to deal with classes of systems. The idea is to deal with sufficiently homogeneous psychological systems, systems in which there is not the unmanagable multiple realizability that seems to characterize intentional psychology and many other special sciences. One would then have theories of beliefs-and-desires-in-such-and-such-systems. There would be no (causally relevant) psychological property of being a belief, or desire, or any such state as could be multiply realizable in a formidable range of supervenience bases. Instead, psychological properties would pertain to restricted classes of systems. With respect to such class-restricted psychological properties, one could formulate bridge laws of sorts: If the system is one of such-and-such a type, then it is in psychological state F just in case it is in physical state G. Kim's hope is that, with suitable specifications of types of systems, one could specify the realizing physical states in a nondisjunctive manner. Presumably such "local reductions" are in order for any theory that is, in principle, Kemeny-Oppenheim reducible but not Nagel reducible. (For example, classical genetics and cellular biology.)

It is important to recognize that Kim is *not* suggesting simply that appropriate macro-level theories must be such that they *could be* fragmented into a set of subtheories for particular classes of systems, where the fragmented results are reducible. Rather, he is suggesting that the special sciences must employ only the results of such fragmentation. After all, it is supposedly the results of such fragmentation that are conservatively reducible theories.

The suggested "local-reductionism" is unworkable. It would prohibit scientists from developing interesting and informative theories employing generalizations regarding systems whose underlying physical realization is subject to substantial multiple realizability. They would be confined to a series of very local observations regarding classes of cases. For example, the biologist would apparently not be allowed to generalize over genes, signal sequences, or any such term having a systemic-functional aspect. Instead, they will need to restrict themselves to theorizing in terms of "gene for such-and-such a feature in so-and-so physically characterized systems" without the benefit of a general notion of a "gene." Even this misgiving probably understates the problem. As Horgan (forthcoming) argues, Kim's local-reductionism underestimates the extent of multiple realizability that is characteristic of abstract special scientific properties such as those of folk psychology. In biochemical terms, the number of possible realizations of a particular belief, even *within* a *single* person may be quite large, as micro-physically distinguishable states of an individual's nervous system may make for psychologically negligible differences and indistinguishable states. All this suggests that the set of systems treated in a local reduction may need to be surprisingly narrow, much below the level of species, to say the least.

But, the problem is not just that the demand that theories be reducible is unworkable. The problem is that this demand is misguided. Kim might acknowledge the difficulties just broached and still insist that he has simply uncovered a tension in our notion of a special science that arises from deeply held scientific norms. I deny this. It is simply a misrepresentation of scientific norms. At least this is so, *provided that we are employing the common understanding of Nagelian reduction, which rules out wildly disjunctive bridge laws*. There are alternative readings of Kim's discussions. Accordingly, in this section, I develop the following indictment of Kim's reduction test: He may be read as adopting the standard, demanding notion of reduction, requiring nondisjunctive bridge laws. But, in this case, he is stuck with the ill-motivated demand for unworkable locally reduced theories, as I have just suggested. Alternatively, he may be employing a particularly undemanding notion of reduction that is compatible with there being multiple (even very many) supervenience bases for the macro-level features of a reduced theory. However, on this reading, it is difficult to understand his insistence on "local reduction" as opposed to global but massively disjunctive reductions. Further, on this reading, the reduction test turns out to be both unexceptionable and uninteresting. Thus, some of Kim's stated views must either be abandoned or treated as relatively trivial (and redundant, given his concern for supervenient causation). Let us review these options more carefully.

It is worth noting up front that one problem for Kim's test may be the notion of reduction he borrows from Nagel. The paucity of conservative reductions has led some philosophers to question whether Nagel's model captures what is really important with respect to intertheoretical relations (for example, Hull 1974; Hooker 1981;

Kitcher 1984; and Rosenberg 1985a.) I admit to sharing their concerns. As Kitcher compellingly argues, typically, the lower-level theory is related to the higher-level theory in a much more focused, piecemeal, manner than portrayed in Nagel's model.

Kim writes of one theory being "reducible" to another, not of the one actually being "reduced" to the other.[13] The reduction test is that if we have good reason to believe that a higher-level theory is Kemeny-Oppenheim reducible but not Nagel reducible, then we should eliminate it in favor of a lower-level replacement. But, is "reducibility" to be understood as reducibility-in-practice or reducibility-in-principle?

There is reason to believe that that the reduction of theories in the special sciences, including psychology, in either Kemeny-Oppenheim fashion or in Nagel fashion, would commonly need to be fabulously complex.[14] Quite probably, it would outrun our expressive and computational resources, and is thus impossible in practice. This is not to say simply that producing the reductions envisioned would not be worth the trouble (although that is probably so as well), but that they may be more trouble than we are capable of. If so, then when Kim's reduction test is understood in terms of reducibility-in-practice, theories in the special sciences, such as psychological theories, meet the test simply by virtue of not being Kemeny-Oppenheim reducible.[15] Of course, one can set aside such concerns for expressive and computational limitations when applying Kim's reduction test, but then one moves from a concern with in-practice reducibility to a focus on in-principle reducibility. In this latter context, we do not pause to worry over the expressibility and computational tractibility of the envisioned reductions.

Thinking of in-principle reducibility makes Kemeny-Oppenheim reducibility a relatively straightforward matter. Given how we are understanding what it is to account for "the same data," if the properties dealt within the higher-level theory do indeed supervene on the properties dealt with in the lower-level theory, then, bracketing concerns over accessibility of initial conditions, expressibility, and computational tractibility, the higher-level theory is Kemeny-Oppenheim reducible to the lower-level theory, provided that the higher-level theory describes supervenient causes. *For a theory to deal with supervenient causes is sufficient then for its in-principle Kemeny-Oppenheim reducibility* (at least to an ideal theory at the level of the supervenience bases).[16]

However, in-principle Nagel reducibility is not so straightforward. If the higher-level theory deals with supervenient causes having multiple realization bases, this may be sufficient to insure its Nagel reducibility to ideal lower-level theories, and it may be sufficient to insure that it is not so reducible, depending on how exactly Nagel reducibility is understood.

As explained above, Nagel reducibility requires bridge laws connecting the lower-level and higher-level properties. To make possible the derivation of the higher-level theory as a special case of the lower-level theory, these bridge laws must be universal biconditionals. However, given the typical multiple realizability of supervenient properties, the characterizations in terms of the lower-level theory employed in the needed biconditionals will need to be disjunctive, even wildly disjunctive. The question becomes whether or not this itself gets in the way of Nagel reducibility, properly understood. That is, the question becomes whether or not such disjunctive reductions are properly taken as cases of conservative reduction. Some philosophers, including both friends of the special sciences such as Fodor (1981) and Kincaid (1990a), and detractors such as Kim (1989b, forthcoming), have thought that proper Nagel reducibility cannot be significantly disjunctive. They differ, of course, on what to make of this. Fodor and Kincaid find no resulting blemish, while Kim, at least in some passages, finds such cases marred beyond acceptibility.

If no limits are placed on the disjunctive complexity of the envisioned bridge laws, then whenever a higher-level scientific theory correctly characterizes supervenient causal relations, this would seem to make it in principle Nagel reducible. Thus, Kim (1990, p. 28–29; 1989b, p. 3) argues that supervenience probably guarantees such disjunctive reduction. He even seems ready to call the higher-level theory "reducible to" the other, at least when the bridge laws involve finitely characterizable infinite disjunctive formulations (Kim 1990, p. 30). Similarly, Rosenberg (1985a, pp. 113–16) argues that, provided the higher-level properties supervene on a finite (although perhaps very large) set of lower-level properties, in principle reducibility is at hand. Whether *we* can comprehend the relevant bridge laws and use them in deriving the higher-level theory from the lower-level one is a matter of our own limited expressive and computational resources. But, for purposes of this discussion of reducibility-in-principle, we are setting aside such limitations. Therefore, for any special scientific theory describing supervenient causes, and with respect to some ideal lower-level theory, reduction of the former to the latter is possible in principle. Thus, *when we are being so lax with what counts as reducibility, I need have no quarrel with Kim's reducibility test for acceptable theories. Theories in a special science dealing well with supervenient causes will pass muster. Indeed they must, for any such theory will be both Kemeny-Oppenheim reducible (in principle) and also Nagel reducible (in principle).*

Again, several philosophers have been understandably dissatisfied with the above modest version of Nagel reducibility. They have insisted that significant reduction requires more in the way of bridge laws than the wildly disjunctive, unmanagable, correlations envisioned above. While they have accordingly been more skeptical regarding the reducibility of theories in the special sciences, they have commonly also been less taken with reducibility as a mark of good special science theories.

Fodor, for example, suggests that significant reduction will be based on biconditionals connecting "natural kinds" as picked out independently by the reduced and reducing theories. Thus, he states that reductionism in the philosophy of mind is committed to there being "natural kind predicates in an ideally completed physics which correspond to each natural kind predicate in any ideally completed special science" (Fodor 1981, p. 131). To be a "natural kind predicate in" a particular theory is, it seems, to be relatively simply formulated in the descriptive vocabulary characteristic of that theory. It is never clear just what constructions on the basic vocabulary of the reducing science are allowed.[17] However, it is clear that disjunctive formulations are thought not to characterize natural kinds. Ideally, the bridge laws of a significant reduction of higher-level theory to a lower-level theory are to hit upon some lower-level characteristic, or set of characteristics, that all and only cases of the higher-level kind have in common. Something like this requirement on significant reduction is needed if in-principle reducibility is to be distinguished from supervenience.

Similarly, despite his arguments in Kim (1990), Kim (1989b, forthcoming) seems to insist that significant reductions must proceed in terms of bridge laws that characterize the reduced property in terms of a nondisjunctive property. This is just what his recommended "local reductions" are to deliver. By fragmenting the higher-level theory into a set of theories each dealing with a restricted class of systems, Kim would avoid the obstacle that he, as well as Fodor, finds multiple realizability to pose for "uniform reduction."

But, notice again how radically this fragments the special sciences. What is reduced is *not* psychological theory, or cellular biology, and so forth, but rather "the psychology of such-and-such a set of systems," and "the cellular biology of such-and-such a set of systems," *where the systems are narrowly enough drawn to make the higher-level properties uniformly realizable.* On Kim's principle, the more general, but irreducible, theories in the special sciences must be eliminated and replaced by local theories that are reducible. But, again, it is all too easy to fail to recognize just how radical this proposal is, by failing to recognize the extent of multiple realizability. After all, as Horgan (forthcoming) points out, common illustrations of multiple realizability in terms of say computers constructed out of differing materials tend to obscure the extent of the problems facing advocates of uniform reductions:

> Multiple realizability might well begin at home. For all we know (and I emphasize that we really *don't* now know), the intentional mental states we attribute to one another might turn out to be radically multiply realizable, at the neurobiological level of description, *even in humans*; indeed, even in *individual* humans; indeed, even in an individual human *given the structure of his central nervous system at a single moment of his life.*

Similarly, Kincaid (1990a) has argued that even a rather low-level cellular biological theory, such as that of the signal sequence, can often be the subject of multiple realization of its central predicates. Now, Kim's suggested reducibility test would seem to require us to abandon such general theories. At the very least, then, local reduction could turn out to be feasible only for very narrowly constrained classes of systems, and many of the special sciences would probably each be fragmented into thousands of "very special sciences," each with its micro-theory. With some understatement, Kim (forthcoming) remarks that his reflections "lead to the further conclusion that if we accept the phenomenon of multiple realization for psychological states, psychology becomes fragmented, losing its unity as a single, integrated science."

Now, before we junk the special sciences for the "very special sciences," we should pause to recall how we got to this point. We have been considering Kim's reduction test: if a theory is Kemeny-Oppenheim reducible, but is not also Nagel reducible, it should be eliminated in favor of a specialized version of the Kemeny-Oppenheim reducing theory. In particular, we are concerned to decide whether this principle is itself well-motivated. Before any headway could be made on this question, we found the principle in need of clarification. The principle proved misguided when reducibility-in-practice was at issue, for that seemed too contingent a matter to reflect what generalizations could be nomic and get at causal factors and patterns of dependency in the course of events. In any case, all, or almost all, special scientific theories seems vacuously to pass this version of the test. On the other hand, when we consider reducibility-in-principle, and place no significant limitations on the complexity of the bridge laws employed in the reduction, then the principle has no force in cases where the theories are antecendently acceptable by virtue of dealing with supervenient causes—all such theories pass. The principle is then plausible, but empty. We have just now been investigating the force of the principle when conceived in terms of reducibility in principle, and when the bridge laws are not allowed to be disjunctive. We find that the principle, so construed, is certainly not empty, but has rather troubling results (I would say almost absurd results). Still, at least we now know what the principle must amount to, if it is not to be empty.

The question now must be: Why should one hold such a principle? Given the rather troubling consequences that it spawns, is there really good reason to hold (the nonempty variant of) Kim's reduction test?

One might propose the reduction test in order to insure that, whatever properties are appealed to in higher-level theories and explanations, these turn out to be causally relevant ones. If the properties could be reduced to causally relevant properties at the lower-levels, this would insure their causal relevance. However, as we have seen, such concerns seem to be addressable by imposing a much less demanding requirement on the special sciences: the requirement that they deal with supervenient causes.

Of course, the classical motivation for reduction requirements has been the concern for a significant "unity of science." This is a worthy concern, and one not to be sacrificed. However, to require strong, uniform, or nondisjunctive Nagel reducibility for theories in the special sciences is a misguided way of pursuing the unity of science. The point has been argued by Fodor (1981), Kitcher (1984), Rosenberg (1985a), Horgan (forthcoming), and Kincaid (1990a). The case that has been compiled against reductionism as a prerequisite to the unity of science is overwhelming. Put simply, the unity of science is best understood as a combination of two claims: (1) the deep logic of explanation and testing in the various sciences is much the same; (2) the various special sciences and the more general sciences are ultimately interwoven in a patchwork of mutually supporting bodies of information regarding the various levels of organization found in nature. The present book stands as a testament to the first claim in application to the human sciences, and this commonly is taken to be the most challenging domain for such claims. But the second claim is the one of most significance in the present context. For it omits any mention of intertheoretic reducibility (in the strong sense).

There are significant levels of organization in phenomena. In describing these levels of organization, and in accounting for phenomena at some levels, we develop special sciences. In developing the special sciences, we commonly formulate "abstract" concepts, for example, concepts that have to do with functional roles within a system. As Horgan (forthcoming) puts it, such higher-level concepts are "strongly realization neutral," which is to say they "are neutral both (i) about *how* they are realized at lower theoretical levels (and ultimately at the level of physics), and (ii) about whether or not they are *uniquely* realized at lower levels (and ultimately the physics level)." This is just what Fodor (1981, p. 133) is driving at when he writes:

> The reason it is unlikely that every kind corresponds to a physical kind is just that (a) interesting generalizations (e.g., counterfactual supporting generalizations) can often be made about events whose physical descriptions have nothing in common; (b) it is often the case that *whether* the physical descriptions of the events subsumed by such generalizations have anything in common is, in an obvious sense, entirely irrelevant to the truth of the generalizations, or to their interestingness, or to their degree of confirmation, or indeed, to any of their epistemologically important properties; and (c) the special sciences are very much in the business of formulating generalizations of this kind.

Because there are such levels of organization describable in abstract, realization-neutral terms, and because such organization gives rise to supervenient causal processes, the special sciences are not to be eliminated, even though the properties on which they focus are commonly multiply realizable in a way that renders them not uniformly reducible.

Such levels of organization provide an objective basis for the special sciences. The special sciences are not simply expedients forced upon us by our own limited abilities to comprehend and reason from magnificently complex arrangements at the level of general physics. Instead, they are the result of our investigations registering regularities at differing levels of organization. To use Fodor's (1981, p. 144) formulation, "there are special sciences not because of the nature of our epistemic relation to the world, but because of the way the world is put together." (On the other hand, we should not ignore the epistemic fallout of these matters, as also reflected in Kincaid's [1990a] discussion of the epistemic as well as objective bases of realization-neutral concepts in the special sciences.)

Still, in the face of the proliferation of special sciences, we can still recognize an important unity of science. The key to understanding what the unity of science comes to is close, careful reflection on actual theorizing on various related levels. Attention to in-principle Nagel reducibility will not yield an appreciation for the unity of the special sciences. For, while the special sciences may be in-principle reducible to more fundamental sciences, given we allow wildly disjunctive bridge laws, this really does not help us understand the unity of science. At most it reflects the concern that the processes posited in the special sciences be physically realizable, be cases of supervenient causation, even though we will commonly find the characterization of the full variety of their possible realizations intractable in practice. On the other hand, the special sciences just are not in-principle Nagel reducible when we do not sanction disjunctive bridge laws. Still, there are, both in principle and in practice, rich interconnections between theories in the various sciences. To appreciate these is to understand the unity of science. This is where the superb work of writers such as Kitcher, Rosenberg, Kincaid, among others, is particularly invaluable.

For example, in a rich and generalizable discussion of classical genetics and molecular biology, Kitcher (1984) characterizes three important sorts of connections between theories at different levels. These fall substantially short of Nagelian reduction. First, lower-level theories can serve to *vindicate* otherwise *problematic presuppositions* of higher-level theories. For example, geneticists took for granted a process of gene replication. How else could genes be passed along? However, they had no account of this process, and the replication of such complicated molecules seemed problematic. Watson and Crick's work then served to vindicate this problematic presupposition. (Further, it did so without providing bridge laws telling us what pieces of the chromosonal material, the DNA, counted as a gene, a different gene, a gene for such-and-such a trait, and so forth. They simply allowed us to understand how the set of genes on a chromosone could be replicated.) Second, Kitcher explains that lower-level theories can induce a *conceptual refinement* in a higher-level theory. Genetic mutations were initially understood in terms of the production of deviant phenotypes. However, when we came to understand the mechanism of replication, and how there can be occasional copying errors there, the possibility of hidden mutations could be recognized. In replication, the addition, subtraction, or substitution of a nucleotide could result in a segment that nevertheless codes for the same protein as was coded for by the original allele, or in a segment that produces a trivially different protein. In either case, we may be said to have a mutation without the production of a deviant phenotype. Now, while the lower-level theory here exercises a significant role in framing the concepts of the higher-level theory, this does not make for the sort of connection needed for reduction. After all, one is not conceiving the higher-level terms solely in terms of the lower-level theory. Rather, the lower-level terms are "mixed into" the higher-level theory to refine its higher-level characterizations. Third, the lower-level theory can provide what Kitcher calls an *explanatory extension* of the higher-level theory. This occurs when the lower-level theory allows one to explain a premise that itself features prominently in an explanation characteristic of many higher-level explanations. For example, molecular biology might account for the connection between a particular genotype and a particular phenotype. As Kitcher notes, this sort of case comes closest to the reductionist ideal. Still, it falls far short in two respects. To begin with, it is typically very local, as it accounts for a particular connection of a sort posited by classical genetics. Additionally, in typical cases, the account is not provided in terms of the lower-level theory alone. Thus, accounting for the production and interaction of particular proteins to produce a given phenotype from a set of DNA codings typically requires a good deal of attention to higher-level context, for example, attention to cytological conditions and developmental context (Kitcher 1984, pp. 367–68).

What we find here is that the special and the more fundamental sciences work together, mutually reinforcing each other. The lower-level sciences vindicate presuppositions at the higher level, sometimes by providing accounts of mechanisms realizing, in particular classes of cases, the processes and capacities presupposed by the higher-level theory. They may even contribute to accounting for, or fleshing out, certain central premises in lower-level explanations. On the other hand, they commonly can do this only when themselves supplemented by attention to higher-level organization that will always to some extent remain nonreductively characterized. That is, we find a "constant shifting back and forth across levels" (Kitcher 1984, p. 371). One might even justifiably talk of theories at different levels being (nonreductively) "linked by, or perhaps incorporated in, an *integrated interlevel* theory" (Kincaid 1990a; see also Maull 1977, Darden and Maull 1977).

I think that it is thus fair to say that the demand for uniform reducibility is not well motivated by the concern for the unity of science. There is a nonreductive unity to science, and that is all. But, if the reducibility test cannot be grounded in the unity of science, then it apparently cannot be grounded at all. As a characterization of the proper relation between theories at different levels, it is misguided and should be abandoned. Let us now review where all this has gotten us.

After noting how many reservations regarding the nomic status of the generalizations in the special sciences, and in psychology in particular, derive from a suspicion that such generalizations cannot deal with the real causal factors, in earlier sections of this chapter I developed the suggestion, found in Kim's own writings (1984), that generalizations appealing to supervenient causes do get at real causal factors. However, we found in Kim's writing an apparently conflicting suggestion that nonreducible supervenience is inadequate. This suggestion is contained in his reduction test for the acceptibility of theories (including theories in the special sciences): if a theory is Kemeny-Oppenheim reducible, then if it is not also Nagel reducible, it should be eliminated in favor of a specialized version of the Kemeny-Oppenheim reducing theory. In order to insure that we are not asking too little of generalizations in the special sciences, we have been considering Kim's reduction test in the present section. In particular, we have been investigating whether this reduction test plausibly adds anything to the demand that the special sciences describe and theorize in terms of supervenient causation at the macro-level. Must theories in such special sciences be reducible to ideal lower-level theories? If so, reducible in what sense?

I have considered a series of reconstructions. If the reducibility of concern in the reduction test is reducibility-in-practice, then the principle has little, if any, application. After all, few special-scientific theories are reducible-in-practice in either of the fashions at issue. In good measure, this may be a function of our limits as information representers and processors. And, it is difficult to appreciate why such limitations should preclude us from using theories that deal with supervenient causes. After all, such irreducibility does not preclude us from accounting for the supervenient causal relation in any one instance. On the other hand, if the reducibility of concern in the test is a matter of reducibility-in-principle, the test is either trivial or leads to absurdly strong and disturbing results. If few limits are placed on the complexity of the reducing-science side of the envisioned bridge laws, then reducibility seems to follow upon a theory's treating supervenient causes. So, if we demand that the special sciences attend to real causal factors, then, insofar as such theories deal with supervenient causal factors, the reducibility test adds nothing. It is then satisfied by all theories that we would independently accept. On the other hand, if significant limits are placed on the complexity or structure of the reducing-science side of the envisioned bridge laws, we get the result that, at best, the special sciences must be fragmented into "the very special sciences" which are, in principle, "uniformly" or nondisjunctively reducible. This is an undesirable result, or so it seems to me. When we then cast about for what would ultimately ground the reduction test, and what might then motivate our swallowing this undesirable result, we find a concern for the unity of science. But we also find that the unity of science can be underwritten by nonreductive relations between the various disciplines. Thus, ultimately, we find the reduction test either trivial or unacceptable. With a free conscience we can rest content in generalizations dealing with supervenient causes.

9

Summary

The work of this book is basically complete; I have developed complementary accounts of interpretation and explanation in the human sciences. Of course, I am under no illusion that I have said anything like all that there is to be said on these fundamental topics, or that I have said it in a way that forestalls all misunderstandings. Along with all authors of books in philosophy, I must admit that some important points stand in need of much further development, and, doubtless, there are points where what I have written is not as clear it should be. Still, I hope that my discussions provide ample reasons for taking seriously the position that I have sought to flesh out. I have sought to give compelling reasons for believing that the combined accounts formulate the basic epistemology of social and psychological inquiry better than do competing accounts. To this end, I have discussed particular interpretive and explanatory work in order to indicate how my account squares with the bases for judgments made by many actual investigators. Accordingly, I offer these discussions as a reflective codification of the practice of inquiry in the social and psychological sciences.

This codification has an important unifying dimension: it exhibits some of the deep continuities that obtain between our inquiries in all realms of knowledge. We are brought to see that what counts as justified belief in the human sciences qualifies on the basis of standards also informing the natural and biological sciences. On the one hand, we find that the justification of interpretation in the social sciences is not sui generis; rather, interpretive understanding is a species of the familiar genus: theory-laden observation of phenomena. On the other hand, the account of intentional explanation advanced here is likewise unifying; intentional explanation, including both rationalizing and irrationalizing explanation, is found to be a species of the common genus: cause-describing answers to why-questions. Such answers draw on nomic generalizations that allow us to appreciate what causally relevant factors in the antecedent course of events made a difference to the occurrence of the event to be explained. Such explanations are themselves found to be complementary to the other genus of explanations, explanations that answer how-questions by analyzing systems. Much work in cognitive psychology can be understood in these terms, it provides answers to how-questions and, in turn, informs rationalizing and irrationalizing explanation as answers to why-questions.

Several chapters have focused on somewhat ancillary issues, supporting or elaborating the central line of argument. While such elaborations and defenses help to fill out the account presented here, it is important not to get one's attention so focused on points of detail, even important detail, that one thereby loses sight of the central lines of argument. So, let me remind the reader of these.

To begin with, I have argued that interpretation is subject to one fundamental constraint: the principle of explicability. This constraint is operative in all theory-laden observation (and all observation is theory-laden): we are to understand what we observe so as to find the phenomena explicable in light of general information regarding what sorts of things there are and how they interact. (Care must be taken so that theory does not become self-vindicating by virtue of this observation-informing role.) Accordingly, when physicists "observe high-energy neutrinos," their results—their observations—are informed by a wealth of theory. "Such neutrinos can best account for such-and-such a sample being extracted from a pool of cleaning fluid one mile below the earth's surface," they might say. This would be to settle on an interpretation, on a set of observations, by reasoning to the best explanation for their sample, given extant physics and chemistry. In much the same fashion, a police officer observing an accident scene interprets long skid marks on dry pavement as reflecting a high rate of speed that contributed to the accident. Again, generalizations (here regarding pavement types and conditions, tire types, car types, and so forth) inform this interpretation, leading to the conclusion that only a high rate of speed could plausibly account for, or explain, the traces observed. The officer can be said to observe that the car had been traveling at a high rate of speed. Similarly, when an anthropologist interprets certain practices, this is a matter of finding what is said and done something one can account for, given what else of a general and particular nature one has (at least provisionally) settled upon.

The principle of explicability enables us to appreciate the

dynamic of controversies regarding particular anthropological interpretations. Thus, for example, we saw how Spiro and Leach argued
for and against interpretations of the Tully River natives by insisting that the favored interpretation made what was believed (and
done) explicable, while the alternative interpretations made what
was supposedly believed (or done) inexplicable.

Further, this understanding of the central constraint on interpretation allows us to account for the limited force of the popular
treatments of interpretation in terms of the principle of charity.
That is to say, we are able to account for why one should interpret
in roughly those ways that are indicated by the principle of charity.
What is more, we are able to provide a principled account of where
we should deviate from charitable interpretation. Adherents quickly recognized that the principle of charity is subject to multiple qualifications: it is progressively less constraining as interpretation
proceeds, and it is subject to a range of qualifications having to do
with sorts of errors and successes. All this might be taken to indicate that the principle of charity is, at best, one among a set of
competing fundamental constraints on interpretation, or, at worst,
subject to ad hoc refinements. However, with the principle of explicability, a more satisfying unitary account proves possible: it provides a deep, principled, motivation of the refinements on the
principle of charity and for its differing force across interpretive
contexts. All that is needed is an appreciation for the way in which
the concern for explicability, characteristic of theory-laden observation, interacts with extant and prospective general expectations
regarding human cognitive functioning and human social life. In
this manner, the principle of explicability provides us with a (refining) reduction of the principle of charity—the principle of charity
comes to be subsumed as a rough, derivative, principle.

The resulting account is, however, more than just an elegant
account of interpretation, although it certainly is that. Its virtues
are not limited to the trading of multiple fundamental principles (or
ad hoc modifications on a single principle) for a single principle
formulating the basic constraints on interpretation. Nor does it
do the view full justice to add that it allows one to account for
nuances of interpretive practice using this one principle (taken
together with our evolving general understanding of cognitive and
social life, of course); although, again, this seems no mean virtue.
Nor is it enough to say that the account even allows us to understand
changes, refinements, in interpretive practice, and in interpretations
across time. Although it can certainly do this, for it leads us to

appreciate how these developments are consequences of refinements in the psychological and sociological expectations that inform interpretation. While the account advanced here thus provides a particularly elegant, simple, unified, yet nuanced, account of interpretation, allowing us to appreciate the constraints on interpretive practice at any given time, and changes in such constraints across time, I think that *the ultimate virtue of this account is that it makes sound epistemic sense.* To view interpretation as theory-laden observation allows us to see the coherence-theoretic sense in the practice of interpretation. The myriad of possible interpretations for a given set of behaviors comes to be narrowed, not by some arbitrary constraints, and not by some imposition that has little to do with what can be expected to obtain in the world as a descriptive fact, but rather by the use of our general knowledge that has to date fared well, and that will be checked further.

As we saw in the third and seventh chapters, the proper use of theoretical resources does not constitute such an imposition on what is observed that the theories employed there are bound to be confirmed, becoming self-vindicating. Enough theory is involved, that the various components of it can serve as mutually checking, in the manner of bootstrap testing. Empirical success is not guaranteed, for there is just no guarantee that we will prove able to adequately model what is observed using our best present theory. (In fact, at this point, success would be shocking.) Rather, what I advocate is the epistemically sound strategy of seeking to fit what is observed within our best descriptive understanding of "how the world is," particularly with respect to the cognitive capacities and social processes of the creatures under study. As I have explained, in this endeavor, we must continually stand ready to make adjustments, either in our particular interpretations, or in our general expectations, or in both. The principles governing when and where to make adjustments are, I take it, familiar, for they are the same as those governing theory building, testing, and application in all scientific domains: simplicity of scheme, relative confirmation of relevant bits of theory, the relative promise of lines of research, and so forth.

The preceding paragraphs reflect what seems to me the telling core of methodological naturalism. If the thrust of these remarks is not assimilated, the insistence that the logic of inquiry in the social sciences is basically the same as that informing the natural sciences will doubtless strike some as intellectual imperialism. It will be wondered why there should be just this one broad approach to the acquisition of knowledge. The answer is that, in the various domains of inquiry, we are faced with choosing the most reliable means for pursuing our goal: veridical information about a certain set of phenomena. In the human sciences, we want to know what people do believe, value, and so forth. We want to know how these states are brought about, how they interact, and to what effect. There are a wealth of important questions to be teased out of these general questions, but they all have to do with matters formulatable in descriptive claims. (This is not to say that we would not want to modify our own ways upon learning of others' ways, or upon learning more about our own ways. We may want to make practical use of the information we garner. We may acquire different values in the bargain. But, this is not the primary business of the social and psychological sciences. First off, we want to get the descriptive story straight.) In light of these concerns, the force of the preceding paragraphs becomes apparent: (1) the logic of inquiry informing the natural sciences is, at base, a matter of *using* our best bets in the way of *descriptive information*, putting them to work in further inquiry in order to get more, or better, information; (2) from the point of view of epistemology, we are well advised to do the same in the human sciences.

The point is similar to that made in connection with rationalizing explanation regarding the sort of information needed to support explanations generally. There I noted that the normative propriety of a course of action or thought had no bearing on the probability of whether of not that course of action or thought is instanced, as long as we have no descriptive information regarding whether that course of action or thought corresponds to human cognitive capacities. So we found that, in explanation, the normative propriety or impropriety of an intentional state or action was strictly irrelevant. By the same token, in seeking to find out general and particular truths about the natural, social, and cognitive world, we are faced with the task of fitting what we can within cohesive bodies of interrelated descriptive knowledge. These *bodies of knowledge are what allow us to pin down* (or at least narrow substantially) *what it could be that we are observing*. Recall the experimental physicist mining for high-energy neutrino-events who employs a range of theory (from chemistry, particle physics, and cosmology) to determine what it is that is plausibly observed. Again, the same sort of investment of provisional descriptive information in the interest of getting more is found in the officer's investigation of an accident scene; and this hypothetical example also reflects the irrelevance of normative principles, qua normative. The officer probably would think the high rate of speed he has uncovered was a violation of a normative principle. But, the normative principle is not employed in judging the speed of the vehicles in question. The officer does not interpret the evidence so as to find the driver in conformity with traffic norms. Absent information regarding the driver's dispositions to conform to certain normative principles, such principles have no bearing on what could plausibly have left the traces confronted. (Of course, if the officer knows the driver, and that the driver was generally inclined to adhere to all traffic regulations, this descriptive information might have a bearing on the officer's observations.)

To borrow Quine's figure, we are faced with rebuilding our ship of theory while remaining afloat in it. Since "the ship" is to deliver to us veridical representations of the world, the relevant materials to employ here are materials that have been fashioned, so far as possible, to deal with the way things are, not the way things ought to be. For the latter claims have, we must admit, a much more attenuated relation to the ways things are. In fact, evaluative positions, or normative principles, have nothing to do with how things are (unless they inform a particular person's actions, in which case their impact is already registered in descriptive information regarding that person's intentional states and psychological dispositions).

The account of intentional explanation presented in chapters 5 and 6 allows us to appreciate the force of such explanations by fitting them into a general account of explanation. Explanations are answers to why-questions and how-questions. Explanations of the two sorts are intimately connected, and these connections are important for an account of intentional explanation.

Systems can exhibit striking properties that call for explanation by raising the question of *how the system manages to realize that property*. Thus we can explain how temperature is realized in gases, or in other states. We can explain how our bodies manage to maintain their temperature, or the concentration of glucose within the blood, within certain narrow limits. Often the property whose realization interests us is dispositional, a matter of systematic responses to inputs or circumstances. Such cases raise the question of *how the system manages to respond in the systematic ways that it does*. Thus, we might wonder how a given radio manages to present us with a range of audible signals, given its settings and impinging electromagnetic radiation. This would call for the analysis of the radio in terms of the interactions between its components in view of their capacities. Such analyses, explaining how a dispositional feature is realized in a system, are called functional analyses. Building on Cummins's work, I have argued that intentional explanations proceed against a background of such functional analyses. Interpretation, as the attribution of contentful states to a system, is understood against a background of a more or less explicit analysis of the cognitive dispositions of the systems of the sort in question. This analysis then supports explanations employing the results of interpretation.

The functional analyses underlying intentional explanation are *interpretive analyses* in which the dispositions of the system are represented by transition laws resembling rules of inference or reasoning. By attending to the interactive realization of simpler dispositions, such analyses allow us to account for how human beings have the capacity to deal with their environment in systematic ways, to arrive at certain conclusions from certain starting points, and so forth. There is no suggestion here that the "capacities" analyzed are themselves optimal or even ultimately desirable. Much contemporary work in cognitive psychology is best understood as attempts to refine our representation of such human cognitive dispositions. Much of "folk psychology" is best understood as also providing a crude representation of such dispositions.

Now, characterizing the dispositions of a system in terms of inputs and outputs gives rise to transition laws for the relevant class of systems. The transition laws spawned by such analyses serve to underwrite a further set of explanations. We commonly are led to wonder *why a system came to be in a certain state*, why it came to have a certain property. To answer such a why-question, we must come to appreciate what it was about the antecedent course of events that, had things been different in those respects, the system would not have ended up in the state that it did, or at least it would have been less likely to have so ended up. To get at these matters, and thus to answer such why-questions, we must draw upon our knowledge of the dispositions of the system, as represented in transition laws. It is in these terms that we understand common intentional explanations. Reflection on particular cases of intentional explanation (such as the hypothetical shark-film cases) is reassuring, as this reveals that such explanations fit the familiar profile of sensitivity to background information characteristic of generalization-based explanations.

As noted, this account is attractive because it allows us to accommodate the range of applications of intentional attributions by reflecting on the interconnections between explanations as answers to how-questions and explanations answering why-questions surveyed just now: (1) by understanding intentional attributions against a background of interpretive analyses as a sort of functional analysis, much work in cognitive psychology is given a philosophical articulation, as is the much less systematic folk-psychological decompositions of decisions and reasoning; (2) by understanding intentional explanations of particular actions and states as singular causal explanations, these also become philosophically recognizable. Thus, the integrated account of explanations as answers to how-questions and why-questions yields an integrated account of the range of intentional explanation and theorizing.

Several important consequences fall out of the account of intentional explanation. To begin with, we see clearly that rationalizing explanation and irrationalizing explanation are, in an important sense, on a par. Attributions of certain forms of irrationality can be, and are, every bit as explanatory as attributions of rationality. Of course, investigators may justifiably tend to think in terms of certain forms of rationality—within limits, they may, for example, approach social phenomena in terms of decision-theoretic rationality. However, if there is to be any such preference for rationalizing over irrationalizing explanation, this must arise from the theoretical background that supports both; it must be a theory-dependent preference. Such preferences can arise from the application of extant theory, or from the relative progressiveness of work on theories within a research program. As argued in chapter 5, such theory-based preferences allow us to account for what concerns for rationality one finds in the social and psychological sciences, while the general account of explanation allows us to understand how we readily reconcile ourselves to, and even seek, irrationalizing explanations in particular cases.

The accounts of intentional explanation and interpretation that have been provided here are clearly complementary. According to the account of interpretation, through the principle of explicability interpretation comes to be informed by the full range of our descriptive information regarding human psychology and social processes. This presupposes that the relevant explanations draw on such information. Further, according to the account of interpretation, attributions of certain forms of irrationality can have a place in an explanatory account just as well as attributions of certain forms of rationality. In such cases, the relevant supporting information must lead us to expect the particular sort of rationality or irrationality attributed. In these respects, the account of explanation supports the account of interpretation. On the other hand, the account of explanation presented here requires that there be nomic psychological generalizations. In this regard, the account of interpretation is supportive, for a recurrent theme in this book has been that there are no special constraints on interpretation that preclude the formulation of nomic generalizations in intentional terms. For example, in chapters 3 and 4, it is found that whatever the minimal level of rationality attributable to others, this is a theory-determined matter, and not some inflexible methodological constraint that might get in the way of formulating empirically fruitful generalizations. In chapter 7, we find that the account of interpretation enables us to understand how even central components of psychological theory could undergo the sort of bootstrap testing, and thus empirical refinement, that is characteristic of nomic generalizations.

Once we have come to terms with these general lines of argument, we can appreciate those chapters that develop ancillary, but important, lines of thought. Thus, while the second and third chapters develop the basic account of interpretation, chapter 4 engages in a bit of elaboration by application. After the principle of charity is shown to be a rough rule of thumb, derivative upon extant theoretical expectations for cognitive and social processes, the now common suggestion that there is an a priori minimal level of rationality attributable to all intentional agents is considered. The suggested constraints are commonly thought to be different in kind from constraints on inquiries in other domains. However, the suggested need to attribute minimal rationality is readily recast as having to do with the centrality of certain expectations within the corpus of contemporary psychological and sociological knowledge. Notably, constraints of this sort are characteristic of scientific inquiry generally. Whatever the minimal level of rationality that is set by central theoretical principles, it provides no basis for seeing the human sciences as significantly different in kind from the other sciences. Thus, chapter 4 can be seen as providing a further defense of the results in the preceding chapters; it shows that the account of interpretation developed earlier can be naturally elaborated to account for the common conviction that attributions of rationality somewhat stubbornly play an important place in intentional interpretation.

Similarly, while the basic account of intentional explanation is set out in chapters 5 and 6, we find that this account presupposes that there are nomic generalizations which can support the explanations called for. The following two chapters then defend this presupposition against several contemporary challenges. Of course, in the course of such defenses, further light is shed on the nature of the envisioned explanations and their supporting generalizations.

Notes

Chapter 1

1. Obviously, this should not be taken to mean that all nomic generalizations must be false, but that there must be ways of subjecting such principles to empirical checks in which the observations used in such tests could, were the generalizations incorrect, indicate this by failing to conform.

2. Actually Davidson provides for nomic generalizations that are not strictly universal. However, on his account, nomic statistical generalizations must be such that, using only the vocabulary of the relevant domain, they could be improvable to a point that could not be further refined with qualifications employing predicates from another domain. For example, the irreducibly statistical generalizations of quantum physics supposedly cannot be improved by qualifying them in chemical, biological, or other terms.

Chapter 2

1. Davidson distinguishes between the sort of theory of meaning he envisions, which takes a structure inspired by Tarski's semantic account of truth, and translation manuals. For my purposes here, the differences are not significant. And, in any case, I have not supposed that what I have called translation schemes will have a characteristic structure that is either different from or like what Davidson is supposing for his theories.

2. Unfortunately it leads Davidson to sketch a idealized unified approach to interpretation that "is not . . . meant to throw any direct light on how in real life we come to understand each other" (1980e, p. 12).

3. Quine would probably not deny this. However, his discussions are not directed to indicating how this fuller set of concerns can be pursued.

4. Turner actually talks of implications within the metalanguage as determining the implications of the interpretive scheme, thus supposing a

Tarskian model (1979, p. 411). However, his discussion shows that he is assuming that the target-language is included in the metalanguage.

5. Paul Roth reminds me that there are important differences between those earlier debates over attributions of rationality and irrationality associated with Winch's (1958, 1964) and the later discussions centering on the principle of charity. Accentuating these differences, one might think that the earlier debates have to do just with what is to count as rational across forms of life, while the later debate has to do with the extent to which one must find rationality (and correctness) under interpretation. However, if taken as more than a characterization of emphases in these philosophical discussions, this contrast is overdrawn. What is emphasized does not exhaust what is said. In Winch's writings, one can find clear commitments to what, within the context of a neo-Wittgensteinian approach to language, amounts to a principle of charity enjoining us to find those we interpret rational in an suitably broadened sense. Winch advances certain interpretations to illustrate how we should go about "understanding a primitive society." Careful attention to how he supports his favored interpretations, and repudiates alternatives, reveals his principle of charity. Roughly, Winch's interpreter must attribute uses, or "points," to activities and utterances within a way of life so that those activities come to be seen as well adapted to their points. When meaning is intimately associated with use, this is a charitable strategy. What people say and do come to be seen as rational, given the uses to which their activity is directed. (For details, see Henderson 1987c; for discussion of the Wittgensteinian roots, see Henderson 1988a.) The manner in which concerns for the constraints on interpretation come to feature in the earlier debate is often reflected in those papers anthologized in Wilson (1970). In particular see Hollis (1970a) and Lukes (1970). Continuity with the later debate is reflected in Hollis and Lukes (1982).

6. Davidson here talks of needing to find others similar to ourselves. On one reading, this may seem to betray a certain ambivalence in Davidson's thinking here. Similarity is a descriptive matter, the same characterization must apply to both ourselves and others, a characterization of the respect in which we are similar. Davidson may thus be counseling us to impose a normative structure on interpretation, and also to find others similar to ourselves as a descriptive matter. On the face of it, these are not quite the same thing. However, these counsels may be reconciled by noting that Davidson (1982, p. 6) also insists that we are, collectively and individually, subjects of our own interpretation, just as others are. Thus, in interpreting others and ourselves, we are bound by the need to impose a normatively derived structure; this, we are told, is the guiding principle. As a result, finding others similar to ourselves becomes a matter of finding others similarly rational in that the structure imposed in both cases is basically that of normative rationality.

7. Transformations in a store of beliefs may be desirable or normatively appropriate in several respects. This is so even when, as here, one focuses

on epistemic appropriateness. Some may be commanded; some may be merely permitted. That is, it may be normatively inappropriate to pass up certain inferences in certain situations, while it may be simply allowable to make certain other inferences. Of course, there are hybrids. For example, it may be allowable to seek to generalize from information about a sample. However, if one chooses to do so, and information bearing on the possible bias of the sample is available, it is inappropriate to pass up making an informed judgment regarding sample bias. Normative rules of all these modalities are glossed here as expressing "desirable transformations in a store of beliefs."

8. To one emersed in the Davidsonian way of understanding interpretation, this last formulation will suggest a way of taking some of the awkwardness out of their position. It will be suggested that there can be no substantial divergence between descriptive generalizations and normative principles (aside from their differing modalities of course). After all, the generalizations must rest on interpreted cases of reasoning. If these must uncover rationality, the generalizations will be little but a celebration of the methodologically insured result. I believe that this obviously fails to do justice to much good work in cognitive psychology. However, a philosophical repudiation of these suggestions will have to wait until later chapters.

9. Stich (1985,1990) seems to break apart this neat package by arguing that folk psychology, and thus intentional idiom, is grounded in a similarity assumption and not, strictly speaking, a rationality claim, yet he also argues that there is a recalcitrant minimal rationality constraint on such idiom. This would seem an untenable approach to intentionality, for if the similarity assumption were really fundamental, the minimal rationality constraint would seem, in principle, a potentially passing artifact of psychological theory (as suggested in my fourth chapter). It is no surprise then, that Stich finds intentional psychology, as he understands it, unworkable.

10. So curious, in fact, that I once charitably understood Davidson differently from the manner here presented (Henderson 1987b).

11. There is at least one notable contributor to the literature on charitable interpretation that does not hold the Standard Conception: Quine (1970, 1987). And it is some indication of the hold the Standard Conception has on the field that Quine's views are commonly misconstrued along the lines of that view. Quine's approach, and common misconstruals are discussed by Henderson (1987a, 1988b). Lukes (1982) may well provide a second exception, by virtue of his defense of an (empirically) flexible bridgehead. However, there is in Lukes's writing some suggestion that explanation in the human sciences requires finding a certain level of rationality. This would seem to transfer the sort of constraints described in the Standard Conception from the domain of interpretation to the domain of explanation. I believe that this would be equally unacceptable, for reasons canvassed in chapters 5 and 6.

12. In this and several other passages, Davidson seems to appeal to

descriptive psychology as informing our modifications of a principle of charity. This seems to me to be incongruous with his insistence, mentioned earlier, that the principle draw on normative principles and that epistemology guide modifications (1984d, p. 169).

13. Here I am implicitly focusing on the more translational dimensions of interpretation by focusing on the interpretation of linguistic productions. This follows a tendency in the literature on charity that I am attempting to survey here. Suspending this focus, I believe we must also recognize particularly simple actions as having a place in the patterns attended to in interpretation. Fetchings, eatings, sleepings, walkings, and so forth, are at least crudely accessible.

14. To begin with, taxonomies may ultimately diverge. The source-language might then have no terms true of all and only what our term 'corn' is true of. Additionally, these early translational moves will tend to "homely" translations, even when less homely translations are open: we will draw on everyday source-language constructions such as the phrase 'corn' in preference to 'cornhood instantiation'. This point is familiar from Quine's (1960, 1970) discussions of the indeterminacy of translation.

15. Hollis understands these charitable aspects of the method operative in the early stages of interpretation to be necessary assumptions or a priori assumptions. Thus he espouses the FMC view of such charity: "I want to insist first that they are *assumptions* and secondly that the anthropologist has no option about making them" (1970b). They are clearly NDS suggestions in his formulations as well.

16. The attentive reader will have noticed what seems to be a tension in Davidson's remarks on interpretation: when discussing refinements on the principle of charity by weighting according to types of error, he seems to point to two different sets of considerations as the sort to inform such a weighting. At points he seems to say that disagreement should be weighted according to the epistemological seriousness of sorts of error (Davidson 1984d, p. 169). Yet in the passages just quoted, he points to psychological information regarding empirical likelihood. Of course, one might attempt to resolve the tension in several ways. For example, one might note that empirical likelihood is supposedly determined in terms of interpretations. Thus, if we initially weight the principle according to epistemological seriousness, empirical likelihood will fall into line. This seems to me a very mistaken way to look at charity in the first place.

Chapter 3

1. This notion of a mistaken assent to an observation sentence can even be given a behavioral construction, as is appropriate when drawing on

Quine's suggestions. By "a mistaken assent to an observation sentence," I understand an assent that would almost universally be withdrawn (within the relevant language community) upon some subsequent stimuli. Consider, for example, the following simple sequence involving a source-language sentence, X, that has roughly the same stimulus meaning as 'Rabbit'. At time t^1 we present the informant with a rabbit-facsimile placed thirty meters off, and in a rabbit-conducive setting. We query, X, and the informant assents. At time t^2, we move the informant much closer, query X, and get dissent. At time t^3, we return to the spot from which the facsimile was viewed at t^1, again query X, and now the informant dissents. This, in effect is to retract the initial assent.

2. This procedure is further complicated (and made less determinate) when we consider abstentions as well as assent and dissent. See Quine 1974, pp. 75–78.

3. It might be objected that any interpretation carries with it an implicit, if somewhat rudimentary, folk psychology, thus an interpretive scheme, by itself, is not strictly vacuous. In one respect, this is to make the point I am most after here: interpretive schemes are never really isolated from psychological accounts. They are constructed against the background of psychological expectations. In other respects, however, I have misgivings. The suggested implicit psychology is hardly sufficient to provide us a notion of empirically adequate interpretive schemes. Additionally, there is an unwelcome conservative aspect to this understanding of interpretation that will be addressed in chapter 4.

4. These responses are mistakes regardless of whether the subject was using the material conditional or a more "natural" rendering of the English conditional (Wason and Johnson-Laird 1972, p. 146). A disjunction can also be used to produce similar results (p. 117).

Chapter 4

1. The distortions that can arise from becoming so enamored with Davidsonian a priori truths that one loses sight of this more extensional view is reflected in Davidson's own worry over whether we can sensibly say that some ancients believed that the earth was flat (Davidson 1984d). Colin McGinn (1977) has usefully criticized Davidson's misgivings.

2. It might be wondered whether I should write of the axioms of measurement theory, rather than the axioms of decision-theory, constraining us here. Of course, both would seem to constrain us. But the latter conform to the requirements of measurement theory. Thus, the concerns expressed by Davidson and Suppes (1957, pp. 5–6), who assert that there are limits

to the "modesty" of a formal decision-theoretic model that are determined by the demand that "conditions for measurement, at least in a limited domain, be shown to exist," can be compared with (Suppes and Zinnes 1963). See also my note 3, this chapter.

3. In Davidson and Suppes 1957, one finds the argument from measurement. There it is noted that common decision theoretic explanations suppose a theory that requires the measurability of subjective probabilities and of attractiveness for individuals. "Provision for such a theory" is said to "amount to placing appropriate restrictions on the patterns or structure of an individual's preferences and expectations" (p. 2). This, in turn is said to require us to "stipulate conditions [axioms of measurement] strong enough to guarantee" measurement on certain sorts of scales (p. 2). While, in view of Richard Jeffrey's work, Davidson may now ask for somewhat less in the scale of measurement than the interval scale sought in 1957, the concerns expressed here do seem to retain some place in his work (Davidson 1980e, pp. 6, 10–11). In view of this continuity, it is plausible to view these early concerns as being incorporated (and in this sense of greater generality, superceded) by Davidsonian concerns for charity in interpretation.

4. This is a somewhat extended notion of intransitivity, since numerically equivalent options are counted as the same option here, although formulated in different verbal terms. However, even if this is not counted as a case of intransitivity, strictly speaking, it is a near kin, and is equivalent for practical purposes.

5. It might be objected that, even in cases of such framing, there remains a significant limited rationality internal to the decision making within each frame. Admittedly, this is so. But it does not rescue from my criticisms the claim that beliefs and desires must be predominantly rational. For, I am supposing that rationality should be judged in terms of our best standards, after all. I readily admit that, if we lower our standards from the best we can formulate to some substantially more limited set, we will find more that passes muster, perhaps a preponderance.

6. It is now common to suppose that at any one time an individual has a extremely large set of standing desires that are together comparable on at least an ordinal scale. But, it might conceivably turn out that the states presently conceptualized along these lines can only be accessed and employed pairwise or in rather small sets, and that any attempt to deal with larger sets induces either an indeterminacy of strength or, amounting to much the same thing, a violation of transitivity as attention shifts across the set of desires.

7. There is a second respect in which anomolous monism would undermine parts of this chapter. Were there no nomic psychological generalizations, then psychology and the human sciences cannot be expected to develop in the way the natural sciences develop. It would then seem that the dis-

tinction between the conceptual and extensional notions of the subject would be out of place in this paper, for there would be no prospect for developing laws that would teach us new and significantly different things regarding a subject (understood extensionally). Thus, my earlier allusions to how in physics we have come to learn new things about subjects, things conflicting with older conceptual a priori truths, would seem to shed little light on what could happen in psychology. (It should be remembered that these earlier remarks were not intended to shed light on what was conceptually a priori, but to clarify what it was to be such, and to call attention to respects in which being so does not ultimately constrain scientific development of views concerning beliefs and desires (understood as an extensional matter.)

8. While it is overly schematic, we might for contrast formulate a summary of what it is to attribute a belief with a certain content to a person:

> To say 'S believes that p' then is to say S has a set of belief states such that, were I to have them, then, given our shared psychological dispositions, one (the putative equivalent in me) would underlie my own assertion of (or assent to) 'p' and together the set of beliefs would produce the range of behavior thought to be equivalent on our interpretive scheme. Thus, our theory and interpretive scheme are allowing us to model what we observe.

Of course, we must add that the theory turns out to be well-confirmed as investigations proceed.

9. For readers curious regarding the more general interpretive context, I suggest that it reduces to the problem of providing interpretive analyses for various classes of systems. (Each analysis being analogous to the analysis, or family of analyses, that we seek for human psychology.) Then interpretation, for certain members of a given class, can be understood as a matter of modeling their actions, with the use of the analysis for the relevant class.

10. Stich's (1984, p. 217) notion of a "different evidential pattern" or a different inferential pattern is not wholly clear. However, his arguments against Quine suggest that the descriptive pluralist need only claim that the overall patterns of others' reasoning does not conform closely to the overall patterns found in Western society. This reading is supported by his reference to the doctrine of prelogicality, carefully elaborated, as apparently one variant of descriptive pluralism which should not be methodologically legislated against (Stich 1990, p. 35). Proponents of such doctrines have typically held that patterns found in the one context are found with much less frequency (and much more restrained) in the other context. Or they have claimed that the difference pointed to reflect different stages of cognitive development, and thus a shared psychology of development. As these remarks indicate, the differences posited by such pluralism are best understood as typically matters of degree, as Stich (1990, p. 13) recognizes.

Chapter 5

1. Having a "pro attitude towards" something with a certain property is to have a favorable propositional attitude towards it in view of that property—for example, to want it or desire it as an instance of that property.

2. This example is suggested by Verba and Nie (1972), where it is shown that the pattern of political activities found in the United States is a good deal more intricate than had previously been recognized. Outside a group of those who are highly politically active, those who seek to influence governmental activities appear to tailor their involvement in ways that are understandable as rational, given their own needs and the different characteristics of types of political activity. Verba and Nie thus apply rationalizing explanation at the level of social aggregates to explain a pattern found among overlapping but distinct groups. One type of political activity that requires a good deal of initiative, individual contacting of officials on particularized problems, is *not* strongly correlated with the general level of political activity of agents. My example is one possible version of such activity.

3. I have been careful here not to bias the issue of whether it is findings of rationality as such that are explanatory. As will become clear, I believe that they are not.

4. Thus, one can typically find authors unself-consciously assuming a measure of both epistemic and practical rationality in accounting for an episode. A nice example is furnished by John Watkins's (1970) reconstruction of a certain naval disaster. Watkins seeks to understand the actions in terms of beliefs that are themselves explicable in context. More explicitly, Phillip Converse (1964) cautiously assumes a limited epistemic rationality in describing the various constraints on political beliefs and values.

5. Cummins refers to the strategy of causal explanation as the subsumptive strategy. This reflects an allegiance to the covering-law model of explanation that I would avoid.

6. This may be too narrow a characterization, for some causal explanations may be devoted to explaining why certain interactions did not produce a certain result. Accordingly, it is perhaps best to think of causal explanation as explaining the development of a system in certain respects.

7. This is not to say that psychologists are, or should be, indifferent to whether their posited psychological capacities can be neurophysiologically realized. Far from it. Rather, the point is that, in their psychological analyses, there need be no suggestion that distinct neurophysiological components are responsible for distinct psychological dispositions, nor is there a suggestion that nondisjunctive neurophysiological components realize what is analyzed as a single psychological disposition. Neurophysiologically salient "black boxes" need not correspond to psychologically salient ones.

8. One may wonder why there is a place for interpretive analysis in addition to descriptive analysis. Epistemologically, a partial answer is not too difficult. In many psychological contexts, we are far from any interesting analysis employing physical descriptions of inputs and outputs. But there is still enough structure to what we can observe that we can be justified in accounting for this regularity in terms of an input and output structure of a sort that makes use of the notion of "information" (and related but less rudimentary notions). Any analysis that specifies inputs and outputs in terms of connections between the environment and states, states and other states, and states and behavior, is likely to employ such notions, particularly when the physical description of the intermediate states is largely unknown.

A significant virtue of interpretive analysis is that, with it, we can afford to be indifferent to variations in the physical realization, or syntactical specifics, of the functional dependencies we manage to study interpretively. These might vary across systems with the same interpretive analysis.

There seems to be a fair amount of confusion on these matters. For example, proponents of a "syntactical theory of the mind," such as Stich (1983) seem to underplay the manner in which syntactic individuation of state-types across physically quite heterogeneous functional systems might involve semantically informed judgments. Or, perhaps better, such judgments may involve information regarding the functional interrelation between states, information that goes beyond syntax proper. Consider, as an instructive analogue, how we might decide that two users of inscriptionally different languages for the predicate calculus are both tokening the universal quantifier sign when one writes '(x)' and the other writes '($\forall$x).' Similar functional concerns inform the positing of internal psychological states with roughly isomorphic transformation-dispositions within two individuals that are potentially quite different neurophysically. Now, when one adds that some of the relevant internal states may be causally tied to variations in the environment, one begins to see how such functional characterizations become more semantical than syntactical. For a related discussion, in connection with Fodor's *Language of Thought* (or LOT) hypothesis, see Crane (1990).

9. I am inclined to call the transition laws causal, insofar as causal laws may be both subject to ineliminable ceteris paribus clauses and nondeterministic. Again, this is characteristic of the special sciences. Free action then must be given a compatiblist reading, if there is to be such freedom. My recognition of the "softness" of psychological laws is then neither wanted or needed for freedom of the will, and beside the point in that context. The sort of softness envisioned here would not make for any interesting freedom of the will, were a compatiblist account unworkable.

10. This is the goal of Good Old Fashioned Artificial Intellegence (GOFAI) with its concern for programmable rules operating at the level of

representations. However, that research program has certainly met with a recalcitrant set of problems, and there is reason to believe that the problem rests, in part at least, with the conception of exceptionless rules that is employed there. This diagnosis is developed in Horgan and Tienson's (1989) discussion of GOFAI's difficulties in dealing with the frame problem (having to do with the recognition and recall of relevant information, that is, determining relevance) and cases of multiple soft constraints (which facilitate human processing but have the opposite effect on GOFAI systems).

11. This is not to say that intentional states are not always subject to some indeterminacy of content.

12. These qualifications are intended to place our ability to follow out logical implications in perspective, in view of its place in reasoning generally conceived in something like the way Harman (1986) does. They are also intended to recognize the importance of factors like "feasibility orderings" of inferences and the structure of memory, as these matters are discussed by Cherniak (1986). In particular, the notion of a "relatively direct implication" is intended to point to the relative difficulty of ascertaining that a certain claim follows from a set of other claims; this is supposedly a function of at least two factors: how difficult certain simple transformations are for a system, that is, "its feasibility ordering" of simple inferences, and the number of such inferences required.

13. I am of course assuming that the home team is having an off year and that the afternoon game falls on a weekday.

14. While the so-called strong programme in the sociology of science is, I believe, a mixed blessing (Henderson 1990b), the account of rationalizing explanation that has been provided here is in accord with important principles that have been much insisted on in classic statements of that approach: the impartiality and symmetry principles (Bloor 1976, 1981).

Chapter 6

1. What I have in mind in this qualification can be elaborated. It seems proper to consider the central explanatory attributions of intentional states to be *de dicto* attributions. That is to say that, within an explanation, the intentional state is most properly taken to be a *de dicto* belief or desire, whose description then constitutes an opaque context. Now, when a causal statement is understood as employing such *de dicto* ascriptions, substitution within such a context may attribute to the agent a belief that is not held. This is obviously a change that could change a true causal statement into a false one. Jimmy may have desired to acquire a dinner date with the most attractive dentist in the town. He may have called Dr. Blood because

of this desire. However, unknown to Jimmy, Dr. Blood may be the most sadistic dentist in the town. It is likely that Jimmy did not desire to acquire a date with the most sadistic dentist in the town. Then it is not true that Jimmy called Dr. Blood because of such a desire. However, *if* some variant of the token-identity theory is correct, the *entire* belief ascription *can* be replaced. The token belief in question would then be identical with a certain neurophysical state. One could then replace the true intentional inscription within the true causal statement with the appropriate neurophysical description of that state and thereby preserve truth.

2. As explained in the previous chapter, explanations come in two (ultimately interrelated) forms corresponding to answers to how-questions (functional explanations) and answers to why-questions. These forms of explanation seem to exhaust the range of scientific explanation. Explanations that account for the occurrence of an event or for an event having a certain aspect (these are typically called singular causal explanations) and explanations that account for nomic regularities in terms of other nomic regularities (what might be called general scientific explanations) are answers to why-questions. Rationalizing explanations seem clearly to be attempts to provide answers to why-questions regarding particular events; thus such explanations are answers to why-questions. (Cf. Cummins 1983; Kincaid 1988, p. 258.) Philosophers of science whose approach to understanding explanation does not make much use of the logic of why-questions need not be alarmed by my own attention to why-questions. What I seek to get from this focus is modest, and any account of explanation will, I think, need to allow as much along these lines. For example, Salmon adopts what he terms an "ontic" conception of explanation, according to which explanation, as an answer to a why-question must provide or rely on descriptive information regarding underlying mechanisms. He (1989, pp. 37–45, 126–28) then conceives of the notion of a why-question as usefully calling attention to the sorts of information needed in an explanation by calling attention to explanations as responses to predicaments roughly like those analyzed by Bromberger (1962, 1966).

3. For example, many everyday explanations, and most in the special sciences for that matter, rest on what Davidson has called "heteronomic generalizations" (Davidson 1980c, pp. 215–25; cf. Rosenberg 1985b). But on strict versions of the covering-law model, such are not nomic.

4. (Woodward 1984, pp. 250–57, 253.) When discussing those clauses that mark out an attribute of an event as an explanandum, Woodward also speaks of the "substitution of identicals" preserving truth (p. 256). However, his examples suggest that this is not to appeal to a notion of property identity. Rather, on his view, the substitution of coextensional terms within causal claims is apparently truth-preserving. He claims that singular causal explanations are extensional "both on the cause-side and on the effect-side" (p. 231). However, he focuses on the effect-side, as I do also.

5. I say many (or some) causal claims are extensional. This is to say that there are such extensional usages, not that all causal claims are extensional. Extensional usages are, I think, also nonexplanatory, for they must make no claim to picking out the causally relevant factors of events. Even so, different accounts of the extensional usages will vary with respect to the scope of the substitutions allowed as they involve different accounts of the relata of causal claims. Suppose that events are the relata in such usages. When events are understood Davidson's way (as I have generally supposed here) there will be a wide range to substitutivity in comparison to what is allowed when events are understood Kim's way, for example.

6. While I have not relied on a counterfactual explication of causation and causal relevance, I have written of understanding what it was about courses of events that made a difference, and I have occasionally employed a formulation in terms of counterfactual dependencies. It remains to indicate roughly how nomic generalizations formulating knowledge of causal relevances support the relevant counterfactual claims. First, in evaluating a counterfactual of the sort appealed to in this essay, the laws are generally to be held constant: (as suggested by Lewis 1973) we are to think in terms of a system that is "running on" from a certain specified set of conditions in the familiar lawlike ways described in our nomic generalizations. (The exception to this rule is the very limited one mentioned below.) Second, we are to suppose that at some time, t, from which the system is to "run on," the world was different in a minimal way stipulated in the antecedent of the counterfactual. However, if (as is likely in some sorts of cases) this involves a violation of laws, this can be thought of as an "isolated miracle" occurring at t, with the system thereafter running on in conformity with the laws. The fundamental thing is just a set of conditions and what our nomic generalizations indicate as the likely outcomes. Thus, in evaluating counterfactuals, the only respect in which the laws are relaxed, or allowed to vary, in setting up the hypothetical system is in that minimal respect necessary for the isolated miracle responsible for the counterfactual antecedent.

7. It is relevant to notice that similar corrections of people's intuitions with regard to sample size, and regression to the mean, seem to be of limited effectiveness (Tversky and Kahnemen 1971; Kahneman and Tversky 1972; Hamill, Wilson, and Nisbett 1980, pp. 587–88).

Chapter 7

1. Actually, one might suggest that the pattern obtained is the product of two utility functions, one having to do with monetary gains and losses, the other having to do with gambling and uncertain situations. However, this plausible suggestion is rendered problematic by the choices obtained in yet a third situation (Tversky 1975, pp. 165–66).

2. In keeping with the general position developed here, such suggestions for possible alternative construals of experiments are themselves based on empirical expectations. Anchoring is an empirically studied effect (Tversky and Kahneman 1974).

3. This statement can be understood or modified to apply rather naturally to hypotheses that are not equations (Glymour 1980, pp. 123–33).

4. These remarks are not meant to suggest that the rudimentary theories used in the earlier stages of interpretation are themselves immune to revision. Revision there is admittedly less likely. But, if efforts at less drastic measures in the later stages are repeatedly unsatisfactory, attention could be focused on the more fundamental expectations used earlier.

5. I do believe that this theory can vary over time. But at any one time the set we would draw on might be reasonably constant.

Chapter 8

1. The class of Horgan and Tienson's soft laws would seem to diverge from the class of Davidson's useful (but non-nomic) heteronomic generalizations. The class that Davidson finds problematic is the class of generalizations with exceptions that can only be systematically treated by turning to a different vocabulary, typically one proper to a more fundamental level of analysis (as when one turns to chemical biology to refine the generalizations of genetics). The class that Horgan and Tienson defend is the class of generalizations (1) with systematic exceptions that are susceptible to formulation at the same level of analysis; and (2) whose exceptions, when treated at this (and perhaps any) level, can never be completely and exhaustively treated. In other words, they defend a set of generalizations whose ceteris paribus clause is never completely eliminable, but can be "cashed out" indefinitely in descriptions at the same level of analysis as the generalization itself. However, it seems to me that any such generalization will have some exceptions that are best treated systematically by moving to a different level of analysis; if so, then the class of soft laws would seem to be a proper subset of the set of heteronomic generalizations. I believe that most worries over the nomicity, or lawlikeness, of generalizations in the special sciences, and in psychology in particular, have centered on heteronomicity rather than on softness. Accordingly, I focus here on heteronomicity worries. Still, this much can be said: it is often thought that although nomic (or law-*like*) generalizations may turn out to be soft, real laws, as the ideal refinements of such generalizations, are not. (To be nomic is to be lawlike, in the relevant sense, not necessarily to be a law.) Accordingly, it is commonly thought that soft generalizations can, at best, be approximations to laws, not laws, strictly speaking. Thus, despite the differences, one can see strong

connections between Horgan and Tienson's concerns and Davidson's worries. (In fact, this understanding of laws, properly so called, is one I attribute to Davidson in the text. This is an aspect of Davidson's thought that is not fully appreciated in LePore and Loewer's [1987] defense of anomolous monism, a defense that appeals to "non-strict laws.") As I say, I believe both heteronomic and soft generalizations can be nomic, and even laws.

2. This aspect of Davidson's thought is just what is missing from LePore and Loewer's (1987) defense of anomolous monism. I do suspect that the position that they advertise there as an unexceptionable anomolous monism is indeed on the right track. However, I am sure that it is not really Davidson's. After all, they write of nonstrict laws, Davidson seems to rule them out. They write of psychological and psycho-physical laws, albeit nonstrict ones. Davidson denies that psycho-physical generalizations can be nomic, and seems to extend the repudiation to cover psychological generalizations: thus the anomolousness that he envisions. I suspect that LePore and Loewer manage to say what Davidson ought to have said, and there is no real anomolousness posited in their account.

3. Classic examples of accidental generalizations include the parochial generalization 'All coins in my pocket contain silver' and the exotic Goodmanian generalization 'All emeralds are grue' (Goodman 1973).

4. But, why might this seem plausible to Davidson? There are probably several influences. It is helpful to notice that Davidson's discussion of heteronomic generalizations comes in the context of his discussion of psychophysical generalizations, generalizations dealing with the physical antecedents and realizations of mental states. Perhaps his special misgivings regarding this special set influenced his thinking regarding the entire set of heteronomic generalization. With respect to this particular subclass of heteronomic generalizations, Davidson believes that he has particularly strong grounds for thinking that they must be non-nomic: he insists that their predicates are "not made for each other" and that this renders such generalizations realistic analogues to 'Emeralds are grue'. I think that Davidson's arguments are unpersuasive on this point, and rest on his misconceptions regarding the principle of charity. For now it is worth noting simply that, at most, Davidson's consideration of the status of psychophysical generalizations provides, at most, a verdict regarding a very limited subclass of heteronomic generalizations, and not (at least not directly) a verdict regarding the whole class (cf. Davidson 1987).

5. In fact, strictly speaking, it may well rely on the claims that heteronomic and thus psychological generalizations are non-nomic. For, as set out above, the view presupposes the Davidsonian claim that there are no strict psychological laws. And this claim seems to be supported by the further claim that psychological generalizations are heteronomic.

6. Of course, this is ignoring all sorts of real limitations on what can

be done with fundamental physics. Limitations having to do with expressibility, computability, measurability, and so on.

7. Thus the vocabulary of physiological biology, strictly construed, is taken to include such classic terms as 'organ', 'heart', 'cell', 'hemoglobin', 'neuron', 'mitochondria', 'dendrite', 'chlorophyll', and 'gene.' But it is not taken to include the biochemical characterization of some of these structures, which, after all, are borrowed from some more fundamental science. ('DNA' and 'RNA' are interesting marginal cases here classed as borrowed, while 'messenger RNA' becomes an interesting hybrid.) Of course, biochemistry is itself a special science, and we can force on it a similar distinction between its vocabulary, strictly construed, and its borrowed vocabulary. I believe that these remarks reflect a significant artificiality in the distinction between "the vocabulary of the special science" and that of the more fundamental science. As I note in the text, some the imports become "second nature" to practitioners of the special science, and are used in what even they take to be rough formulations of some of their central generalizations. This, in turn, suggests a certain artificiality to the distinction between heteronomic and homonomic generalizations. This is fine with me, for I believe that the distinction is vastly overrated and has little metaphysical gold to yield. Kincaid's (1990a) description of molecular biology as an inherently "mixed theory" would also seem to point to troubles for Davidson's attempt to get much of interest from the notion of heteronomic generalizations. See also Maull (1977) and Dardin and Maull (1977).

8. In fairness to Davidson, we should notice that he does continue these remarks in a way that seems to refine the suggestion in an important way:

> But if we combine this observation with the conclusion that no psycho-physical statement is, or can be built into, a strict law, we have the Principle of the Anomalism of the Mental: there are no strict laws at all on the basis of which we can predict and explain mental phenomena (1980c, p. 224).

However, we now seem to have the suggestion that heteronomic generalizations cannot be nomic when they deal with open systems and the relevant exogenous factors interact with the system (as characterized in the special science) in ways that cannot be specified in nomic generalizations. With such qualifications in place, it is rather difficult to see how Davidson's concern for such special cases bare on his general thesis regarding heteronomic generalizations. Additionally, I find it difficult to appreciate how these qualifications are to be hooked up with the concerns we uncovered earlier regarding heteronomic generalizations not picking out causal factors.

9. I find that the notion of dependence is particularly unclear. At one point Kim suggests that dependence might be understood in terms of the "independent assumptions" to which explanations commit us. But, it seems

to me that supervenient explanations, which Kim takes not to be independent, may commit us to independent assumptions not made in the lower-level explanations. For example, the generalizations employed in a supervenient explanation may have to do with a class of systems not all of which are covered by the particular generalizations in the lower-level explanation of the particular case. Additionally, explanations that appeal to distinct events within the same deterministic causal process may be wrongly taken to be independent on this proposal.

10. For purposes of Kemeny-Oppenheim reduction, what counts as explaining the same datum? To apply to the range of cases that Kim intends, one must understand the matter loosely enough to apply in cases in which the two theories have different, but closely related, domains (and different vocabularies), say one is intended to explain bodily motion and the other to explain actions. I think that the following is a rough but acceptable way of understanding the matter: the two explain the same datum if there is some description of the relevant events in the one theory such that the properties ascribed to those events by that theory supervene on the properties ascribed in the descriptions of the events rendered in the other theory. The idea is to allow theories providing us causal accounts (at the micro- and macro-levels) of a given supervenient causal transaction to be said to explain that causal sequence as a datum (rendered in somewhat differing ways). Here the datum must be taken to be the token causal event-pair. Supposedly something along these lines is involved when one says, as Kim does, that a neurophysiological theory and an intentional psychological theory might account for the same phenomenon (a particular instance of a person's climbing a ladder, a person's bodily motions as they ascend a particular ladder) in compatible terms (a certain set of beliefs and desires, a certain complex neurophysiological state) (Kim 1989a, p. 77).

11. Admittedly, in some contexts, Kim insists that supervenience, and supervenience causation, is sufficient for reducibility. However, in those contexts, Kim is conceiving of reduction in terms of a undemanding version of Nagel reduction in which the bridge laws employed can be wildly disjunctive. Yet, in connection with the application of his reduction test, Kim seems to insist that the relevant form of Nagel reducibility requires bridge laws that are not wildly disjunctive, and maybe not disjunctive at all. More on this will follow.

12. Curiously, Kim (1989a, p. 101) also asserts that the proper application of his principle of explanatory exclusion leads to such reductionist constraints. But, if supervenient explanations, as set out above (and in Kim 1984), do not require that the respective theories be Nagel-reducible, and if supervenient causal explanations nevertheless are not in violation of the exclusion principle, then the reductionist result does not follow from the exclusion principle. For these reasons, the explanatory exclusion principle should not commit us to reductionism.

13. It is significant that the historical cases Kim mentions as applications of his dictum involve theories from the same science. Stahlian and Lavoisier's theories were both theories in what then passed as fundamental chemistry. They were theories intended to account for chemical combinations in terms of what basic materials there were. Impetus theory and dynamical theory were both meant to provide fundamental accounts of the causes of motions. This is no accident, for Kim's dictum must at the very least be qualified so as to apply only to theories within a single science. In any case, it is somewhat doubtful that the central scientific choices regarding what theories to tentatively adopt and develop are made by comparing extant theories. It seems plausible that such choices are rationally made by comparing research traditions in terms of their recent history of problem solving (Laudan 1977). Thus, it is not clearly permissible to attempt to read lessons about theoretical virtues from historical choices in the simple way Kim's discussion sometimes suggests.

14. I am presupposing here that reduction, including Nagelian reduction, is understood so as to allow disjunctive bridge principles. This does not bias the ensuing argumentation, for I am here only concerned to point out that, if one were concerned with in-practice reducibility, few if any higher-level theories would be either Kemeny-Oppenheim reducible or Nagel reducible. Thus the reduction test, understood in such terms, really has little, if any, bite.

15. Or, if a very few theories are Kemeny-Oppenheim reducible in practice, they will almost certainly still fail to be Nagel reducible in practice, if for no other reason than the limitations of our cognitive capacities. This seems a rather capricious basis for rejecting higher-level theories. It has no connection with either their truth or usefulness.

16. I am not considering the more complex situation of investigators faced with deciding what to do when working with various theories no one of which is ideal. Were we to attend to this situation, this would lead to yet further restrictions and qualification on the reduction test.

17. Assuming that Fodor is not attacking reductionism as a straw man, it presumably must also allow for macro-level characterizations describing statistical characteristics of ensembles with regard to the lower-level properties mentioned in the reducing theory. For example, mean kinetic energy of the molecules in a sample of gas. While I do sympathize with Fodor's misgivings regarding wildly disjunctive bridge laws as a basis for interesting reduction, I do not find the notion of a lower-level "natural kind" particularly helpful in this regard.

Bibliography

Agassi, J. (1963). *Towards an Historiography of Science, History and Theory: Studies in the Philosophy of History*, Vol. 2. The Hague: North Holland Publishers [Middletown, Conn.: Wesleyan University Press, 1967].

Barden, G. (1972). "Method and Meaning." In A. Singer and B. Street, *Zande Themes: Essays Presented to Sir Edward Evans-Pritchard*. Totowa, N.J.: Rowman & Littlefield, pp. 105–29.

Beattie, J. (1964). *Other Cultures*. New York: The Free Press.

Black, M. (1979). "Wittgenstein's Language-games." *Dialectia* 33: 277–89.

Bloor, D. (1976). *Knowledge and Social Imagery*. London: Routledge and Kegan Paul.

———. (1981). "The Strengths of the Strong Programme." *Philosophy of Social Science* 11: 199–213.

Bromberger, S. (1962). "An Approach to Explanation." In R. Butler, ed., *Analytical Philosophy—Second Series*. Oxford: Basil Blackwell, pp. 72–105.

———. (1966). "Why Questions." In R. Colodny, ed., *Mind and Cosmos*. Pittsburgh: University of Pittsburgh Press, pp. 86–111.

Brown, H. (1987). *Observation*. Oxford: Oxford University Press.

Burge, T. (1979). "Individualism and the Mental." *Midwest Studies in Philosophy* 4: 73–121.

Cherniak, C. (1986). *Minimal Rationality*. Cambridge: MIT Press.

Churchill, J. (1983). "The Coherence of the Concept 'Language-Game.'" *Philosophical Investigations* 6: 253–54.

Collingwood, R. (1956). *The Idea of History*. Oxford: Oxford University Press. (Originally published 1946, Clarendon Press.)

Converse, P. (1964). "The Nature of Belief Systems in Mass Publics." In D. Apter, ed., *Ideology and Discontent*. New York: Free Press, pp. 206–61.

Crane, T. (1990). "The Language of Thought: No Syntax Without Semantics." *Mind and Language* 5: 187–211.

Crocker, J. (1977). "My Brother the Parrot." In J. Sapir and J. Crocker, eds., *The Social Uses of Metaphor: Essays in the Anthropology of Rhetoric*. Philadelphia: University of Pennsylvania Press.

Cummins, R. (1975). "Functional Analysis." *Journal of Philosophy* 72: 741–60.

———. (1983). *The Nature of Psychological Explanation*. Cambridge: MIT Press.

———. (1989). *Meaning and Mental Representation*. Cambridge: MIT Press.

Cummins, R., and Schwarz, G. (1991). "Connectionism, Computation, and Cognition." In T. Horgan and J. Tienson, eds., *Connectionism and the Philosophy of Mind*. Dordrecht: Kluwer, pp. 60–73.

Dallmayr, F., and McCarthy, T., eds. (1977). *Understanding and Social Inquiry*. Notre Dame: University of Notre Dame Press.

Dardin, L., and Cain, J. (1989). "Selection Type Theories." *Philosophy of Science* 56: 106–29.

Dardin, L., and Maull, N. (1977). "Interfield Theories." *Philosophy of Science* 11: 43–64.

Davidson, D. (1980a). "Actions, Reasons, and Causes." In Davidson, *Essays on Actions and Events*. Oxford: Clarendon Press, pp. 1–19.

———. (1980b). "Causal Relations." In Davidson, *Essays on Actions and Events*. Oxford: Clarendon Press, pp. 149–62.

———. (1980c). "Mental Events." In Davidson, *Essays on Actions and Events*. Oxford: Clarendon Press, pp. 207–25.

———. (1980d). "Psychology as Philosophy." In Davidson, *Essays on Actions and Events*. Oxford: Clarendon Press, pp. 229–44.

———. (1980e). "Towards a Unified Theory of Meaning and Action." *Grazer Philosophische Studien* 11: 1–12.

———. (1982). "Paradoxes of Irrationality." In R. Wollheim and J. Hopkins, eds., *Philosophical Essays on Freud*. Cambridge: Cambridge University Press, pp. 289–305.

———. (1984a). "Truth and Meaning." In Davidson, *Inquiries into Truth and Interpretation*. Oxford: Clarendon Press, pp. 17–36.

———. (1984b). "Radical Interpretation." In Davidson, *Inquiries into Truth and Interpretation.* Oxford: Clarendon Press, pp. 125–40.

———. (1984c). "Belief and the Basis of Meaning." In Davidson, *Inquiries into Truth and Interpretation.* Oxford: Clarendon Press, pp. 141–54.

———. (1984d). "Thought and Talk." In Davidson, *Inquiries into Truth and Interpretation.* Oxford: Clarendon Press, pp. 155–70.

———. (1984e). "On the Very Idea of a Conceptual Scheme." In Davidson, *Inquiries into Truth and Interpretation.* Oxford: Clarendon Press, pp. 185–98.

———. (1987). "Problems in the Explanation of Action." In P. Pettit, R. Sylvan, and J. Norman, eds., *Metaphysics and Morality: Essays in Honour of J. J. C. Smart.* Oxford: Basil Blackwell, pp. 35–49.

Davidson, D., and Suppes, P. (1957). *Decision Making: An Experimental Approach.* Stanford: Stanford University Press.

Dretske, F. (1972). "Contrastive Statements," *Philosophical Review* 81: 411–37.

Elster, J. (1982). "Belief, Bias, and Ideology." In M. Hollis and S. Lukes, *Rationality and Relativism.* Cambridge: MIT Press.

———. (1984). *Ulysses and the Sirens: Studies in Rationality and Irrationality.* Rev. ed. Cambridge: Cambridge University Press.

Evans-Pritchard, E. (1937). *Witchcraft, Oracles and Magic Among the Azande.* Oxford: Clarendon Press.

———. (1956). *Neur Religion.* Oxford: Clarendon Press.

Festinger, L. (1957). *A Theory of Cognitive Dissonance.* New York: Harper and Row.

———. (1961). "The Psychological Effects of Insufficient Rewards." *American Psychologist* 16:1–11.

Festinger, L., Riecken, H., and Schachter, S. (1956). *When Prophecy Fails.* Minneapolis: University of Minnesota Press.

Firth, R. (1964). *Essays on Social Organization and Values.* London School of Economics Monographs on Social Anthropology, no. 28. London: Athlone Press.

———. (1973). *Symbols: Public and Private.* Ithaca, N.Y.: Cornell University Press.

Fodor, J. (1981). "Special Sciences." In J. Fodor, *Representation.* Cambridge, Mass.: Bradford Books, pp. 127–45.

———. (1987). *Psychosemantics.* Cambridge: MIT Press.

———. (1989). "Making Mind Matter More." *Philosophical Topics* 17: 59–79.

Føllesdal, D. (1979). "Hermeneutics and the Hypothetico-Deductive Method." *Dialectica* 33: 319–36.

———. (1980). "Explanation of Action." In R. Hilpinen, ed., *Rationality in Science: Studies in the Foundations of Science and Ethics*. Dordrecht: D. Reidel, pp. 231–47.

———. (1981). "Understanding and Rationality." In H. Parret and J. Bouveresse, eds., *Meaning and Understanding*. Berlin: de Gruyter.

———. (1982). "The Status of Rationality Assumptions in Interpretation and in the Explanation of Actions." *Dialectica* 36: 301–16.

———. (1985). "Causation and Explanation: A Problem in Davidson's View of the Mind." In E. Lapore and B. McLaughlin, *Actions and Events: Perspectives on the Philosophy of Donald Davidson*. Worcester: Blackwell, pp. 311–23.

Geertz, C. (1973). *The Interpretation of Cultures*. New York: Basic Books.

———. (1973a). "Religion as a Cultural System." In *The Interpretation of Cultures*. New York: Basic Books, pp. 87–125.

———. (1983). *Local Knowledge*. New York: Basic Books.

Gellner, E. (1973). *Cause and Meaning in the Social Sciences*. London: Routledge and Kegan Paul.

Glymour, C. (1980). *Theory and Evidence*. Princeton: Princeton University Press.

Goldman, A. (1969). "The Compatibility of Mechanism and Purpose." *Philosophical Review* 78: 468–82.

———. (1970). *A Theory of Human Action*. Englewood Cliffs, N.J.: Prentice-Hall.

Goodman, N. (1973). *Fact, Fiction, and Forecast*, 3d ed. Indianapolis: Bobbs-Merrill.

Habermas, J. (1984). *The Theory of Communicative Action*. Vol. 1. Trans. Thomas McCarthy. Boston: Beacon Press.

Hacking, I. (1983). *Representing and Intervening*. Cambridge: Cambridge University Press.

Hamill, R., Wilson, T., and Nisbett, R. (1980). "Insensitivity to Sample Bias: Generalizing from Atypical Cases." *Journal of Personality and Social Psychology* 39: 578–89.

Harman, G. (1986). *Change in View: Principles of Reasoning*. Cambridge: MIT Press.

Haugeland, J. (1985). *Artificial Intelligence: The Very Idea*. Cambridge: MIT Press.

Hempel, C. (1965a). "The Logic of Functional Analysis." In Hempel, *Aspects of Scientific Explanation and Other Essays in the Philosophy of Science*. New York: The Free Press, pp. 297–330.

———. (1965b). "Aspects of Scientific Explanation." In Hempel, *Aspects of Scientific Explanation and Other Essays in the Philosophy of Science*. New York: The Free Press, pp. 331–496.

Henderson, D. (1987a). "The Principle of Charity and the Problem of Irrationality." *Synthese* 73: 225–52.

———. (1987b). "A Solution to Davidson's Paradox of Irrationality." *Erkenntnis* 27: 359–69.

———. (1987c). "Winch and the Constraints on Interpretation: Versions of the Principle of Charity." *Southern Journal of Philosophy* 25: 153–73.

———. (1988a). "Wittgenstein's Descriptivist Approach to Understanding: Is There a Place for Explanation in Interpretive Accounts?" *Dialectica* 42: 105–15.

———. (1988b). "The Importance of Explanation in Quine's Principle of Charity." *The Philosophy of the Social Sciences* 18: 355–69.

———. (1989). "Rationalizing Explanation in the Social Sciences: Its Role and Limitations." *Canadian Journal of Philosophy* 19: 267–88.

———. (1990a). "An Empirical Basis for Charity in Translation." *Erkenntnis* 32: 83–103.

———. (1990b). "On the Sociology of Science and the Continuing Importance of Epistemologically Couched Accounts." *Social Studies of Science* 20: 113–48.

Hollis, M. (1970a). "The Limits of Irrationality." In B. Wilson, ed., *Rationality*. Worcester: Basil Blackwell, pp. 214–20.

———. (1970b). "Reason and Ritual." In B. Wilson, *Rationality*. Worcester: Basil Blackwell, pp. 221–39.

———. (1982). "The Social Destruction of Reality." In M. Hollis and S. Lukes, eds., *Rationality and Relativism*. Cambridge: MIT Press, pp. 67–86.

Hollis, M., and Lukes, S. (1982). *Rationality and Relativism*. Cambridge: MIT Press.

Hooker, C. (1981). "Towards a General Theory of Reduction." *Dialogue* 20: 38–59, 201–36, 496–529.

Honderich, T. (1982). "The Argument for Anomalous Monism." *Analysis* 42: 59–64.

———. (1984). "Smith and the Champion of Mauve." *Analysis* 44: 86–89.

Horgan, T. (1989). "Mental Quasation." In *Philosophical Perspectives*. Vol. 3. *Philosophy of Mind and Action Theory*, pp. 47–75.

———. (1990). "Actions, Reasons, and the Explanatory Role of Content." In B. McLaughlin, ed., *The Philosophy of Fred Dretske*. Oxford: Basil Blackwell.

———. (forthcoming). "Nonreductive Materialism and the Explanatory Autonomy of Psychology."

Horgan, T., and Tienson, J. (1989). "Representations without Rules." *Philosophical Topics* 17: 147–74.

———. (1990). "Soft Laws." *Midwest Studies in Philosophy* 15: 256–79.

Horton, R. (1970). "African Traditional Thought and Western Science." In B. Wilson, ed., *Rationality*. Worcester: Basil Blackwell.

———. (1973). "Paradoxes and Explanation: A Reply to Mr. Skorupski." *Philosophy of Social Science* 3: 231–56.

———. (1982). "Tradition and Modernity Revisited." In M. Hollis and S. Lukes, eds., *Rationality and Relativism*. Cambridge: MIT Press.

Horton, R., and Finnegan, R., eds. (1973). *Modes of Thought: Essays on Thinking in Western and Non-Western Societies*. London: Faber and Faber.

Hull, D. (1974). *The Philosophy of Biological Science*. Englewood Cliffs, N.J.: Prentice-Hall.

Humphreys, P. (1989a). "Scientific Explanation: The Causes, Some of the Causes, and Nothing But the Causes." In P. Kitcher and W. Salmon, eds. *Scientific Explanation. Minnesota Studies in the Philosophy of Science*, Vol. 13. Minneapolis: University of Minnesota Press, pp. 283–306.

———. (1989b). *The Chances of Explanation: Causal Explanation in the Social, Medical and Physical Sciences*. Princeton: Princeton University Press.

Jarvie, I. C. (1964). *The Revolution in Anthropology*. London: Routledge and Kegan Paul.

Johada, G. (1982). *Psychology and Anthropology: A Psychological Perspective*. New York: Academic Press.

Johnson-Laird, P., and Wason, P. (1972). "A Theoretical Analysis of Insight into a Reasoning Task." In P. Wason and P. Johnson-Laird, eds. *Psychological Reasoning: Structure and Content*. London: Bratsford, pp. 143–57.

Kahneman, D., and Tversky, A. (1972). "Subjective Probability: A Judgment of Representativeness." *Cognitive Psychology* 3: 430–54.

Kemeny, J., and Oppenheim, P. (1956). "On Reduction." *Philosophical Studies* 7: 6–19.

Kim, J. (1984). "Epiphenomenal and Supervenient Causation." *Midwest Studies in Philosophy* 9: 257–70.

———. (1989a). "Mechanism, Purpose, and Explanatory Exclusion." *Philosophical Perspectives* 3: 77–108.

———. (1989b). "The Myth of Nonreductive Materialism." *Proceedings and Addresses of the American Philosophical Association* 63: 31–47.

———. (1990). "Supervenience as a Philosophical Concept." Report No. 23. 1990 Research Group on Mind and Brain, University of Bielefeld.

———. (forthcoming). "The Disunity of Psychology as a Working Hypothesis."

Kincaid, H. (1988). "Supervenience and Explanation." *Synthese* 77: 251–81.

———. (1990a). "Molecular Biology and the Unity of Science." *Philosophy of Science* 57: 575–93.

———. (1990b). "Defending Laws in the Social Sciences." *Philosophy of the Social Sciences* 20: 56–83.

Kitcher, P. (1981). "Explanatory Unification." *Philosophy of Science* 48: 507–31.

———. (1984). "1953 and All That. A Tale of Two Sciences." *Philosophical Review* 43: 335–74.

———. (1989). "Explanatory Unification and the Causal Structure of the World." In P. Kitcher and W. Salmon, eds., *Scientific Explanation. Minnesota Studies in the Philosophy of Science.* Vol. 13. Minneapolis: University of Minnesota Press, pp. 410–505.

Knox, R., and Inkster, S. (1968). "Postdecision Dissonance at Post-time." *Journal of Personality and Social Psychology* 8: 319–23.

Kripke, S. (1982). *Wittgenstein on Rules and Private Language.* Cambridge: Harvard University Press.

Kruglanski, A., and Freund, T. (1983). "The Freezing and Unfreezing of Lay-Inference: Effects on Impressional Primacy, Ethnic Stereotyping, and Numerical Anchoring." *Journal of Experimental Social Psychology* 19: 448–68.

Kruglanski, A., and Mayseless, O. (1987). "Motivational Effects in the Social Comparison of Opinions." *Journal of Personality and Social Psychology* 53: 834–42.

Laudan, L. (1977). *Progress and Its Problems*. Berkeley: University of California Press.

———. (1984). *Science and Value: The Aims of Science and Their Role in Scientific Debate*. Berkeley: University of California Press.

Leach, E. (1954). *Political Systems of Highland Burma: A Study of Kachin Social Structure*. London School of Economics Monographs on Social Anthropology, no. 44. G. Bell and Sons, 1954. Reprint. London: Athlone Press.

———. (1961). "Golden Bough or Guilded Twig?" *Daedalus*, pp. 371–87.

———. (1969). "Virgin Birth." In E. Leach, *Genesis as Myth and Other Essays*. London: Jonathan Cape.

LePore, E., and Loewer, B. (1987). "Mind Matters." *Journal of Philosophy* 84: 630–41.

———. (1989). "More on Making Mind Matter More." *Philosophical Topics* 17: 175–91.

Levin, J. (1988). "Must Reasons be Rational?" *Philosophy of Science* 55: 199–217.

Levi-Strauss, C. (1966). *The Savage Mind*. Chicago: University of Chicago Press.

Lewis, D. K. (1973). "Causation." *Journal of Philosophy* 70: 556–72.

———. (1974). "Radical Interpretation." *Synthese* 23: 331–44.

Little, D. (1991). *Varieties of Social Explanation*. Boulder: Westview.

Loar, B. (1981). *Mind and Meaning*. Cambridge: Cambridge University Press.

Lukes, S. (1970). "Some Problems about Rationality." In B. Wilson, ed., *Rationality*. Worchester: Basil Blackwell, pp. 194–213.

———. (1982). "Relativism in its Place." In M. Hollis and S. Lukes, eds., *Rationality and Relativism*. Cambridge: MIT Press, pp. 261–305.

Lycan, W. (1988). *Judgement and Justification*. Cambridge: Cambridge University Press.

Mackie, J. L. (1974). *The Cement of the Universe*. Oxford: Clarendon Press.

Malcolm, N. (1968). "The Conceivability of Mechanism." *Philosophical Review* 77: 45–72.

Malinowski, B. (1931). "Culture." *Encyclopaedia of the Social Sciences*. London: Macmillan.

Maull, N. (1977). "Unifying Science Without Reduction." *Studies in the History and Philosophy of Science* 9: 143–62.

McClosky, H. (1964). "Consensus and Ideology in American Politics." *American Political Science Review* 58: 361–82.

McDowell, J. (1985). "Functionalism and Anomalous Monism." In E. LaPore and B. McLaughlin, eds. *Actions and Events: Perspectives on the Philosophy of Donald Davidson.* Worcester: Blackwell, pp. 389–98.

McGinn, C. (1977). "Charity, Interpretation, and Belief." *Journal of Philosophy* 74: 521–35.

Mill, J. (1974). *A System of Logic Ratiocinative and Inductive.* Toronto: University of Toronto Press. (Originally published 1843.)

Miller, R. (1987). *Fact and Method.* Princeton: Princeton University Press.

Nagel, E. (1961). *The Structure of Science: Problems in the Logic of Explanation.* New York: Harcourt, Brace, and World.

Nisbett, R., and Ross, L. (1980). *Human Inference: Strategies and Shortcomings in Social Judgment.* Englewood Cliffs, N.J.: Prentice-Hall.

Pinch, T. (1986). *Confronting Nature.* Dordrecht: D. Reidel.

Popper, K. (1950). *The Open Society and Its Enemies.* Princeton: Princeton University Press.

Prothro, J., and Grigg, C. (1960). "Fundamental Principles of Democracy: Bases of Agreement and Disagreement." *Journal of Politics* 22: 276–94.

Putnam, H. (1975a). "Language and Reality." In Putnam, *Mind, Language and Reality.* Cambridge: Cambridge University Press.

———. (1975b). "The Analytic and the Synthetic." In Putnam, *Mind, Language and Reality.* Cambridge: Cambridge University Press.

———. (1975c). "The Meaning of Meaning." In Putnam, *Mind, Language, and Reality.* Cambridge: Cambridge University Press.

———. (1978). *Meaning and the Moral Sciences.* Boston: Routledge and Kegan Paul.

Quine, W. V. O. (1953). "Two Dogmas of Empiricism." In Quine, *From a Logical Point of View.* Cambridge: Harvard University Press.

———. (1960). *Word and Object.* Cambridge: MIT Press.

———. (1970). "Philosophical Progress in Language Theory." *Metaphilosophy* 1: 2–19.

———. (1974). *The Roots of Reference*. La Salle, Ill.: Open Court.

———. (1986). *Philosophy of Logic*. 2nd edition. Englewood Cliffs, N.J.: Prentice-Hall.

———. (1987). "Indeterminacy of Translation Again," *Journal of Philosophy* 84: 5–10.

Rabinow, P., and Sullivan, W., eds. (1987). *Interpretive Social Science: A Second Look*. Berkeley: University of California Press.

Railton, P. (1978). "A Deductive-Nomological Model of Probabilistic Explanation." *Philosophy of Science* 45: 206–26.

———. (1981). "Probability, Explanation, and Information." *Synthese* 48: 233–56.

Ricoeur, P. (1981). "The Task of Hermeneutics." In J. Thompson, ed. and trans., *Hermeneutics and the Human Sciences*. Cambridge: Cambridge University Press, pp. 43–62.

Root, M. (1986). "Davidson and Social Science." In LaPore, ed., *Truth and Interpretation: Perspectives on the Philosophy of Donald Davidson*. Worchester: Blackwell, pp. 272–304.

Rosenberg, A. (1985a). *The Structure of the Biological Sciences*. Cambridge: Cambridge University Press.

———. (1985b). "Davidson's Unintended Attack on Psychology." In E. LePore and B. McLaughlin, eds. *Actions and Events: Perspectives on the Philosophy of Donald Davidson*. Worcester: Blackwell, pp. 399–407.

———. (1988). *Philosophy of Social Science*. Boulder: Westview.

Ross, L., Lepper, M., and Hubbard, M. (1975). "Perseverance in Self-Perception and Social Perception: Biased Attributional Processes in the Debriefing Paradigm." *Journal of Personality and Social Psychology* 32: 880–92.

Roth, P. (1985). "Resolving the Rationalitatstreit." *Archives of European Sociology* 26: 142–57.

Roth, W. (1903). "Superstition, Magic and Medicine." *North Queensland Ethnographical Bulletin* 5: 242–61.

Salmon, W. (1978). "Why Ask 'Why?'—An Inquiry Concerning Scientific Explanation." *Proceedings and Addresses of the American Philosophical Association* 51: 683–705.

———. (1984). *Scientific Explanation and the Causal Structure of the World*. Princeton: Princeton University Press.

――――. (1989). "Four Decades of Scientific Explanation." In P. Kitcher and W. Salmon, eds., *Scientific Explanation, Minnesota Studies in the Philosophy of Science*. Vol. 13. Minneapolis: University of Minnesota Press.

Shapere, D. (1982). "The Concept of Observation in Science and Philosophy." *Philosophy of Science* 49: 485–525.

Shweder, R., and LeVine, R., eds. (1984). *Culture Theory*. Cambridge: Cambridge University Press.

Simon, H. (1957). *Models of Man*. New York: Wiley and Sons.

――――. (1979). "Rational Decision Making in Business Organizations." *American Economics Review* 69: 493–513.

Skorupski, J. (1973). "Science and Traditional Religious Thought." *Philosophy of Social Science* 3: 97–115, 209–30.

――――. (1976). *Symbol and Theory: A Philosophical Study of Theories of Religion in Social Anthropology*. Cambridge: Cambridge University Press.

Skyrms, B. (1986). *Choice and Chance: An Introduction to Inductive Logic*. 3d ed. Belmont, Calif.: Wadsworth Publishing.

Slovic, P. (1972). *From Shakespeare to Simon: Speculations—and Some Evidence—About Man's Ability to Process Information*. Oregon Research Institute, Research Bulletin, Vol. 12.

Sosa, E. (1984). "Mind-Body Interaction and Supervenient Causation." *Midwest Studies in Philosophy* 9: 271–82.

Spiro, M. (1966). "Religion: Problems of Definition and Explanation." In M. Banton, ed., *Anthropological Approaches to the Study of Religion*. London: Travistock, pp. 85–126.

――――. (1968). "Virgin Birth, Parthenogenesis, and Physiological Paternity: An Essay in Cultural Interpretation." In *Man*. N.s. 3: 242–61.

Stich, S. (1983). *From Folk-Psychology to Cognitive Science*. Cambridge: MIT Press.

――――. (1984). "Relativism, Rationality, and the Limits of Intentional Description." *Pacific Philosophical Quarterly* 65: 211–35.

――――. (1985). "Could Man Be an Irrational Animal?" *Synthese* 64: 115–35.

――――. (1990). *The Fragmentation of Reason*. Cambridge: MIT Press.

Sullivan, J., Piereson, J., and Marcus, G. (1982). *Political Tolerance and American Democracy*. Chicago: University of Chicago Press.

Suppes, P. (1985). "Davidson's View of Psychology as a Science." In B. Vermazen and M. Hintikka, eds., *Essays on Davidson: Actions and Events.* Oxford: Clarendon Press.

Suppes P., and Zinnes, J. (1963). "Basic Measurement Theory." In R. D. Luce, R. R. Bush, and E. Galanter, eds., *Handbook of Mathematical Psychology.* Vol. 1. New York: Wiley.

Taylor, C. (1985). *Philosophy and the Human Sciences.* Cambridge: Cambridge University Press.

Tienson, J. (forthcoming). "The Private Life of the Brain in a Vat."

Turnbull, C. (1977). *The Mountain People.* London: Picador.

Turner, S. (1979). "Translating Ritual Beliefs." *Philosophy of Social Science* 9: 401–23.

———. (1980). *Sociological Explanation as Translation.* Cambridge: Cambridge University Press.

Turner, V. (1975). "Symbolic Studies." *Annual Review of Anthropology* 4: 145–61.

Tversky, A. (1969). "Intransitivity of Preference." *Psychological Review* 76: 31–48.

———. (1975). "A Critique of Expected Utility Theory: Descriptive and Normative Considerations." *Erkenntnis* 9: 163–73.

Tversky, A., and Kahneman, D. (1971). "The Belief in the Law of Small Numbers." *Psychological Bulletin* 76: 105–10.

———. (1974). "Judgment under Uncertainty: Heuristics and Biases." *Science* 185: 1124–31.

———, and Kahneman, D. (1981). "The Framing of Decisions and the Psychology of Choices." *Science* 211: 453–8.

van Fraassen, B. (1980). *The Scientific Image.* Oxford: Clarendon Press.

———. (1983). "Theory Comparison and Relevant Evidence," in J. Earman, ed. *Testing Scientific Theories, Minnesota Studies in the Philosophy of Science.* Vol. 10. Minneapolis: University of Minnesota Press, pp. 27–42.

Verba, S., and Nie, N. (1972). *Participation in America: Political Democracy and Political Equality.* New York: Harper and Row.

Wason, P. (1972). "Self-contradictions." In P. Wason and P. Johnson-Laird, *Psychological Reasoning: Structure and Content.* London: Bratsford, pp. 114–28.

Wason, P., and Johnson-Laird, P. (1972). *Psychological Reasoning: Structure and Content.* London: Bratsford.

Watkins, J. (1970). "Imperfect Rationality." In R. Berger and F. Cioffi, eds. *Explanation in the Behavioral Sciences.* Cambridge: Cambridge University Press, pp. 139–52.

Wilson, B. (1970). *Rationality.* Worcester: Blackwell.

Winch, P. (1958). *The Idea of a Social Science and Its Relation to Philosophy.* Atlantic Highlands, N.J.: Humanities Press.

———. (1964). "Understanding a Primitive Society." *American Philosophical Quarterly* 1: 307–24.

Wittgenstein, L. (1958). *Philosophical Investigations.* English text of the third edition. Trans. G. E. M. Anscombe. New York: Macmillan.

Woodward, J. (1979). "Scientific Explanation", *British Journal for the Philosophy of Science* 30: 41–67.

———. (1984). "A Theory of Singular Causal Explanation", *Erkenntnis* 21: 231–62.

———. (1986). "Are Singular Causal Explanations Implicit Covering-Law Explanations?" *Canadian Journal of Philosophy* 16: 253–80.

Wylie, A. (1986). "Bootstrapping in the Un-Natural Sciences: Archaeological Theory Testing." *Proceedings of the Philosophy of Science Association 1986.* Vol. 1, pp. 314–21.

Name Index

Subject Index